GOOD EVENING,
FRIENDS

A Broadcaster Shares His Life

DAVE WARD

WITH JIM MCGRATH

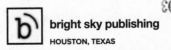

bright sky publishing

HOUSTON, TEXAS

Disclaimer: Although the author, co-author and publisher have made every effort to ensure that the information in this book is accurate, many events, locales and conversations are recreated from memories and are the sole opinion and responsibility of the author. The publisher does not assume liability for any errors or omissions.

---

 bright sky publishing
HOUSTON, TEXAS

2365 Rice Blvd., Suite 202
Houston, Texas 77005

ISBN: 978-1-942945-76-5

10 9 8 7 6 5 4 3 2 1

Library of Congress Cataloging-in-Publication Data on file with the publisher.

Editorial Director: Lucy Herring Chambers
Editor: Aries Ann C. Jones
Designer: Marla Y. Garcia
Cover photo courtesy of Gittings Photography for LCA Houston
International Society News

Printed in Canada by Friesens

For my beautiful Laura,
without whom I would not be here.
She saved my life, quite literally,
on several occasions.
I will love her forever.
DAVE

For Paulina, Anna, Caragh and Jack
JIM

CONTENTS

FOREWORD

Barbara and I were delighted to hear the news that Dave had decided to write this book about his life and legendary career as a broadcaster because, first of all, he has an important and fascinating story to share. But more than that, we have listened and watched since he started on the air in Houston in 1962. The man is a broadcasting institution—that trusted voice and face we turned to almost every night to tell us about our city and world.

When you get down to it, Dave's career has mirrored Houston's own story. He chronicled so many of the people and events that inspired and drove the Bayou City's rise from a sleepy southwestern oil town to the fourth largest city in America. Along the way, his own career took off, not unlike the space program he covered so diligently.

The fact is, Dave was, and remains, so popular that looking back I am more than a little relieved he never decided to get into politics. Who could compete? There's never been another news broadcaster like him, and I honestly can't see how anyone will ever replicate what he has done in his career again.

To be clear, I am not just talking about his Iron Man-like longevity at the same TV station. Just as importantly in my view, if not more so, Dave Ward is one of the most trusted and capable news reporters I have ever met.

I'll let you in on a little secret: despite my sincere efforts to be kinder and gentler, I did not always enjoy the warmest relationship with the news media. As a group, the Beltway media "pack" as I called them always seemed to find something in me or my policies they could question or criticize. As for my side of the story, I guess you might say some of their constant second-guessing would grate on anyone's nerves—especially if you were also trying to deal with the breakup of the Soviet Union, strong-willed Allies, and Saddam Hussein.

But if I saw Dave Ward was on the schedule, I knew I was dealing with a true professional—a reporter who would ask the direct questions any public figure should expect, but also one who was fair and impartial in a way many reporters merely *think* they are.

If our media friends, especially in Washington and New York, are open to a suggestion from someone who has been around the track a few times, I would encourage every reporter to study Dave's singular career and then try to emulate his sterling example. If they did, American journalism might regain much of the credibility and respect it has shed over time.

As Dave Ward tells you in the pages that follow, it's not rocket science: "Just the facts, ma'am."

George H. W. Bush
Houston, Texas
August, 2017

With my mother, Mary, and my sister Mary, sometime around 1943.

PREFACE

Good evening, friends. I can't begin to count the times I have greeted you this way—on the air, as your emcee, or when we have had the chance to meet. And every time I say it, it reinforces the feeling I have about my work as a broadcaster: no matter our ages, races, religions, or beliefs, we are a community. I have been blessed with the opportunity to discover and share the news that impacts us all, and it has created a deep sense of connection in me. Over the years, many of you have told me that, since you invited me to bring the news into your homes every night for so many years, you feel the same connection.

How did I come to see our relationship this way? And how did this greeting become so much a part of who I am? I hope the stories that follow will show you.

This might be an unusual way to start telling the story of my life, but let me tell you about Ron Stone. Best-known as the news anchor at KPRC-TV Channel 2 in Houston from 1972 to 1992, Ron was the finest television news anchor the city of Houston ever saw. I admired him greatly, and though we were technically rivals for much of our careers, he was also my dear friend.

I had known and watched Ron since 1962. We had both recently arrived in Houston; I was at KNUZ radio, and he had been recruited by Dan Rather to join KHOU-TV Channel 11. Because KNUZ had no television affiliate, and Channel 11 had no radio affiliate, our news departments regularly worked together on stories. We'd call each other and occasionally meet. He always impressed me as a total gentleman, and very knowledgeable.

As a TV news anchor, Ron had a folksy style of delivery that I found engaging. He always opened his TV newscasts saying, "Howdy, neighbors." And at the end of each newscast, he routinely said, "Good night, neighbors." It had a ring to it that I liked, so much so that, when I got the chance to anchor the news at KTRK-TV Channel 13, I wanted to find an opening line that created the same feeling.

I decided "friends" had the same warmth as "neighbors," so I chose it. That's how I came up with the expression that has become such a part of me that loved ones tease it should be on my tombstone. "Good evening, friends."

What I want to share with you here, though, is not the genesis of a phrase—basically borrowed from a friend I admired—but the way that it has come to represent the life story of an ordinary man who has had the opportunity to forge a career in the very extraordinary business of radio and television news reporting. So many people in recent years have asked me to share my stories that not only did I feel obligated to write them down, but I have also thoroughly enjoyed the process. It is a daunting task to try and capture your life in words, but working on this project over the past few years and reflecting on the journey have also reminded me just how blessed I have been—to have experienced it all, and also to have lived to tell the tale!

In 2007, I won an Emmy Award—my only one, in fact—for a special program I put together on my fellow Houstonian and dear friend Steve Tyrell, who also happens to be a brilliant music producer and singer. We called that report "Steve Tyrell: A Houston Standard," but for reasons I will detail in the pages ahead, I had originally wanted to call it "Steve Tyrell: The Accidental Singer."

Well, that's how I feel about my life story—*Dave Ward: The Accidental Anchor*. Especially early on in my life and career, so many twists and turns brought me to Houston when they could just as easily landed me in Austin, or Dallas, or some other far-flung place around the world as a member of the United States Navy. Each time something might have happened to veer me off the path that led to Houston, something happened to keep me on track—something quirky, I might add.

Was it destiny? Serendipity? The hand of providence?

Friends, as you read, you get to decide.

Whatever it was, I could not be more fortunate—or grateful. I have been extremely lucky to succeed for sixty years in a highly competitive industry. I have also been fortunate to do it in what I consider the greatest city in the world, with some of the best colleagues at all levels. Like others, I have worked very hard at my craft, but I am also well aware that had it not been for the radio listeners and television viewers who continued to tune me in, I would have been out of a job long ago.

Accordingly, I owe each of you who watched our newscast a tremendous debt of gratitude. Though the magic of television, after gathering as much important and timely information as our team could, I sat in a studio and faced you. Over time, the pictures and sound we sent into your house created a deep and enduring bond, and let me assure you: it was a two-way street.

For the majority of my years as an anchor at KTRK, I went to work on most holidays to be with you—my broadcast family. After all, I consistently spent more hours in the day with all of you and cherished our time together. It just seemed natural to share the holidays. So we did.

We have been through so much together over so many years. Because of your loyalty and trust, I had a front row seat to history—meeting the people and witnessing the events that shaped who we are as Texans and Americans.

I was on the air on KNUZ Radio when President John F. Kennedy was assassinated in 1963. The utter shock and horror of that national tragedy scarred our nation and all who were alive at that time. I was there fifty years later in Dealy Plaza to help memorialize those horrific events for future generations.

Then it was on to the national political conventions in 1964—where I first met George H. W. Bush, who would later become Vice-President and then President of the United States in his own right.

I shared the tragic news with you of the assassinations of first Dr. Martin Luther King Jr. and then that of Senator Robert F. Kennedy.

In the early 1970s, we went to Managua, Nicaragua to witness the aftermath of a huge earthquake that resulted in an outpouring of love and supplies from the people of Houston.

Together we witnessed the amazing highs, and devastating lows, associated with our space program.

I never thought I would be able to report on the end of the Vietnam War; it seemed like we were forever into that thing. But the opportunity finally came.

And, similarly, I never thought I would share the news with you that the Cold War had ended, or the Soviet Union had dissolved.

And I really never dreamed I'd report on either the start, or the end, of the Space Shuttle Program.

By the magic of television, I was able to take you onboard the *USS Houston*, a nuclear attack submarine far below the surface of the Pacific Ocean.

We flew in several U. S. Navy, Air Force and Air National Guard jet fighter planes—and even took the controls on some.

I had this front row seat on the most significant events of our lives only because of you—the viewers and listeners who kept me on the air. With that privilege came the responsibility to provide you with the best information available and to communicate it as clearly as possible. And as I carried out that responsibility to the best of my abilities, a relationship of trust and care developed to a degree that humbles me as I recall your love and support through the highs and lows of my career and personal life.

I have always deeply admired Walter Cronkite. Recently, I was walking out of a drug store in Houston when I had a moment similar to one he recalled in his life story. A guy came up to me and said, "Pardon me, sir, but didn't you used to be Dave Ward?"

You could have knocked me over with a feather.

I said, "Yes. Well, actually, I'm what's left of him, yeah."

As for the rest of me, I've tried to put it right here in these pages. I'm not claiming to be Uncle Walter, but I am one of the lucky few who experienced the heyday of broadcasting. If you enjoy reading these stories half as much as I did living them, that's the only accolade I need.

So, let's get started.

GOOD EVENING,
FRIENDS

A Broadcaster Shares His Life

*If my wife, Laura, had not saved my life on November 30, 2016,
you would not be reading this story.*

1

LUCKY I WOKE UP

November 30, 2016, was not a good morning. Around 5 a.m., I stirred awake in bed—prodded by an uncomfortable, pressure-like feeling that was building in my chest and shooting down both arms. It wasn't a horrible pain, just uncomfortable, so initially I thought it was a mild case of heartburn.

Maybe if I just lie here a minute it'll go away...

But the irregular sensation persisted. Lying there in the pre-dawn darkness, I started to sense something was terribly wrong, so I decided to wake Laura, my wife. "Sweetheart, I don't know if I'm having a heart attack or what, but I feel terrible," I told her. "I feel like an elephant is walking on me—I could be having a heart attack. Would you get me an aspirin?"

Laura sprang immediately into action. She initially struggled with the aspirin bottle due to the childproof cap, so she smashed it open on the counter sending pills flying all over the bathroom. Quickly, she gave me a pill with some water. Then she suggested calling an ambulance, but I knew there was an emergency clinic near our home—and something inside was telling me we didn't have a lot of time to wait on an ambulance to arrive. So, I suggested she drive me there, which she did, at a very high rate of speed—with her flashers on and her arms waving to try and flag a policeman we never saw. Between the moment I woke up and the moment I walked into that clinic, a mere thirteen minutes had elapsed.

I have no doubt that Laura's quick response saved my life.

We rolled right into that clinic parking lot, with Laura practically parking the car up on the curb. A nurse came out, and as Laura was explaining that her husband was having a heart attack the nurse saw me and said, "Oh my gosh! Mr. Ward! What are you doing here?" Laura, exasperated, said, "*That's* the husband I was telling you about, the one who is having a heart attack!"

I wanted to walk into the clinic, but they insisted on putting me in a wheelchair and taking me into one of the exam rooms where they immediately gave me a little nitroglycerine pill. Within about five minutes, the worst of the symptoms were completely gone and, feeling much better, I told Laura it was time to go back home.

Wrong.

Just then, the attending doctor came into my room and announced, "Mr. Ward, you are in the middle of an active heart attack. We've already alerted your doctors at Methodist Hospital, and we're going to send you there right away." Despite my feeling a lot better, the doctor and Laura convinced me that this was more serious than it felt. As they got me ready for transport, I gave Laura my wallet, house keys, wedding band, and a few other items, and they put me in an ambulance bound for Methodist, which, in my view, is the greatest hospital in the greatest medical center in the world.

Arriving at the hospital around 7:30 a.m., my cardiologist and friend Dr. Mohammed Attar was already there with his team. They wheeled me in and did their tests, which confirmed that I was, in fact, in the middle of an active heart attack—meaning my heart was receiving insufficient blood flow. In my case, one artery leading into my heart was ninety-nine percent blocked.

In the U.S., one in every five heart attacks is classified as being "silent," meaning the damage is done without the victim even being aware of it. Many people in my position would have died in their sleep.

I was lucky I woke up. I guess the good Lord wasn't through with me yet.

Diet and lifestyle can be contributing factors to having a heart attack, and the truth is I have never had the greatest diet. I am also not too big on exercise. And as much as I hate to admit it, I still smoke. So that artery didn't get blocked by itself, or overnight.

But on that late fall morning in 2016, I was also feeling quite a bit of stress. The very last newscast of my fifty-year career at KTRK-TV Channel 13 was scheduled for Friday, December 9th, just over a week later. I hated the idea of leaving the station, the people and the work I loved; but, at that time, the station's management and I could not find a mutually agreeable way of extending my contract. I was frustrated and upset. I felt that after a half century doing my job at a high level, I would recognize when I was not good at my craft anymore, or our ratings would show that I was no longer connecting with our audience. But now it seemed like the station saw something I didn't.

I never wanted to be one of those folks who didn't know when it was time to hang it up. I had talked on more than a few occasions with Dave Strickland, KTRK's fantastic news director until 2014, about *not* wanting to stay on the anchor desk too long. Dave and I had the kind of relationship where we could be honest with each other— brutally honest when needed. But, Dave had left KTRK in July of 2014, five months before I was taken off the 10 p.m. newscast.

In August of 2016, the station's management announced they were also taking me off the 6 p.m. newscast at the end of the year.

I was heartbroken.

I have always known that TV news is a business, and to be successful, it has to operate as such. Referring to my job as news anchor, I had often told friends, "It's the company's sandbox. I'm just allowed to play in it," and, over the decades, as competition increased, I had seen the increasing challenges of the business firsthand. We live in an environment today where some employment contracts for TV reporters run only thirteen weeks. Through my long career, I have always respected the authority of the management, even when I have not agreed with some of their decisions.

In 2016, our ratings were still very good, and I still felt I was doing good work. As that last newscast on December 9th approached, I became increasingly dismayed. Although my life has included more than a fair share of mishaps and accidents, when I look back at this period in late 2016, it's like watching a slow-motion car wreck. My life seemed to be spinning out of control, and I felt there was nothing I could do to avoid the coming collision.

The heart attack was only the start of a series of significant medical setbacks that would sideline me for months. Since 2005, Dr. Attar had been monitoring a heart murmur caused by a narrowing in my aortic valve. After examining me that fateful morning, he determined that, in addition to the heart attack, my aortic valve also was hanging on by a thread. With such a serious set of delicate challenges, "Mo" (as we called Dr. Attar) wanted the best heart surgeon in the world, Dr. Gerald Lawrie, to perform the operation. There was just one problem: everyone wants Gerald Lawrie—who was born in Australia and with Dr. Attar studied under and worked with the amazing Dr. Michael DeBakey—doing their surgery. Dr. Lawrie was not free that day, so they sent me to a hospital room to wait. I was under strict orders not to have caffeine, or food, or anything else that could over-stimulate my blood pressure. My situation was apparently that precarious.

Later that day, they finally let me have some food. Laura had elevated my head so I could eat a chicken salad sandwich, drink a Coca-Cola®, and visit with some friends and family when Mo walked in the room.

"David, are we having some kind of party?" he asked, clearly not pleased. "Put your head back down, give me that Coke®, and I'm going to have to ask everyone to leave—we cannot have any stimulation like this." Right around that time, another doctor in scrubs walked into the room: it was Dr. Lawrie. Thankfully, they had somehow found room on his schedule for him to do my surgery the next morning, and he came to explain exactly what was going to happen.

After a restless, sleepless night, Dr. Lawrie performed the bypass on my right coronary artery that caused the heart attack, and replaced the damaged aortic valve with a natural prosthetic valve taken from a cow. (Insert your own joke here if you want; but in the hotly contested medical debate pitting "porcine valves versus bovine valves," the experts I consulted say cow valves are superior to pig valves.) The recovery that followed started with eleven days in the intensive care unit, with Laura constantly by my side.

I will spare you the gory details, but I had several massive complications in the immediate aftermath of that big operation—including one involving "uncontrollable, inexplicable bleeding." Both Dr. Attar and Dr. Lawrie were somewhat mystified, but that bizarre and very serious issue eventually resolved itself.

I was still in ICU and not fully out of the woods when Laura invited my dear friend and co-worker Melanie Lawson to visit. At that point, I was not in a coma, but I had not been very responsive, awake or alert. When Melanie, who shared a cubicle at the TV station with me and Art Rascon, sat down next to me, something special happened.

Melanie pulled the TV show *Jeopardy* up on her smartphone. When that familiar theme song came on my eyes shot open.

"C'mon Dave," she said sweetly. "Let's play *Jeopardy*."

Melanie and I had a habit of watching that show every afternoon together. Clearly that memory, the human connection of that, helped snap me out of whatever lethargic funk had me so sleepy. After that, I stayed awake most of the day, but there would be a few more daunting setbacks before the road ahead got smoother.

A few weeks after my open-heart surgery, for example, I came down with pleural effusion, meaning I had accumulated so much fluid around my lungs that the lungs themselves could not fully inflate. As a result, it felt as if I could barely breathe –a truly horrible feeling. I was increasingly panicked over the quickly deteriorating situation, because it felt as if I was drowning. But when the doctors and nurses checked my complaints, the ultrasound tests did not show any accumulation of fluid—so they quite understandably didn't feel they could take any proactive measures.

Once again, my Laura intervened on my behalf. She went to the top hospital manager to make sure they were aware of the gravity of the situation. That day, Christmas Day 2016, Dr. Manuel Bloom came in to my hospital room and performed a thoracentesis—a procedure where a needle is inserted through the back to draw off excess fluid. He did one lung that day; and the other lung, the next. Altogether, they pulled 2.5 liters of fluid out of my lung cavities.

With each breath I was finally able to draw, I felt like I was sucking life back in, and it was such a relief. I knew that if Laura had not stepped in and demanded more treatment for me, I wouldn't have survived. It was the second time in three weeks her tenacious love had most certainly saved my life.

A few days later, they moved me to a floor where I was expected to start physical therapy. I was still so weak and out of sorts that my interest in any form of exercise was non-existent. Not to be daunted by my lack of motivation, Laura called in reinforcements, starting with Jeff Bagwell, former Houston Astros star who would soon after be elected to the Hall of Fame.

Jeff, who is a dear friend of ours, told Laura not to worry. "Rachel and I will be there this afternoon…I'll come kick his ass." When Jeff arrived, he didn't politely say "hi" or "how are you?" Instead, he looked straight at me and commanded, "Get up out of that bed!" Then Jeff and the physical therapist walked me up and down that damn hospital hallway three or four times. When I complained at one point about getting tired, Jeff shot back, "I'll be the judge of that. I think you *can* walk some more." So onward we went.

As he was leaving, Jeff gave me one more piece of tough love. "Dave," he said, "your hair looks like crap. Do something." Only someone who knows me well, and cares enough to confront me, could do what Jeff Bagwell did that day. As Melanie had a few weeks before, Jeff knew what I needed to get me up and going. I will always be grateful to both of them for recognizing, as Laura did, that I needed their strong spirits to challenge rather than coddle me. What if they had all let me lie in the bed feeling sorry for myself?

Despite the powerful intervention of this tough love, a couple of weeks later my heart rate was still pretty slow and irregular. After a few more tests, Dr. Attar determined that I needed a pacemaker. He referred me to another terrific doctor for that procedure, Nadim Nasir, whom Dr. Attar called his "heart electrician."

I felt as if I had been run over by a truck—a feeling I actually have experienced and will tell you more about in the next chapters. But even as painful and life-threatening as all of these heart and lung-related interventions were, what really rang my bell was the hernia operation that came last. The recovery from that hurt like the dickens! It was far more grueling than anything that came before it.

In the span of a few months, I had gone from feeling like an expert in my field with the ability to call the shots in my life, to feeling like the my future was uncertain at best. Five serious medical setbacks—one right after the other—were more than I could ever have imagined handling. And, as my initial lackluster efforts to recover show, doubt filled me as it never had in my entire life.

But as 2017 progressed, and I got further away from that terrible spell, I got to thinking. How lucky I was to be alive after all the risky things that I've done in my lifetime. How lucky I was to have a strong woman like Laura by my side and good friends to fight for me when I thought I was too weak to fight for myself. Spending so much time in the hospital, and coming face-to-face with my mortality, gave me a new perspective. My priorities changed, and what mattered most to me came more clearly into focus.

I realized that, if there was nothing to be done about my time as the news anchor at KTRK ending, I would find something else to do to engage with my viewers and help our community. Before my heart attack, I had already planned to become increasingly more active with the Crime Stoppers organization, as I have been since the program's inception in 1981. I wasn't sure what other opportunities I would discover when I left KTRK, but I knew they were out there, and I was darn sure going to continue using my talents to give back to our wonderful city.

In a way, it was another wake-up call.

Thanks to my great doctors and just the right balance of tough love and TLC from head nurse Laura Ward, by Tuesday, May 2nd, 2017, I had recovered well enough to make that familiar drive back to the KTRK studios to work my final 6 p.m. newscast as anchor. Near the end of the broadcast, I was given a rare opportunity to address my loyal viewers to tell them how much their trust and friendship through the years had meant to me.

While there are no words and not enough time to ever sum up what this era of my life meant to me, here is some of what I said to my television family that evening:

> *You have kept me grounded, my feet planted securely. When I tripped up, you forgave me. When I achieved successes, you applauded me. When I was ill, you comforted me. And when I've been distraught, you embraced me. You gave me far more than I could have ever hoped for… It's hard to identify a time over these last fifty years that I didn't feel loved and accepted by each and every one of you, and I thank you. I hope I have fulfilled your expectations and delivered the news in a fashion that kept you informed and made you feel safe. I have not taken my responsibility to do that lightly, and I have done my best. I have always leveled with you and told you the truth—good or bad. That has been my focus throughout my years: to report trusted content, and to get it right…*
>
> *…You know, they say the last goodbye is the hardest, so let me be clear: I am not saying goodbye. I am simply leaving this anchor chair. I don't intend to ever say goodbye to you. I will always be part of this city, and serve the people… This hasn't been just a career for*

me; it's been my life's purpose. And I look forward to continuing our journey together…

Emotionally, I kept it together pretty well, and near the end paid tribute to two of my broadcasting heroes: Ron Stone and Walter Cronkite. But when it was time to say "Good evening, friends" for what I thought might be the last time, my voice caught. I was incredibly touched seeing dozens of the station's reporters and crew members starting to gather around me, applauding. These were my colleagues and friends with whom I had worked for so long, and whom I would miss very much.

Just months before, in November, 2016 when I hit my fiftieth anniversary, the station had thrown me the most lavish party—during which they named me "anchor emeritus" and erected a plaque to that effect in the newsroom. Around that same time, the Walt Disney Company, which owns KTRK today, flew Laura and me out to Burbank, California for an elegant award dinner hosted by CEO Bob Iger—along with Mickey Mouse. In fact, when Mr. Iger called me up to the podium that night to receive a unique bronze of Snow White and the Seven Dwarves marking my fifty years of service, Mickey was standing right there. I reminded him: "You know, Mickey, you and I both went from black-and-white to color."

Then the day after my final broadcast as anchor, on May 3, 2017, I was invited down to Houston's City Hall for a special celebration with Mayor Sylvester Turner and Harris County Judge Ed Emmett in front of a very nice crowd. There, they gave me the key to the city with an overly generous proclamation on behalf of Harris County. Their sentiments and the celebration were a real highlight, and it helped me to keep my concern about the future at bay.

So, it was a heck of a send-off, but I still find myself wondering just where all that time went.

Fifty years had passed, just like that. My broadcast family had come to mean so much to me, and now the challenge of staying in touch with them in new ways had begun. The reflections that had begun with my time in the hospital had given me new perspective, and I soon found myself looking back to the very beginnings of my journey.

Receiving my 50th anniversary company gift, a bronze Snow White and the Seven Dwarves, from Bob Iger, CEO of the Walt Disney Company, and two special friends.

My grandfather and namesake, Rev. David Ward.
He died a quarter-century before I was born.

KEPT THE FAITH

Of course, before I had a broadcast family, I was part of the extensive Ward family—blessed with a mother and a father, and grandparents, and two sisters who raised me and taught me basic values like respect for other people. My family was not well-off in terms of finances, but we were wealthy in other ways. I never had to look over my shoulder wondering if I had their support. The love, encouragement, patience and discipline they offered in equal measure was the foundation on which I sought to build a meaningful life.

So, who were the people who built the family that provided me with such a strong foundation? I'll take you back a few generations to give you a feel for my people. It fascinates me how many traits they had that came together in my eventual career.

There's an old saying that those who were not born in Texas got here as quickly as they could. Well, in reviewing our family history, it's clear the Wards took the scenic route. In 1830, my great-grandfather Jesse Henley Ward set out from his native Alabama for Illinois, traveling by a pioneer "mover's wagon" with his parents and five siblings. Six years old at the time, Jesse was the fifth of George and Elizabeth Ward's nine children. How he—or anyone in those days—survived what must have been an incredibly difficult journey is beyond me. The terrain they covered was inhospitable at best. One account I've read of a similar journey described the experience this way: "The party followed a track through land that was primeval: dense forest, untamed rivers and streams. After heavy rains, the rivers were largely not fordable. There were swamps to cross and hills that tested the strength of both man and beast."[1] I imagine how challenging it must have been for my great-grandfather to make this trek as a child.

My Ward forbearers were part of the great westerly migration of pioneers, made possible by the Louisiana Purchase, and inspired by the fertile soils and opportunity they saw in the Mississippi River Valley. It was common during that period of our history for groups of pioneering families to migrate together, not only for the sake of safety, but also to share the immense burden. They had all of their worldly possessions with them as they sought to start and build a new life. They had to manage the livestock needed to help pull the wagon. They had to make camp each night in hostile territory, and deal with Lord knows what else.

George and Elizabeth Ward and their family eventually settled in southern Illinois, in what is present-day Williamson County. There, they started farming, but then relocated to the northwest part of Jackson County, also in Illinois, in 1837, after the death of my great-great-grandfather George. By then, his wife Elizabeth had re-married, and my great-grandfather Jesse was ready to strike out on his own. Unlike his older brothers Samuel, Anderson and Jeremiah, who in time ventured across the Mississippi River into Missouri, Jesse put down roots in Jackson County. On January 21, 1842, the eighteen-year-old Jesse married Nancy Murden, whose father, David, was one of the oldest settlers in the area. Together, over the next twenty years, Jesse and Nancy had nine children—seven of whom survived into adulthood.

I got my name from their second child, David, my grandfather who was born in March, 1844 in Campbell Hill village that was, thankfully, in northwest Jackson County. I say "thankfully" because, while Jackson County abuts the Mississippi River on its southwest border, Campbell Hill sits some fifteen miles from the mighty waterway. Three months after my grandfather was born, the Great Flood of June, 1844 ravaged the low-laying bottom lands on both sides of the Mississippi. In some spots, the river reportedly swelled to a width of fifteen miles across, destroying crops, obliterating warehouses, wiping out dwellings, sweeping away fences and barns. Had it not been for the willingness of neighbors and settlers to help

---

[1] https://www.alabamapioneers.com/alabama-to-texas-moving/

each other in the wake of that catastrophe, it is believed a famine would have ensued throughout the region.

In 1855, thirty-one-year-old Jesse bought a farm three miles south of Campbell Hill and eventually began buying grain, raising stock and selling "agricultural implements." He continued to rise as a respected man within his community. An 1876 profile in *History of Jackson County, Illinois* described him this way:

> *Mr. Ward is a man who stands high with his neighbors, as a man of fair dealing and scrupulously honest in the every-day transactions of his life…he has, by re-election, been continued in the responsible office of Justice of the Peace and is now Police Magistrate of the Town of Campbell Hill. In politics, he has always been a staunch supporter of the principles of the Democratic party…His first vote for President was cast for James K. Polk, and he has never missed voting at a presidential election since…His son, Francis M., served for a time as a soldier in the late war.*

His son Francis, my grandfather's older brother, served for three years as a soldier for the Union Army during the Civil War. The politics of the region at that time and my great-grandfather Jesse's steadfast devotion to the Democratic party make this an interesting development. At the outset of the war, it was not known where the loyalties of the citizens of "Egypt" (as the sixteen southernmost counties in Illinois were called at the time) might fall: to the Union, or the Confederacy. President Lincoln was concerned enough about the southern half of his home state that he appointed Congressman John A. McClernand, an anti-abolitionist Democrat with strong political ties throughout southern Illinois, as a General in the Union Army to help keep the region with him and the Union cause.

Added to that, the southernmost city in Illinois, Cairo (pronounced Kay-ro by the locals), sits at the confluence of the Ohio and Mississippi Rivers—and as such was of great strategic importance. Early on in the Civil War, the Union sent several regiments to fortify their hold on Cairo. What happened in "Egypt" in the early 1860s mattered greatly.

A critical tipping point in the conflict came on August 19, 1861, when Colonel John A. Logan, who earlier that year had resigned his seat in the U. S. House from southern Illinois to join the fledgling war effort, addressed a large crowd of citizens in nearby Marion. Earlier in his political career, as a member of the Illinois statehouse, Logan had helped pass a law prohibiting African Americans—even if free— from settling in Illinois. He went on to have a widely admired career as a soldier and U.S. Senator, but his early legislative record was not without controversy.

But in Marion that fateful day, then ex-congressman Logan, whose former district covered 18 counties including Jackson, climbed in the back of a wagon in the city square and eloquently, boldly, and effectively declared: "The time has come when a man must be for or against his country ... I, for one, shall stand or fall with the Union." The assembled crowd responded with cheers, and several recollections suggested a wave of patriotism washed over the audience. In his memoirs, President U. S. Grant later praised Logan's leadership and war recruitment efforts for the Union. Logan's former congressional district, Grant wrote, "had promised at first to give much trouble to the (federal) government, (but) filled every call made upon it for troops, without resorting to the draft."

As it was, my great uncle Francis Ward was one of 137 men recruited by Captain Asgill Conner of Carbondale to volunteer in the original Companies "H" and the "New Company C" in the 18th Illinois Infantry. On October 12, 1862, he mustered into duty in Jackson, Tennessee. The regiment remained there for the rest of the year under the command of Lieutenant Colonel D. H. Brush, drilling, performing tactical instruction, and guarding the critical railroads and bridges needed for the movement of troops and supplies against attack or destruction by the Confederate rebels. At that point in the war, the 18th Infantry totaled 930 men, and it had lost 65 in combat with another 30 dying from wounds received in battle. Disease, perhaps the deadliest foe most men on either side faced, claimed 117 more of their troops, and 164 had been discharged for wounds or disability.

On the whole, the "Old Eighteenth," as it was known, saw limited action. On December 20, 1862, for example, they marched towards Lexington and Trenton, Tennessee to intercept the rebels who were attacking the Union troops guarding the railroads. They returned to Jackson on January 7, 1863, after a few brief skirmishes, during which time they marched more than 125 miles in snow, rain, mud, over hills and rocky roads, and through ice-cold streams. Later in 1863, in June and July, the regiment joined the campaign led by General Ulysses S. Grant that captured control of Vicksburg, Mississippi. Any Civil War buff will tell you that was one of THE Confederate strongholds, and its loss—which basically split the Confederacy in half and ceded control of the Mississippi River valley to the Union—proved a pivotal turning point in the war.

Despite the absence of sustained, savage combat experience, Francis Ward's regiment was nevertheless no stranger to the horrors of war. On August 31, 1863, a unit assessment of the 18th Infantry found that fewer than 200 troops were able to perform their duty. Their numbers were so depleted that Colonel Lawler was re-assigned to another unit, owing to the fact that a regiment so small was not entitled to such a high-ranking commander. The Old Eighteenth remained in Arkansas for the remainder of the war, stationed principally at Pine Bluff, Duvall's Bluff and Little Rock. On December 16, 1865, the Regiment was mustered out at Little Rock.

Col. John A. Logan's wife Mary recounted in her book *Reminiscences of a Soldier's Wife* that "exclamations of joy rang out" from the households of returning Civil War servicemen as they entered their hometowns and came into view, whereas "cries of distress were heard" from the families whose loved ones were not seen or found. Families in this latter category were eventually permitted to search the returning trains and wagons "among the wounded, dying or dead… with tear-dimmed eyes, blanched faces, and quivering lips ... [moving] cautiously from one to another." Mrs. Logan summed up such scenes by saying: "All the pomp and circumstance of chivalry and military display" at the outset of the war had given way to "the agony of pain and terror of death."[2]

After the war, whichever side they had supported, families in the area faced the new tragedy of living without the loved ones lost in the horrific conflict. The Wards were among the fortunate. Francis Ward arrived back home in Jackson County shortly after New Year's Day, 1866. I can only imagine what a homecoming that must have been.

Still very much a frontier farming community, the northwest part of Jackson County, including Campbell Hill and Ava where much of the Ward family settled, was a sparsely populated community

---

[2] https://thesouthern.com/civil-war-timeline/article_1de4361e-8e20-11e0-b5a2-001cc4c002e0.html

with one church, the Freewill Baptist Church, located at the corner of Washington and Second Streets. In 1860, Rev. Henry Gordon and Rev. William Bradley founded the church with twelve original members. Four years later, the newly ordained Reverend George D. Ward—my great-grandfather Jesse's younger brother, who was born in 1831 during the family's westward trek to Illinois—took over as pastor. Jesse and Nancy Ward lived on their forty-acre farm two miles from the church, and they joined the congregation shortly after brother George became its leader.

The ordination of Uncle George was an important milestone: over the next century the Ward family would have a circuit-riding Baptist preacher among our ranks. I sometimes think that I, too, was genetically predestined to talk for a living.

My grandfather David Ward entered the Baptist ministry in 1872 and was ordained in 1876. He served as pastor in Elk Prairie in the northeast part of Jackson County from 1884 to 1894 and accepted several other appointments around the county. He married Mary Hiser in 1870, and together they had twelve children—seven boys and five girls. My father, Henry Martin Ward, the youngest of the dozen, was born in a log house in Ava on August 25, 1895. At the time, my grandfather David was fifty-five years old, and my grandmother Mary was forty-four.

Ward family lore says that my grandmother Mary cried when she learned she was pregnant with my father, and after eleven children who could blame her? Henry Ward was largely raised by his older sister, Bessie, and they remained very close throughout his life.

When he turned ten, my father's family moved to the coal-mining town of Willisville, Illinois, and he entered the public-school system in third grade. He graduated from eighth grade in May of 1911, and eventually started working in the mines as a day laborer. It was dangerous work for anyone, no matter what age. Records show that, on December 19, 1910, twenty-two-year-old George A. Ward (of unknown relation) from nearby Murphysboro, Illinois was riding the tail chain of a loaded coal car down a slight incline out of the Gus Blair Big Muddy Coal Mine when his foot slipped, and he fell in front of the car. He was rolled between a prop and the car, and instantly killed. Hundreds of other unfortunate men of all ages died through the years from falling stone, or mishandled explosives, or other horrible accidents, and the shadow of these dangers added to the grimness of the miners' hard lives.

My grandmother Mary constantly tried to get my father to attend church on Sundays, but early on he rebelled, preferring to take whatever money he had to a nearby bar where he would double, or sometimes triple, his money shooting pool. He was that good. I only saw him shoot pool one time at one of his nephew's homes in Murphysboro. They had a pool table in the basement, and my cousin and I were down there going at it. When my dad came downstairs with his nephew to watch us, his nephew asked him: "Uncle Henry, when was the last time you had a pool cue in your hand?"

"It's been *years*," Dad answered. Whereupon he took a pool cue and, with surgical precision, ran the table—not missing a single shot.

Dad's pool-playing days came to an abrupt halt in April, 1913, when he was seventeen. He attended a rousing religious revival hosted by the charismatic evangelist Billy Sunday, who at that time was one of the most famous Americans, the Billy Graham of his era: "The former big-league baseball player (for the Chicago White Stockings) turned born again 'fighting saint' preached to the common man, and as such employed colloquial language, an earthy touch that shocked the more erudite men of the cloth," according to one memory of him. "He also gesticulated wildly on the pulpit; ran from one end of the stage to the other; tossed about chairs and other furniture in fits of religious excitement; and occasionally slid into an imaginary base, as if beating a throw from the devil himself. He railed against not only alcohol, but agnosticism, card playing, college professors, dancing, movies, philosophy and even reading novels."[3] And of course, shooting pool.

Billy Sunday's theatrics and message spoke to my father in a compelling way and changed his life. Dad later told me that he felt like the Spirit of the Lord spoke directly to him saying, "You've got to change your ways, and help spread the Word in any way you can." Inspired, he attended several more revivals, and he eventually started studying music and singing.

My father was starting to receive his call to preaching just as his preacher-father, in turn, was called home to heaven. On March 30, 1914, David Ward died at home in Willisville after being in poor

[3] https://www.pantagraph.com/news/local/evangelist-billy-sunday-rocked-bloomington-in/article_30c3e4c0-15f6-11e0-a788-001cc4c002e0.html

health for a few weeks. He was seventy. His obituary noted that Rev. Ward had been a member of the International Order of Oddfellows in Elkville, a recent member of Missionary Baptist Church in Willisville, and "lived a consistent Christian life." His tombstone in Percy, Illinois is inscribed: "I have fought the good fight. I have finished my course. I have kept the faith."

When World War I broke out, Dad was in the middle of his music and vocal studies, but he registered to support the war effort and was inducted into the U. S. Army at Louisville, Kentucky on October 4, 1917. He was assigned to the 84th Infantry Division, Company C, 333rd Infantry and received five months schooling on automatic weapons and poisonous gases. He eventually attained the rank of Sergeant and became an automatic weapons instructor.

In early September of 1918, the 84th Infantry—which was known as the "Lincoln" division in World War I because it was comprised of national guard and other recruits from Illinois, Kentucky and Indiana—landed in southern France. Sgt. Ward was assigned to Group 31 with the non-commissioned officers and was marching to the western front in the Metz area in northeast France (200 miles east of Paris) on November 11, 1918, when the Armistice was declared.

My father and his compatriots could not have been more fortunate in terms of the timing. The Allied Expeditionary Force—under the command of U.S. General Jack Pershing—had scored an important string of victories against the Germans that summer, before launching what proved to be the pivotal Meuse-Argonne offensive in the fall of 1918 with an opening fusillade, including mustard gas and phosgene shells. That would explain why they needed personnel with my father's specialized training.

As it was, that offensive had the Germans in full retreat. Arriving U.S. reinforcements like my father's unit had time to advance some thirty-two kilometers before the general armistice was announced. If that war had gone on for another couple of weeks, my sisters and I might not ever have existed.

Sgt. Henry Ward returned from France to New York in April 1919, was discharged in Illinois a month later, and became licensed to preach at the Missionary Baptist Church in his hometown of Willisville a month after that. He threw himself into furthering his education and his evangelical pursuits as a gospel singer, which led him, on

January 1, 1920, to attend the Moody Bible Institute in Chicago. He graduated as president of his class in April 1922, now known as H. M. Ward, a civilian.

Shortly thereafter, another evangelist, L. C. Bauer, recruited my father, who had a beautiful voice, to help manage the music at the revival meetings Bauer conducted traveling across the United States. *The Daily Free Press* in Carbondale covered the 1923 annual assembly of the Illinois Baptist State Association taking place in Creal Springs in the southern part of the state and noted that "the music at the assembly will be in charge of Prof. Henry M. Ward of Willisville, who has varied experience in revival work."

In 1924, my father married Helen Irene Symonds of Skene, Mississippi. She was a gifted piano player, and I have been told she also performed with "Brother Bauer" (as my father called him) at his revivals. Early in 1925, the newlyweds set out for the first of his two associate-pastor assignments in southern Illinois at the First Baptist Church in Herrin, just east of his birthplace in Jackson County.

Williamson County was dotted with coal mines, and the accompanying mining camps, outside of any local jurisdiction and law enforcement, could be very rough places to live. As a result, Williamson County at the time was, in one recent assessment, "the most lawless county in Illinois, perhaps in the entire nation."[4]

When my father entered the scene, Herrin had recently been rocked by a massacre that erupted in June of 1922. Striking union coal miners attacked and gunned down replacement workers (known derogatorily as "scabs") who had crossed their picket line. The union strikers had reportedly marched some fifty of these men at gunpoint a few miles outside of Herrin, lined them up against a barbed wire fence, and then ordered the captives to run for their lives as they opened fire. Several who managed to escape were lynched. In the immediate aftermath, regular townspeople were witnessed spitting on the corpses of the strike-breakers. The wounded who survived feared for their lives even as they recovered in the hospital.

In all, twenty-three men died over a forty-eight-hour period in the "Herrin massacre." It remains the deadliest mass murder stemming from a labor conflict in U.S. history—a shocking outburst of anarchy

[4] https://www.nbcchicago.com/blogs/ward-room/The-12-Most-Corrupt-Public-Officials-In-Illinois-History-S-Glenn-Young-136674698.html

that went unpunished at the time and remained a topic largely avoided and unrecognized in what was still a union town until just a few years ago.

Not only was Herrin a place of great labor strife when my father arrived, it was also constantly roiled by the newly rising Ku Klux Klan. With the onset of Prohibition, the Klan was running rampant throughout southern Illinois, riding a wave of anti-alcohol, anti-Catholic and anti-immigrant fervor. The Klan saw themselves as self-appointed defenders of public morals and launched numerous raids against boot-legging operations and speakeasies in the region.

Of course, the Klan's crusade to rid the world of drink pitted them against local bootleggers like the rival Shelton and Birger gangs, who were locked in a vicious struggle to control the black market for booze. Books touching on this particularly violent period in the region refer to this part of southern Illinois as "Bloody Williamson"—the county that encompassed Herrin and the county seat Marion where it all was centered.

Making matters worse, in 1923, the KKK recruited a former Treasury Prohibition agent named S. Glenn Young who had been fired from his federal job not only for killing a man during a raid on a still operation, but also keeping the $157 he confiscated for personal use and traveling with his mistress while on official business. Quite a guy. In addition to joining the Klan, Young was simultaneously deputized by the local Prohibition Commissioner, whereupon he continued to conduct violent raids against illegal bars and still operations—and make hundreds of arrests.

After an anti-Klan riot in Herrin left a Klanman's son dead, Young also arrested the sheriff and assumed all local law enforcement powers unto himself—acting on behalf the Klan. It was a local coup in essence and the power clearly went to Young's head for in short order he was indicted for multiple abuses including false imprisonment, conspiracy, kidnapping, assault with attempt to murder, assault with deadly weapons, falsely assuming an office, robbery, larceny, riot and malicious intent. Even the ne'er-do-wells in the Klan tired of Young's extreme actions and sidelined him. The "klan dry raider" as he was known was later shot dead in a Herrin cigar store on January 24,

1925—in the same room where he had staged his first booze raid some four years prior.

My father had been fortunate to avoid armed conflict in World War I, but now he was thrust squarely into the middle of another battlefield in southern Illinois. Open cultural warfare raged between the moralists and nativists on one side, and the economic opportunists— immigrants legally offering cheaper labor and bootleggers seeking and selling illegal liquor—on the other.

Just before my father arrived, the Ministers' Association of Williamson County had issued a lengthy joint statement. It underscored the lawless and dangerous state of affairs in and around Herrin, saying, in part:

> *The imprisonment of innocent men upon unfounded charges must cease. The persons guilty of these outrages must be brought to justice without favor or partisanship. Honest witnesses must not be so cowed that they will fear to give evidence. The courts must dispense justice punishing the guilty and protecting the innocent. To do that, we need a State Attorney who will enforce the law and a Sheriff who will apprehend real criminals. We have neither.*

I imagine what it must have been like to be a man preaching morality and peace in a lawless, dangerous place like Herrin. He persevered, but the dark times brought him not only incredible professional challenges, but also personal tragedy. On September 29, 1925, he and Helen suffered the stillborn birth of a baby girl. They named her Jewell Eloise and buried her the next day in the Herrin City Cemetery, where, three years before, 16 victims of that union coal strike massacre were put in unmarked graves. Only just recently was it learned that these massacre casualties were buried in Block 15 of the cemetery, which was once a "potter's field" or section reserved for the unknown, the poor and the unwanted. I believe Jewell was buried there too.

In April 1928, my father completed his second associate pastoral assignment in nearby Marion, the county seat of Williamson, another town rocked by unrest. After his ordination as a full minister, the couple moved to north Texas and the city of Troup—where Dad had received a unanimous call to serve as pastor in his own right there. The Wards had arrived in Texas at last.

Compared to the chaos and danger the couple had experienced in southern Illinois, Troup, Texas was a far more welcoming and civil community. It had about 1,800 residents in 1930; as the next decade unfolded, the oil boom in east Texas made it a key railroad stop and added to the pace of economic activity.

Troup was a far better place to raise a family. On June 15, 1931, Dad and Helen welcomed my half-sister Shirley Sue Ward. Shirley was born in what was then known as the "Baptist Hospital" in Houston. What they were doing so far from Troup, I have no idea. It might have been because that Baptist Hospital in Houston was the very first Baptist healthcare institution in Texas and had already developed a national reputation for the quality of its care. By 1920, it had 200 beds, and by 1946 it had become known as the Memorial Baptist Hospital. Today, we know it as Memorial-Hermann Hospital—another one of the great medical institutions in the Texas Medical Center.

Their excitement and joy soon yielded once more to grief. Helen Ward was diagnosed with chronic myeloid leukemia—an exotic disease at the time, for which there was no known cure. She went south to Nan Travis Hospital in Jacksonville, Texas for treatments, but slipped quickly away—dying on November 18, 1935, after eleven years of marriage. Dad had escaped the horrors of war and the conflicts of southern Illinois, but he had not been able to find lasting joy. He had already buried one child; now, he had lost Helen and had a motherless baby daughter. How dark those days must have seemed to him.

Just the next year, however, while earning an advanced degree at Baylor University in Waco, my father met Mary Warren, an undergraduate student from Dallas. He was forty-one; she was twenty-four. Later in her life, my mother confided to me that their friends were initially not enthusiastic about the union—and my mother's parents were *definitely* against her marrying such an older man with a child. They relented, however, and the couple was married on October 17, 1937, at Cliff Temple Baptist Church in Dallas.

A year after his second trip down the aisle, my father received a calling to relocate from Troup to Mineola in East Texas to become pastor of the Baptist Church there. "It would have done your heart good to see unanimity in that meeting, and you see they were of one mind and one spirit," his letter of invitation read. "We do not think there is any doubt that the Lord wants you on this field, and this church is prepared to meet any condition you might set up."

So, Rev. Henry M. Ward, together now with Mrs. Mary Ward and seven year-old Shirley Ward, was on the move again—and their traveling road show was about to add an act.

Sgt. Henry Martin Ward during World War I. Had that conflict lasted longer, I might not ever have been born.

With my maternal grandfather, Jesse Warren, who was a streetcar motorman in Dallas for over 40 years. Note the matching uniforms.

3

DINOSAURS

"**E**XTRA!! Pastor HM Ward Summoned in the Night" screamed the May 6, 1939, headline of the special bulletin printed on the back of *The Builder*, the newsletter of the First Baptist Church of Mineola, Texas. It went on to read:

> *Our pastor received a peremptory summons at 3:30 Saturday morning to appear immediately in Dallas, Texas. A young preacher, who upon his arrival in that City, assumed the name of David Henry Ward, claimed to be close kin to our pastor; therefore he secured the services of Mr J.T. Warren to send such summons. Upon arriving in Dallas, Pastor Ward went immediately to the appointed meeting place, but was kept waiting with quite a deal of anxiety until the hour of 'High Twelve' before the stranger made his appearance. The pastor declared forthwith and immediately that he had never seen the Stranger before; however, after much observation and discussion by a score of Genealogists, the decision was reached that the young man's claim is only half-true, owing to the fact that a marked resemblance to Mrs Ward can very easily be detected. He has round face, long fingers, and pretty little mouth, all of which are very much like Mrs Ward; but by further study it was found that he has ten fingers, ten toes, two ears, and one nose, very much like the pastor; also, he is somewhat bald, has a thin layer of light blonde hair, and is possessed of a good tenor voice...*

With such a birth announcement, it seems I was fated to go into the news business.

Many people have told me that you can't remember things that happen before you are two years old, but I distinctly remember the parsonage where we lived on East Kilpatrick Street in Mineola, Texas in 1941. It was a two-story house near the town square, with big columns on the front and a cement porch where I would ride my tricycle up and down, backwards and forwards, over and over and over. It was a wonderful time.

I also have clear memories of my father taking me with him on his walks through the downtown area in Mineola, which was about the size of a postage stamp, and how our housekeeper, Hattie, loved me and took care of me.

In September of 1941, we moved to Huntsville, Texas, because my father was named the pastor of the First Baptist Church. There, we had an old hound dog—strictly an outdoor dog—named Bozo. He was always lying around the backyard, or off to the side, usually sleeping most of the day. Meanwhile, our neighbors down the bottom of the hill had a big, red chow dog they kept in a cage. One morning, when I was about four years old, I was in the front of the house playing in the sand in the yard when that chow dog had managed to get out. He came up the hill and was on the other side of the street when I first saw him. I remembered what my parents told me: "Son, if an animal is anywhere near you, you just freeze. Be very still."

That's exactly what I did. I went absolutely still, but that chow dog saw me and came charging across the street. I started screaming, but before I knew it that old chow dog had me down on my back. I was flailing away at that thing, and saw my poor, horrified mother coming out of the front door with a dish rag in her hand.

Right about that time, POW! Bozo hit that big chow dog from the side and knocked that thing about ten feet. Bozo just lit into that chow dog and finally chased it off. My mother brought me in the house and cleaned the dirt off and the little scratches that I had. I was really not hurt at all—just stunned and scared more than anything.

That night, my mother had planned to serve a big steak for our dinner, but don't you know Bozo got that sirloin.

Who could argue with that?

On Sunday, December 7, 1941, our family attended church as usual, after which my mother prepared a big lunch. Around three o'clock in the afternoon, the phone suddenly started to ring off the hook. People were calling and telling us they had heard the startling news that Japanese air forces had attacked the U.S. Naval Station in Pearl Harbor. Before long, people started coming over to our house.

Later that afternoon, my father called the local radio station, KSAM in Huntsville, and had them announce that the First Baptist Church was going to open—and we would have radios there where people could listen to the news. Then we went back down to the church, where we remained well into the night, very much in shock. I had seen my mother cry before that day, but that was the first time I saw tears streaming down my father's cheeks. As President Roosevelt said, it was a date which would live in infamy.

Like millions who lived through that defining moment in world history, over my lifetime I have tried to learn as much as I could about World War II. I am endlessly curious about what caused such a global conflagration, such as how the Japanese Navy was able to get so close to Pearl Harbor without being detected. To this day, I still read everything I can about that war. I've read so many stories about it, I almost feel like a World War II veteran. I don't think that anyone alive during that horrible time could ever forget it. Nor can I forget that my father, then forty-six, registered for the draft—even though the cut-off age was forty-five.

At an early age in Huntsville, I made four really good friends: Jody Kirk, George Evans, Sandy Lowery and George Marshall Ricks. We lived within a quarter mile of each other—and in short order we got to be so tight that our mothers made a deal where each mother would take all five boys one day of the week, Monday through Friday. Such an arrangement would give each mother four days "off" during the week. It was a great idea. We boys had a ball, and our mothers enjoyed having four days when they did not have to manage five innocent but unruly boys.

It being the World War II era, our little gang all had fake wooden rifles and pistols. We would get together, stage our own war, and pretend like we were attacking the enemy. Behind George Evans' house there was a heavily wooded area, and we would play like we were on an island in the Pacific Ocean, shooting at the enemy.

There was also a little pond back in that wooded area where we would go and catch crawfish. We'd put a little piece of bacon on a string, pull the crawfish out, then we would pinch the pinchers off of them and race the things! It's funny: none of us at that time, back in the 1940s, ever thought about eating a crawfish. Years later, thanks to my wife Laura's fabulous cooking, crawfish became one of my favorite dishes.

If torturing crawfish was not your cup of tea, at that time you could go to the movies for nine cents. The Life Theatre, about a block down from the main square in Huntsville, showed all of the serious films. Across the street at the Avon Theatre, they offered double-feature cowboy movies on Saturday afternoons where we saw western stars such as Gene Autry and his wonder horse, Champion; Roy Rogers and his horse, Trigger; and Dale Evans and her horse, Buttermilk. I don't remember Lash LaRue's horse, but I do recall that he didn't carry a gun. He carried a bull whip instead, which is where he got the nickname "Lash." Also, Hop Along Cassady. All of them had faithful side-kicks along with them, but my favorite was Fuzzy St. John, a bearded old guy with a weird way of walking.

Around the corner from the movie theatres in Huntsville was a drug store where you could get a soda for a nickel. The comic books there cost a dime, and don't you know I wish I still had some of those old comic books today. They would be worth a fortune! When I was nine or ten, on Friday and Saturday evenings, I had a paper route right around the Square in downtown Huntsville. I would stand on the corner in front of the Café Texan and sell the evening *Houston Chronicle*.

Technically, that was my first job in the news business.

Another friend of mine, Rowland Floyd, lived just down the street. His father, Dr. Willis W. Floyd, was a physicist, and Dr. Floyd spent quite a bit of time during the World War II years at a facility in Tennessee. We didn't know why he was there, but he was working on the Manhattan Project—to develop a nuclear weapon. As we soon discovered, he and his co-workers were successful in that endeavor. Dr. Floyd and his group helped us win the war, which makes them bona fide heroes in my book.

One day, Rowland and I decided we would build a small house—like a tree house, but on the ground—out of some old packing crates and wooden boxes. We worked at cobbling it together on the side of his house, and finally one night we wore our mothers down enough to get permission to spend the night in it. I would sleep on the bottom, and Rowland would climb up and sleep in the top area. At least, that was the idea.

Well, when we tried to do that, we found out that that little house was too short. We could not stretch out in those boxes. But being stubborn kids, we decided we would try to stick it out. About three o'clock in the morning, we finally gave up and went back into the house to get some sleep. Knowing when to let reason overcome my pride and enthusiasm was an important lesson that I would keep learning as the years went by.

Rowland and I had lots of adventures together. I remember one in particular that could have had a tragic ending. Down at the bottom of the hill on the same street where he lived is today's Sam Houston Park; it still includes the old steamboat house—a two-story house built to look like a steamboat. It was in that house that the Father of Texas a nd the hero of San Jacinto, Sam Houston, died. There was also a small log cabin there—I think it was a replica of the first cabin that Houston built. Also in Sam Houston Park is a small lake built in the shape of Texas.

Rowland and I were walking through that park one day, up near what must have been the panhandle area of that little lake. It was overgrown with weeds and grass, and it looked like solid ground to me. So I walked towards it and of course I fell into the lake. The water was over my head; I had to keep jumping off the bottom just to breathe. Rowland turned around, ran to his home—around three hundred yards away—and got his father. Dr. Floyd ran down to the lake and pulled me out of the water. Thank goodness I did not get caught in the weeds and pulled under.

Although I would grow up to have some very serious accidents as an adult, I don't remember any other close calls as a child—scrapes and bruises were routine for kids who played hard back then, but they were unremarkable. When I turned five years old, I got pneumonia and spent about a week in the hospital there. I remember my mother being constantly by my side because I had to get a shot of penicillin— which they had only just started using to treat infections—every three or four hours. While she must have been terrified, I don't have any memories of my life being threatened at the time.

Other memories of that time are strong. When I started school, in September of 1944, my mother drove me to the schoolhouse. I clearly recall that the last thing she said to me before I got out of the car was, "David, if anyone asks you, we are English." That was fine with me. I didn't think much more about it—especially since nobody asked.

Fast forward about thirty years. I was at my parent's home, which was then in Jacksonville, Texas, for a Thanksgiving dinner. I don't know how it came up, but at one point I said, "Of course we are English." My mother looked at my father, and then they both looked at me. "Where did you get that idea, son?" she asked.

I replied, "You told me on the first day of school. When I got to school, you said if anybody asks, we're English. But nobody asked."

They laughed in disbelief! My mother said, "Son, we have a strong dose of German heritage on both sides of the family." Back in September of 1944, in the middle of World War II, she explained, it wouldn't have been good to be considered German. So, I was full-blooded English…at least until I was about thirty-five years old.

While we lived in Huntsville, my father drove a maroon, four-door 1939 Chevrolet. It was known as the "preacher's car." Whenever he came down the street, the neighbors would all say, "Here comes Brother Ward." Our family spent a lot of time in that car, mostly going to and from church.

I was in the back seat of that car in August of 1945 when the breaking news came over the radio that World War II was over. This was a week after U.S. forces detonated atomic bombs at Hiroshima and Nagasaki in Japan, a devastating and decisive blow. "Japan surrenders, Japan surrenders," came the urgent report, crackling across the radio on the Mutual Broadcast System. "Now repeating the entire bulletin: The Japanese government has accepted the Allied formula embodied in the note dispatched to Tokyo by the United States…"

With Germany surrendering earlier in May of 1945, the news of Tokyo's capitulation meant the Allies had prevailed. Good had defeated evil, as we saw it.

I was in the back seat listening and could sense something important was happening. But at the age of six, I was trying to make sense of it all. "Well, who won?" I finally asked.

My mother and father both said, "We won. America won the war."

"I know that," I replied, "but I mean WHO won the war?" As a child, I thought there would be one person, one man, who won the war for us. Now, after having broadcast the news for so many decades, I have such a clear understanding of how complicated world events are that the innocence of that question amazes me. I didn't understand very much back then, but I definitely had the desire to learn more and the willingness to ask questions to get to the bottom of things.

It was also in that 1939 Chevrolet that my father drove us to Navasota to catch the train to and from Dallas, to see my mother's parents. The Southern Pacific "Sunbeam" had a steam locomotive with a silver front; it pulled red, orange and black passenger cars and ran from Houston to Dallas. Those trips started my love affair with trains which continues to this day.

Once we arrived in Dallas, it only got better: there I got to ride on the streetcar with my grandfather. Jesse Thurman Warren drove a Dallas streetcar for forty-two years, and my sister Mary and I basically grew up on those streetcars. We loved them, and our grandfather's daily riders got to know us. When I was about four years old, my grandmother Alice Viola "Ola" Warren made me a child-sized streetcar motorman's uniform, fashioned from one of my grandfather's old uniforms.

My grandfather could probably drive a streetcar up a flight of stairs if he had to, but he wasn't worth a flip at driving a regular car because you had to steer the thing. I can clearly remember my grandfather driving us someplace in their car, and my grandmother Ola constantly saying, "Thurman, watch out!"

When Dallas retired all those streetcars in 1956 and took them off the streets, my grandfather told me they were making a huge mistake. The bus makers, oil comapnies and tire companies all wanted to sell their products to people who drove normal cars—not the streetcar— and they finally made it happen. But, my grandfather was right: the silent electric streetcars now are making a comeback in both Dallas and Houston, and in other cities as well in the form of light rail. I still think they should be called streetcars.

On my seventh birthday, in 1946, my grandparents gave me a Lionel electric train. It was a steam engine with three passenger cars. The passenger cars had lights inside, as well as automatic couplers—a new feature at the time from Lionel. It was also the first year that they used metal to make toys. After World War II was over in 1945, they added an oval track to it.

I played with that train like crazy, adding track and trains over the years to the extent that, years later in Houston, I converted a third-floor bedroom of my condo to a train room. I had trains running all around and up and over bridges. Here, there, everywhere. So, yes, I thoroughly enjoyed my trains.

On my ninth birthday, as a present, my mother drove me and my childhood friend Bud Scarborough to Navasota, where we caught the Southern Pacific Sunbeam to Dallas. It was just me and Bud on that trip, traveling all by ourselves. I felt great.

I had been on trains before, but Bud had not—so I was the seasoned traveler between us. When we arrived in Dallas, my grandparents picked us up at Union Station, and we spent the night with them. The next morning my grandfather drove us to the train station, and we caught the Missouri Pacific Texas Eagle. It ran from Dallas to St. Louis, but we got tickets to Marshall in East Texas: that's where my Aunt Bessie Carter lived.

My grandmother packed us a sack lunch—one sandwich for each of us. Around noontime, I said, "Come on, Bud, we're going to the dining car." After they seated us at a table, we pulled out our little sack lunch. The other passengers on the train got quite a kick out of this—two little boys sitting there. Each of us ordered a glass of milk, and we split an order of French fries. The total bill came to two dollars. Bud and I dug into our coin purses, and each put a dollar on the tray. The waiter came back, picked it up, looked at it, and just turned his head toward the ceiling of the dining car and he said "Uh, oh." Immediately, it hit me he was upset.

"Oh no, Bud," I said. "We didn't leave him a tip."

So we both dug in our coin purses again, and each put a quarter on that tray—a fifty-cent tip on a two-dollar tab. The waiter looked down and saw it, and this time he happily uttered, "Mighty fine, mighty fine."

Arriving in Marshall, my Aunt Bessie picked us up, and we spent the night with her. She ran the dining hall at East Texas Baptist College there in Marshall, which gave her the authority to work the freight elevator. You would have thought we had died and gone to heaven, Bud and I had such a ball just riding up and down on that elevator. The next morning, Aunt Bessie took us back to the train station, where we boarded the Missouri Pacific Texas Eagle again. This time, we got off in Phelps—about 12 miles east of Huntsville—where my mother picked us up. After my first solo trip on a train, I felt like a world traveler.

As a result of those happy childhood experiences, I wanted more than anything to become a steam locomotive engineer and drive trains for a living. Well, I might as well have fallen in love with a dinosaur. By the time I grew up, all the steam locomotives were gone. I did get one chance to "drive" one in 2014, when Union Pacific brought one of its big 4-8-4 northern-type steam locomotives to Texas. I got to ride up in the engine cab and blow the whistle all the way into Houston. I even got to pull the throttle open and start the train at one stop. It was quite a ride. While I wasn't able to be a railroad engineer, over the years I would find myself in many other fast machines, not always with the happy endings of these early train trips.

Along with trains, I also fell in love for the first time with an actual person while living in Huntsville. Malynn Hardy was in my second grade class. On our last night in Huntsville, my sister Shirley drove me over to Malynn's house, and we sat on her living room couch. For the first and only time, I held her in my arms and gave her a kiss. When my sister came to pick me up, I floated across her front lawn down to our car, and distinctly heard in my mind the song, "I Only Have Eyes for You."

> *Are there stars in the sky,*
> *maybe millions of people go by,*
> *but they all disappear from view,*
> *for I only have eyes for you…*

When I got home, my mother was in the kitchen. As I walked passed her, my head still in the clouds, I said, "Oh Mommy, isn't love wonderful?"

"Yes, it is David," she replied. "Yes, it is. God is love."

Years later I saw Malynn in Houston, but it just wasn't the same. There can only be one first love.

Incidentally, Malynn had been present a year earlier when we had a class picnic in the spring—in a big field out to the south of Huntsville. After lunch, we chose up sides to play softball. I was one of the first ones at bat, and I hit the ball pretty good. I ran around the bases and made my way to where I thought we had put third base, but instead stepped into a big pile of cow droppings there. My feet slid out from under me, and I fell right into it.

One of the teachers took me home in her car, but since I was covered with that cow excrement, she made me ride standing up in the back of her car. When I got home, my mother was horrified. She stripped those clothes off, threw them away, and made me take a long, hot bath. That was one of my most embarrassing times ever in front of all my little friends in the fifth grade.

All the while, my mother and father stayed very active in the church. Dad continued to preach there and around Texas. My mother sometimes played the piano at Sunday services. They sang very nicely together, too.

But in a family blessed with a lot of musicality, it was my half-sister Shirley who was the most talented. She started playing piano around age three, and by the time she was ten she was playing revivals around Texas with my father, as well as meetings and concerts of all kinds.

In July of 1941, for example, *The Wood County Democrat* in Quitman, Texas (just north of Mineola) ran a story with the headline "Miss Shirley Ward Amazes Friends with Knowledge of Piano," in which they reported she "amazed a group of friends here Monday night after the revival meeting had dismissed with her uncanny knowledge of the piano and musical tones."

The *Wood Country Democrat* story continued:

> *While a few friends lingered for a moment of conversation after the services, Miss Shirley began to run her tiny fingers over the piano keyboard, and one of the ladies asked her if she could play. It turned out that she had been playing since the age of about three years, and in the manner of a real genius.*

My sister Mary to this day believes that Shirley was such a fine piano player she would have been good enough to compete in, and win, the Van Cliburn International Piano Competition had it been started by that time. Shirley routinely tackled and mastered some of the hardest pieces by Sergei Rachmaninoff, Beethoven and other top-notch composers.

In May of 1948, *The Paris News* northeast of Dallas featured a photo and lead story of Shirley on their Society page, announcing she would be playing there as part of a twenty-concert series before entering Baylor that fall. Shirley was very much a child prodigy, and looking back, I feel a little sheepish that my sister Mary and I used to annoy her with some regularity as she diligently practiced in the living room of our home.

One day, from another room, I heard Shirley playing, followed by my father's distinct voice singing a love song to my mother. Curious, I crawled to the door that was right next to the piano and peeped through. From that vantage point, I could see Shirley's face at the piano as well as my mother's and father's. Shirley was crying, very silently, as she played that love song—the pain of loss and longing so evident on her face. Her mother had died when she was barely four years old, and it moved me very much to see her so sad playing for our father to sing to a person who, to her, was another woman.

Shirley started at Baylor University in Waco in 1948 and played flute in the band. That fall, my dad and I attended a football game there—and saw Shirley perform, which was fun. After the game was over, we got in the car to go back to Huntsville. When we got to the edge of Waco, just out of town, my father pulled over to the side of the road and said, "David, you get in the driver's seat and you drive us home to Huntsville."

I couldn't believe it. I had driven our car backwards and forwards, up and down our driveway there in Huntsville a number of times, so I knew how to work the gears. So I got behind the wheel and drove that car all the way home. At night. I was all of nine years old.

When we got home, I went running in the house. I couldn't wait to tell my mother. "Mommy, I drove the car home from Waco!"

She wasn't as excited as I was. "Henry, is that true?" she asked.

"Yes, he did," Dad replied. "And he did very well."

My mother was furious! Perhaps she had a sense of the trouble that cars would cause me later, or perhaps she was just aghast at the idea of a nine-year-old driving across Texas.

*The Ward family circa 1945, still living in Huntsville. That's my big sister
Shirley standing next to my father—her early career as a
piano phenom had already taken off.*

Growing up in Huntsville, I had a group of four great friends
with whom I had fun, played war and tortured crawfish.
Top: George Marshall Ricks – Jodie Kirk
Bottom: Sandy Lowry – George Evans – David Henry Ward

The passenger train Wabash Cannonball ran daily from Detroit to St. Louis.
I would see it almost every afternoon while we lived in Granite City, Illinois.

4

PLENTY OF TROUBLE

On January 1, 1949, the first and only TV station in Houston at the time—KLEE-TV, which was re-named KPRC-TV a year later after the Hobby family bought it from original owner Albert Lee—made its inaugural broadcast. They signed on around 9:30 p.m. on New Year's Day after a technical delay of a few hours. The very first words heard on air reportedly came from the chief engineer, Paul Huhndorff: "There's been trouble, plenty of trouble."[5] From that somewhat inauspicious start, they began airing a variety of music and entertainment programming Monday through Friday evenings to the two thousand people in Houston, and anyone else in the region, who had a TV set. There was no local news at this time, though I seem to recall they produced a sports report every so often.

Seventy miles to the north, in Huntsville, the only person who had a television set was Doctor Black. One of his sons, Roland Black, was a classmate of mine in elementary school. One day he invited a bunch of us guys out to his house to see this new-fangled contraption. I remember the Blacks' model featured a very small, round screen, about ten inches, in a big box on the floor. It was quite the draw.

Since there were no daytime programs, the station put up a black-and-white test pattern with an old Indian chief's head and lines all around it. At the time, I had no idea what that meant. Nevertheless, we'd sit there and just stare at that damn test pattern. To think that that picture was somehow flying through the air all the way from Houston was just amazing to me. In a way, it still is.

---

[5]   https://www.houstonarchitecture.com/haif/topic/4728-back-when-houston-had-just-one-tv-station/

In the Spring of 1951, my father was called to another church, and we moved from Huntsville to Granite City, Illinois—right across the Mississippi River from St. Louis. That's where and when the Wards got our first television set, which sat in the living room. It was a Westinghouse, with a black-and-white screen that was very small—especially by modern standards: it was a twenty-inch.

One night, I remember my sister Mary and I were watching the Milton Berle show alone. As my mom and dad came in the room, Uncle Miltie introduced his next act. It featured a woman, I think they called her Dagmore. Anyway, she started doing an imitation of a striptease. "Da ta da da" and all. Well, one look at that, and my mother and father were horrified.

"Oh my God!" Dad exclaimed as he turned the TV off. "That was terrible; you should never watch anything like that."

"Dad, Mary and I, we had nothing to do with that," I explained to him, truthfully.

"Okay, well, when something like that comes on the television, you turn it off," he instructed us. Happily, our TV privileges were not revoked. In the afternoons, like so many other kids, Mary and I could still rush home from school to watch "The Howdy Doody Show," featuring Buffalo Bob and his puppet Howdy Doody.

My father had been called to be the pastor of the Third Baptist Church in Granite City. My father hated that place, and so did I. We were so unhappy there. My father rarely if ever listed it on his resume or any other accountings of his life's story, and I really did not want to revisit those memories as I reflected on my own life for these pages.

Two years before, when I was ten, my father drove home in a brand new, 1949 four-door, green Packard. That was a huge step up from the old '39 Chevy we had been driving. I am pretty sure Dad made a deal with the Packard dealer there in Huntsville and got it for a substantial reduction in price. Dad loved that big, beautiful Packard, but it led to trouble at the church. Before long, word was getting around that the members at First Baptist in Huntsville thought their pastor was getting a little "uppity."

During the trip drive from Huntsville up to Granite City, my father discovered that his big, beautiful Packard that caused him so much trouble was also a lemon. He had to put a quart of oil in the thing every hundred miles, and as it was, it only got about eight miles per gallon of gasoline. But, he continued to drive it around Granite City, because we had no choice.

Adding to our collective misery, the congregation in the Third Baptist Church of Granite City turned out to be almost fanatics. Not only did they not approve of Dad's fancy car, they also were shocked that the preacher would let his children go see movies. And they were doubly shocked that the preacher and his wife also went to the movie theatre. It's like they preferred living in the dark ages.

Another interesting development that I am sure did not please the congregants at Third Baptist Church was the fact that, while we lived in Granite City, my mother took a job with the St. Louis Streetcar Company. To be sure, my father was not at all happy about it, either. He thought the husband's role should be to provide for his family. My mother had worked at the Dallas Railway & Transit Company when she was younger, but this was the first time she had not so much as asked or suggested *but told* my father she would be taking the job in St. Louis. My father was so upset they didn't really speak for about a week, but he got over it.

Just as there was no air conditioning anywhere in Huntsville, there was also no central heating in Granite City, either. Our home was heated by a coal-burning furnace, and it was my job, along with my sister's, Mary, to go down in the basement and shovel coal into that furnace about once every other day during the winter season. A coal truck would come deliver coal to our house once a week and dump it right through a window in the basement that went to the coal bin.

During the one full winter we spent in Granite City, we woke up one morning to find thirteen inches of snow on the ground. Snow was everywhere. Mary and I were excited. We had never seen snow like that. We wanted to go out and build a snowman, but my father shot that down. "No, you have to go to school," he said. "Up here they don't turn out school for snow. They go to school come rain or shine."

Well, I trudged the blocks to our school through all the snow, and when I got there, I was the only child there. The janitor said, "Are you kidding? It's snowed out here. We got over a foot of snow. School is closed."

No one was more relieved than me. All the schoolkids there called me "Tex," no doubt owing to my high, squeaky, childhood Texas drawl. Looking back, it seemed like I was in a fight every two or three days.

That snow was on the ground for about a week. The first day or so, it was kind of pretty—very white and pristine. But with the air pollution up there from all the steel mills and furnaces, within three days that snow had turned gray. By the time it all melted away at the end of the week, it was almost black.

As far as I was concerned, the only redeeming value of Granite City was the railroad tracks about ten blocks from our home. Six different railroads had their main lines from Chicago to St. Louis running through Granite City. I would ride my bicycle over there most every afternoon after school, just to watch the trains go by. There was a train, freight or passenger, every eight minutes or so.

I particularly liked the afternoons when the Wabash Cannonball came through—that famous train the Carter Family and later Roy Acuff sang about. It would be followed by another Wabash train, I don't remember the name, about five minutes later. One day the Wabash Cannonball would have a big, black steam engine on it, and the train that followed would have a diesel engine. The next day, the Cannonball would have the diesel engine, and the train behind it would have a steam engine. This was the transition period when railroads were going from steam to diesel, and it was interesting to me how those two trains seemed like they traded out engines every day.

My father had a hard time in Illinois when he was starting his ministry, and my own experience there was difficult, too. They say that we block out painful memories, and that might explain why the trains are the only thing I remember strongly from that unhappy time. Luckily, my parents felt the same way I did about Granite City, and my dad was working hard to make things better for the Ward family.

*I am not sure where or why Dad was fussing with this mule,
but clearly he was as determined as it was stubborn.*

At home in Mineola with Dad and my sister Shirley.

5

SUMMER BREEZE

After a year-and-a-half in Granite City, we were all ready to get the hell out of there. To go anywhere.

Anywhere but there.

In the fall of 1952, Dad had been working for some time to try and secure a new assignment, and he had developed a pretty good lead in Cisco, Texas—about fifty miles east of Abilene, and one hundred miles west of Fort Worth. One Sunday afternoon, he came to me with tears in his eyes. "David," he said, "I was expecting a call today from the pulpit committee in Cisco…" His voice was slow, soft, sad.

He removed his glasses to wipe away the tears and continued "…but that call hasn't come, and I don't think it's going to come."

I tried to reassure my father as best I could, but this news left me as disappointed and frustrated as he was. Ten minutes later, however, the phone rang—it was the call my father had been expecting, and the news was good. We would soon be Texas-bound!

You've never seen four happier people than the Ward family that day.

Once in Cisco, the fancy but impractical Packard disappeared very quickly, replaced by a 1952 four-door Ford. It had been a demonstrator, and I learned to drive that thing. I even got my driver's license at the age of fourteen. You could do that in Texas back in those days.

The next year, I bought my first car. It was a 1928 Model A Ford Coupe, with a rumble seat. I paid just thirty-five dollars for it. It had no front fenders, and no exhaust system: the exhaust came right out of the manifold. There was no ignition key in this old Model A, either: just two wires sticking out of the dashboard that you used to start the car. It sounded like a tractor coming down the road, but it did have a factory-installed 1928 AM radio—and most importantly, that radio worked!

Every morning during the school year, I would drive Mary to her junior high school—and most afternoons, if I didn't have band practice, I would pick her up, too. Of course, that was long before the days of cell phones, so it was hard to change plans suddenly if needed.

In March of 1953, before we set out for school, I was glued to the TV watching NBC's pioneering broadcaster Dave Garroway as he hosted the fairly new *Today Show* from Yucca Flats in Nevada. They were covering an atomic bomb test on live TV—or at least trying to do so. For whatever reason, maybe poor weather, they scrubbed the test for several days running, Finally, on March 17th, they were able to proceed.

As a way of trying to calm public fears about nuclear testing, the test itself was open not only to Garroway and his NBC crew but also to the general news media. Some six hundred reporters and Defense Department personnel gathered to view the historic occasion from the so-called "News Nob," an area about seven miles south of the actual testing site.

At 8:20 a.m., Eastern time, a 2,700-pound weapon exploded on top of a 300-foot detonation tower. Even though I was watching on a black-and-white television, I was stunned by what I saw next. Oh, my Lord God in Heaven, what immense power. Growing up during World War II, I never—ever—had any sympathy for the Japanese until I watched that live blast. I realized how horrific it must have been to be in Hiroshima and Nagasaki back in 1945. Just to imagine all those people, civilians, babies, children under that thing because of what was then a blood-thirsty government in Tokyo—it was truly tragic.

I have one other vivid memory from that experience: Dave Garroway, another disc jockey-turned-anchor, closed that and every other *Today Show* telecast he hosted by simply raising his right hand, and saying "Peace." It seemed particularly fitting that day after watching that ominous mushroom cloud rise eerily from the desert floor. That memory was just one of the impressions that eventually would help me develop my own on-air persona in the years to come.

But at the time I wasn't focused on my eventual career, because I was fully engaged being a Texas high school boy. In Cisco, I met the guy who would become my best friend over the next three years. His name was Daryl George Crofts. He had a twin sister named Dorothy. Everybody shortened her name to "Dot," so Daryl became "Dash." Dash and I first got to know each other in the school band. He played drums and I played trumpet.

Dash and I went everywhere together. We went to the movies. We went hunting. We went on double dates. On some of those dates, I would be able to drive my dad's Ford, but on others we'd have to ride in my old Model A. Dash and his date would sit in the rumble seat. Those girls did not like climbing into that rumble seat.

My mother did not like Dash Crofts one bit, but I did. It was with Dash that I started smoking cigarettes (which I do not recommend to anyone). My parents hated that. At night, I had to be home no later than 10:30, and my mother would routinely walk by me and sniff me. "You've been smoking again," she would say, disappointed.

In 1954, Dash and I drove a couple of dates to Abilene in my father's Ford to see a concert by a relatively unknown singer named Elvis Presley. There was a popular drive-in restaurant on the west side of Abilene where we went to eat an early dinner before the concert. Parked out front was a big, pink Cadillac that had a bass fiddle strapped to the top of it. We thought, "My goodness, that's got to be Elvis' car!"

We went inside to get a couple of hamburgers. Elvis was not in there, but there were some young men that we figured must have been in his band. Sure enough, we saw them on stage a little later that night backing up Elvis, who was young and very slender. When he came out on the stage and started singing and gyrating, all the girls started screaming hysterically. Dash and I really couldn't understand what this fascination was.

Another time, Dash and I and a friend were driving around Cisco in that other boy's Buick. We had bought some little penny balloons and filled them up with water and went driving along looking for any of our friends to attack. At one point, we saw a friend's car coming the other way. We stopped that Buick, jumped out, and inundated that other car with water balloons. The driver rolled down the window, and wouldn't you know it, it wasn't our friend! It was his father, so we apologized profusely. The man, though clearly perturbed, said, "That's all right" and drove away.

We were still driving around downtown Cisco when we came upon that same father, only this time he was in a police car—and pointing us out to the officer. I was sitting in the back seat when I saw what was happening and started smashing water balloons just as fast as I could—trying to get rid of the evidence. When the officer walked up and told us to get out of the car, I opened the back door of the car and watched helplessly as water came pouring out. Obviously, we were guilty.

That police officer issued us a ticket and told us to be in the Mayor's office the next day. Right around noon, we walked down to City Hall. The Mayor fined us two dollars each for the water balloons. We then asked him, "Please, Mr. Mayor, since we're out of school and don't have an excuse, would you please call the school or write us an excuse so we can get back in school?"

He said, "I'll do better than that. I'll call the school principal." The Mayor then picked up the phone and told Buck Overall, the principal—that's right, a principal named Buck Overall—what had happened. Finally, he said rather ominously, "I hope you will take care of these boys."

Well, I didn't like the sound of that one bit. None of us did.

We walked back to the high school and, sure enough, Principal Overall was waiting for us. He took us into his office, gave us a lecture, and then gave each of us two big swats on the butt with a big wooden paddle he called the "Board of Education." I stood there and took my two licks, and it hurt like the dickens. When Dash received his swats, he went down on one knee. As we walked out, he said, "Oh, that was terrible, David. How did you manage not to collapse? I mean, he hit us pretty hard!"

That was the last time that we went water ballooning in Cisco.

In my old Model A, we also used to go out in the country and hunt jackrabbits, which were abundant in that area of west Texas. With its big balloon tires, the Model A was perfect for it. We could go off road and just take it across a field. We wouldn't go fifty feet or so before we'd scare up a jackrabbit. And at night, I could kind of herd those things because they kept trying to run to the dark. When they would turn and try to run to the right, I would turn to the right. If they tried to run to the left, I'd turn to the left a little.

For these nighttime expeditions, there usually would be two guys in the rumble seat, standing up and leaning over the top of that Model A with 22-caliber rifles. Dash usually sat in the right-hand seat with a rifle as well. When we took off after a jackrabbit, it sounded like a tank coming across the prairie. We killed a bunch of jackrabbits, threw them in the back of that car on the rumble seat, and took them to a guy on the northeast side of Cisco who would pay us twenty-five cents for each rabbit. What he did with those jackrabbits I have no idea, but we'd pick up two or three dollars a night, which was enough to put gas in that old Model A.

One night, Dash and I had our rifles out near Lake Cisco. The front headlight on that old Model A would usually swivel because it was loose, and I would turn that thing to where it pointed up and to the right. Then, we'd drive down this dusty road out there in the forest, and that light would shine up in the trees. That night, we saw these eyes looking back at us through the light. We stopped, got out, opened fire on that tree, and down came two raccoons. Dash taught me how to skin those raccoons, and I took those skins home and placed them on the cement porch to show my mother and dad.

Looking back, I now realize I was acting like the family dog or cat who kills something in the yard and brings it to the door seeking the approval of its master. That never goes well. My mother was less than impressed. "Get those things off of my porch!" she shrieked. So, I picked them up, and Dash took them home. The stain those two skins left was still on that porch when we left Cisco to move to Jacksonville a year or two later.

In the fall of 1955, our high school chartered a special train to take the football team and the band—and anyone else who wanted to go—to a town about eighty miles west of Abilene. I forget which town it was, but it was for a district playoff or a bi-district playoff football game. That train was packed full of people, as if half the town of Cisco went with us. I remember this special train had an old black steam engine on it. We rode it out there during the day, played the football game that night, and then got on the train and rode back to Cisco all night long. We arrived back early, early the next morning. While I don't remember the town or who won or lost the football game, I distinctly remember that train.

I have so many memories of Dash. Another time, out south of Cisco, he and I discovered an earthen dam across this little creek that a farmer or rancher had built. It formed a very sizeable pond that was also very deep, and it became our swimming hole. We would go skinny dipping out there after school and in the summers.

We would find old fence posts that had been discarded, they were about four inches square and six feet long—throw a few of them in the pond and go swimming with them. Well, one day, the Missouri Pacific Railroad unloaded a bunch of new crossties down near the railroad station in Cisco. It was a huge stack of crossties. These were eight inches square, and must have been seven, eight, maybe nine feet long. Dash and I were very excited when we saw them.

One night, we stole one of those crossties, put it in the back of his pick-up truck, and lugged it all the way out to our little swimming hole. We dragged it through the brush, threw it in the pond, and jumped in to go swimming with it. It had enough mass to hold both of us up. We could lie up on that big crosstie, and swim across the pond. I remember in the middle of the pond, we'd turn it up on one end and shove it down as far as we could under the water. That little pond was so deep, it never hit the bottom , but it would then come up shooting out of the water like a rocket. We had so much fun playing around with that crosstie.

There was, however, one thing we did not figure on. Those new crossties were soaked with creosote, a preservative that the railroad used to make their wooden crossties last longer. That creosote got all over us, and we came down with the most horrible rash on our chests, on our backs, on our legs and arms, all over. As a result, we spent many agonizing hours, over two or three days, getting over that.

I figure we paid for the sin of stealing that crosstie.

In later years, Dash played in a country band that had gigs around the Abilene area. Another player in that band was Jimmy Seals. Eventually, they got together with Danny Flores, known as Chuck Rio, who wrote the song "Tequila," and they became part of his group called The Champs—which also included Glen Campbell. They traveled all over the world playing rock 'n' roll tunes.

In the late 1950s, I got a postcard from Dash when I was living in Tyler, and The Champs were playing in Tokyo. The picture on that post card showed the beach in Galveston with the old Pleasure Pier in the background, and down on the beach, very small, you could see two boys and two girls. It turns out, I was one of the boys in that picture. I had driven to Galveston with a friend and our dates, and we were on the beach when a photographer up on Seawall Boulevard yelled down and said, "Look at the camera." We posed for him. How Dash got that postcard in Tokyo I will never know. When I talked with Dash a few years ago, he didn't remember either.

Years later, in 1969, Dash and Jimmy Seals formed their own group, Seals and Crofts. I'm sure you have heard their songs on the radio including "Summer Breeze" and "Hummingbird." I had, too, but I didn't make the connection to Dash at first. I thought they were saying "Seals and Cross." Quite some time later, someone told me, "No, that was Jimmy Seals and Dash Crofts." I was stunned to know that the singer of those popular songs was my old friend Dash.

Along with all the fun we had in Cisco, I also got my first real jobs. The first one was working in a service station. It was just to the west of the main downtown traffic light. My job was to pump gas, clean windshields, and all the general stuff that a young kid would do. I only worked there on the weekends, which meant only Friday evenings and Saturdays since my father would not allow me to work on Sundays.

My next job in Cisco, one that I had full-time during the summer, was working at a factory that made work gloves. The owner and operator usually hired one student to work a summer job there, but this particular summer he hired two of us—me and another young boy named Bobby Cluck. The gloves were made inside out because all the stitching on all the fingers was on the inside of the glove. Our main job, for which we were paid seventy-five cents an hour, was to turn the gloves right side out.

We would take a glove, right-handed or left-handed, stretch it over tubes that stuck up out of the middle of a machine. When we got the glove pulled down over it, we would press a button and plungers would come down from above and push those fingers down into the hole. Then we would pull the glove off of those tubes, and it would end up right side out. We had quotas to meet, and the old man told us that none of the students who had worked there before us had ever reached their quota.

Well, Bobby Cluck and I started competing against each other in that sweltering hot factory to see who could turn the most gloves out in a day. As a result of that competition, we both beat our quotas by the end of that summer. The general manager, as you can imagine, was just delighted, and we got a bonus.

I always felt poorly for the men who had to work in that factory full-time. Most had no education and struggled trying to get a job doing anything else. I could sense they were a bit jealous of Bobby and me, especially after we made our quotas, because they had to meet their quotas all the time. It was an interesting experience, and it began to develop a sense of empathy in me for people in different circumstances than my own. It also made me want to learn more about other people's lives. These early feelings of how important it is to understand and connect with the broader community would expand once I began broadcasting.

In Cisco, I played football one year, making the B team; the only time I carried the ball, I fumbled it. The A team always wore black jerseys with gold numbers. The B team, meanwhile, had to wear gold jerseys with black numbers. For the last game of the season, the coach let us all wear the black jerseys with gold numbers—everyone, that is, except one little boy everybody called "Pee Wee." Pee Wee got the only gold jersey, so he mildly complained to the coach.

"Pee Wee, I'm sorry," the coach explained, "but we just don't have enough of the black jerseys. You're stuck with that gold jersey."

Well, little Pee Wee was so distraught he started to cry, at which point our starting quarterback Benji Lipsey stood up, brought his black jersey over, and said, "Here, Pee Wee, you wear my jersey. I'll wear yours." While Pee Wee was probably not going to see any playing time, whatever his jersey color, Benji then became the only player on the field with a gold jersey. Now the other team could really concentrate on sacking the quarterback. It was truly an unselfish act. Leadership is never all glory, and strong teams are formed when we are willing to make sacrifices for each other—even if it means making ourselves a target. I will never forget that young man, the leader of our team, letting Pee Wee wear his A team jersey.

During one game in high school, I was playing in the band, and we were standing down behind the end zone getting ready to perform at halftime. The Cisco Lobos had the ball on their own two-yard line, and Benji Lipsey, of course, was at quarterback—this time in his regulation black jersey. He called a quarterback sneak just to get a few yards out to where they weren't in danger of getting a safety in the end zone. And then he ran that thing ninety-eight yards. Touchdown! Every one of us in the band, and in the stands, just went crazy. Benji was a real football hero—both on the field and in the hearts of the team.

I have such fond memories of the idealism and passion of high school. Amid the excitement of football games, band practices, and clowning around with Dash and our friends, there was of course room for romance. I met my first real girlfriend in the Lobo band. Her name was Sandra Turknet, and she played the clarinet. A very lovely red-headed young lady, Sandra ran around with Dash's sister, Dot, and she fit right in with our crowd. We'd go to movies, or swimming out at Lake Cisco. Sandra, however, did not like my Model A very much, so when we'd go on a date, I always had to try to borrow my parents' car. I wanted everything to be perfect for my girl.

Under the moonlight by the lake, I had all kinds of romantic dreams about Sandra and me, but my preacher dad would have been relieved to know that they were just dreams. When my family left Cisco in the middle of my Junior year of high school to move to Jacksonville and I had to say goodbye to Sandra, I was still firmly a virgin. My introduction to the joys and complications of mature love would not come for a couple of years.

My Cisco buddy Dash Crofts, on the right, with his partner Jimmy Seals in their heyday. Dash remains a good friend.

I was blessed with the love and devotion of a really great mother.

I am thankful my loving parents gave me such a good start in this life.

After driving my old Model A, getting my grandfather's
1937 Chevy was a great improvement.

6

ENOUGH TO LAST
A LIFETIME

In the middle of my junior year in high school in 1956, my father was called by the Baptist General Convention of Texas to become the district Missions Secretary of an area covering seventeen East Texas counties and all the Baptist churches in it. His promotion meant another move for us, this time to Jacksonville, Texas, just south of Tyler.

Not only did I have to say goodbye to my beautiful clarinet player before we left Cisco, I also had to sell my old Model A Ford. By then, the vehicle didn't run, and it had two flat tires. But I still got thirty-five dollars for it, exactly what I had paid for it two years earlier. Not bad, especially considering all the fun I had in that thing.

At that time, my mother had bought me a red jacket. I was very proud of that jacket and wore it to my new school with blue jeans. It made me feel kind of like Jim Stark, the James Dean character in the movie "Rebel Without a Cause." When Stark was the new kid in school, the other students didn't like him at all and teamed up against him. In my case, most of the students at Jacksonville High School were very kind and gracious. However, there were a few that didn't like this new guy, the new trumpet player, coming in to Jacksonville— into "their" school. There was one guy who even picked a fight with me, which ended in a draw.

At first, we lived in a rent house while my father met with a homebuilder in the First Baptist Church there, and they designed and built our very first house. It was a solid house, made all of salmon-colored brick, and it even had air-conditioning. Having now been a

Houstonian for so many years, it is hard for me to imagine that I never lived in a house with air conditioning until I was seventeen years old!

Another perk of this new house was that it had a carport big enough for two cars. I had been a little worried that the sale of the Model A would put a crimp in my freedom, but I didn't have much time to mope about that. My maternal grandfather, Jesse Thurman Warren, the street car driver, retired from the Dallas Railway and Terminal when they took them off the streets there in 1956. My grandparents, Jesse and "Ola," decided to move to Jacksonville to live with us. My father built an additional little house behind our house that had their bedroom, and my grandfather gave me his green 1937 Chevrolet two-door sedan.

This was a dream come true—quite a step up from that old Model A Ford, I'll tell you. My love of cars and trains, and anything that moved fast, only continued to grow over the years. You have to imagine, friends, what it was like to be a young man at this time—the war to end all wars was over and America had emerged as the world's superpower. At home, we were rapidly moving from a world of coal heat and fans to central air, trains were getting sleeker and faster, air travel was becoming standard, television was broadcast all day long— and I had a car I did not need a clothespin to start.

In particular, the trains that connected the country held a magic for me that has never faded. I distinctly remember the Missouri Pacific Texas Eagle coming through Jacksonville from St. Louis headed to Houston. Every night I could, I would chase it southbound out of Jacksonville in my old '37 Chevrolet. The railroad ran parallel to the highway to Palestine there for about three to four miles. Those trains had a big old Alco diesel in the front, and they were beautiful. Of course, this was after all the steam engines were dead, but I would chase that train out of Jacksonville every night that I was available. And I loved every minute of it.

Around this time, my father bought a 1957 two-door Buick Special. It was yellow- and gold- colored. I think it was a demonstrator, so he got a real good deal on it. That Buick was my father's pride and joy. One Saturday, I washed that car thoroughly, from bumper to bumper, as teenage boys did for their families back then. On Sunday morning, when it was almost time to go to church, my father told me: "David, back the car out of the carport so your mother and Mary can get in."

I did as instructed and went back in the house. A few minutes later, my father and I walked outside and over to the car, and I saw this massive bird dropping right on the hood of the car. When my father saw that, he exasperatedly said, "Oh look, David, a bird done shit on the car!"

I just stopped, frozen. He looked me directly in the eyes and got a little grin on his face. Then he said, "You never heard me say shit before, have you son?"

"No, sir, I never have."

He replied, "And you never will again."

As usual, my father was good for his word. That incident showed me that every little word we use can matter. We have to use respectful language if we want to be respected. How important that idea became to me when I entered broadcasting and my words flew beyond even the range of the trains, landing on ears I had never seen.

Life in Jacksonville held many of the same charms and challenges of my time in Cisco. In addition to fiddling with our cars, playing the trumpet and all the other school and church activities, I also found work. I was still far from the broadcast field, but in hindsight, every experience I had seemed to be teaching me lessons I would need once I discovered what I had been put on this Earth to do.

My first summer in Jacksonville, I worked with a contractor who put tile in bathrooms and kitchens in new houses. I thought that would be easy, because my job was to mix the cement, or "mud" as we called it, that they used to put the tile in. How hard could that be?

Only one problem: our first project that summer was the dormitory for women at Lon Morris Junior College in Jacksonville. It was five stories tall, and of course, we started at the very top floor. This meant I had to haul that mud in ten-gallon buckets all the way up to the fifth floor. I figured out that it was actually more efficient to only fill those buckets half full –but still I think that's one reason why my arms are so long!

We got through that summer, and my next job was at the Nichols Pistol Factory. They made toy cap guns, probably the best of their day. One of my jobs was to ladle the molten-hot metal—over 800 degrees Fahrenheit—out of the furnace into the molds. Then when they cooled, I had to separate the parts. The left half of the gun would go in one box, the right half and the cylinder for the bullets would go in another, and the bullets were individual bullets that held a cap inside the shell there. They were very authentic, probably too authentic for children, but back in those days before widespread consumer reporting, there was not such an awareness of potential dangers in products as there is now.

In my senior year, as I was getting ready to graduate from high school, I got the itch to see the world and travel. Where did all the trains go, and who lived at the end of the lines and beyond? I had heard of foreign countries on the radio since my earliest memories of WWII reports, and television was bringing images of exotic lands into our home. But how did a preacher's son from Jacksonville, Texas, get himself to these places? Laying tile and filling cap guns weren't skills that would take me abroad.

The only way I figured I could possibly see the world was to join the Navy. On June 21, 1957, I got in my Chevy, headed to the recruiter in Tyler and joined up. There was another kid from Jacksonville who tried to join the Navy too, but for some reason they wouldn't take him. He wanted me to wait until he could re-apply, but I was too eager to get going. "Sorry, pal," I told him, "but I'm going in now."

The recruiter sent me to Dallas for further processing, and one of the first steps was the physical exam. They had all of us new recruits standing there buck naked, and one of officers in charge came up and said, "Alright, anyone who's had any kind of major surgery in the last six months step forward."

I stepped forward. Earlier that year, in February, I had developed a pilonidal cyst on my tailbone, and Dr. Travis in Jacksonville operated to remove it. With that kind of surgery, however, you don't sew it up. It has to heal on its own. It had been incredibly painful when that anesthesia wore off, but I was able to get back to school quickly.

Now, that officer during the Navy exam came over to me and asked, "What kind of surgery?"

I told him, "A perinoital cyst on my tailbone."

He laughed and said, "You mean a pilonidal cyst." Then he added, "Alright, turn around, bend over, and spread your cheeks."

This was not how I had imagined my indoctrination into the Navy would go. I did as instructed. The area had developed a little infection, and he commented that the cyst might be coming back—but they would send me on out to San Diego anyway and let them decide. So, they flew us out to San Diego, and in the receiving area where recruits first arrive there had to be 400 guys. The first night I was out there, moreover, two of the recruits got into a knife fight. I thought, "Wow, these sure aren't Texas boys."

The next day, the same exam scene played out when the head recruiter asked anybody who had recently had a surgery to step forward. After examining me, he said, "This cyst looks like it has grown back. We need to have a doctor look at this." So, they sent me to the base sick bay. The doctor there ordered me to have sitz baths twice a day, sitting in a tub of water with epsom salts.

Being in that sick bay, I was considered to be "walking wounded." So they put me on kitchen duty every day, serving the other sailors coming through for their meals—and making trays for sailors too sick to get out of bed. This went on for over two weeks. Finally, they said my repaired cyst was not healing properly, and they sent me to Balboa Naval Hospital in San Diego. When I first enlisted, they told us not to bring anything other than the clothes on our backs and a toothbrush and a razor if you shave, so that meant I had to put my civilian clothes back on, which were the only other clothes I had.

Once at Balboa Hospital, a Navy doctor looked me over and declared I needed another surgery. "We can do the operation here, and then when you recover you can start your basic training," he explained. "Or, since this was a pre-existing condition, we can give you an honorable discharge from the Navy, you go back to Jacksonville and have your doctor do it and then you can re-enlist."

It took me about one-tenth of a second to make that decision. Maybe all of that kitchen duty had soured me, but by then I'd had enough of the Navy to last me a lifetime. I told the doctor, "I'll take the discharge, have my doctor do it, and then we'll talk about re-enlisting."

When he heard that, he gave me this lecture about how much money the Navy had already spent on me. He also noticed my civilian clothes and asked, "Why aren't you in dungarees and navy?" I informed him that no one had issued me any kind of uniform. So he called an orderly and said, "Give this man a sea bag when he gets back to base."

When I arrived back at sick bay, I had a full sea bag—uniforms, shoes, my sailor cap, everything. I'll never forget putting on those dungarees, which looked like blue jeans really, because I had to walk somewhere outside. As I was walking down the sidewalk, two officers walked by heading the other way, and I saluted. It was the first and only time I ever saluted anyone. After they passed, I couldn't help but crack up. Those two officers just looked back at me as if to say, "What's wrong with that recruit?"

Long story short: they flew me back to Dallas, and I took a bus to Jacksonville. As I walked up to our house, carrying my duffle bag, my grandmother Ola was in the kitchen looking out of the big bay window facing the carport. When she saw me walking up, she smiled and started shouting, "It's David! It's David! David's home!"

The prodigal son had returned from the Navy after just over a month. It has to be one of the shortest Navy careers in recorded history. With my respect for the work our armed forces do, there is a part of me that wishes I had been able to actually serve in the Navy. But the good Lord obviously had other plans for me. I just wasn't aware of them yet.

The next day, I went to see my hometown physician Dr. Travis. "Those doctors in the Navy told me the cyst had grown back, and I need surgery again," I explained. The doctor took one look, chuckled, and said, "That's amazing. That cyst has not grown back; this is just a little infection." He put silver nitrate or some kind of solution on there and, man, that set me on fire! It burned like crazy! But within two days, that thing had healed up and has never bothered me since then.

If I hadn't had that surgery, I would have been enlisted in the Navy. Had I ended up in the Navy, who knows where I would be. Reminds me of that line from the Billy Joel song *Piano Man*: "…he's talking to Davey, who's still in the Navy, and probably will be for life."

This would not be the first time that one seemingly insignificant decision would change my path. I can't tell you what would have happened if I had chosen to have the Navy doctors treat the cyst. But one thing is sure: I would certainly not be here today.

Another shot here with my sister Mary. Being the son or daughter of a circuit-riding Baptist preacher kept us on the move growing up.

*Getting ready to graduate from high school and launch one
of the shortest Navy careers in recorded history.*

"AND NOW,
MUSIC LOVERS..."

I've mentioned my trumpet to you a few times, friends, but let me tell you a little more about how important music has been in my life. It was not just a way for me to meet girls in the high school band. After growing up with parents who sang and played the piano, and a half-sister who was undoubtedly a prodigy, music just became a part of who I am.

When I was about six or seven years old, my father said, "Son, you need to learn how to play a musical instrument. What instrument would you like to learn to play?"

When I first suggested I might like to learn the saxophone, my father surprised me by saying, "No, you will not. The saxophone is the devil's instrument. You will learn how to play a trumpet."

Which I did, and over time I got pretty good at it.

In Cisco, I had been first-chair, the lead trumpet player, in the school band. But at Jacksonville High School, Butch Stapleton was first-chair trumpet; I became second chair. Butch had a bad left leg, but he could still march—and march pretty good at that. His sister Cathy was a cheerleader, and I dated her while I was in my junior and senior years. The trumpet may have been more respectable than the sax in my dad's eyes, but there is no doubt that it provided a high school boy like me opportunities for temptation, too.

During my senior year at Jacksonville High, a man named Edwin Fowler, who was known as "Pinky," came to listen to our band. He was not only the registrar at Tyler Junior College, but also the director of the Tyler Junior College Apache Band—who played for the world-famous Apache Belles. Well, of course, they weren't world-famous, but they were in direct competition with the Kilgore Junior College Rangerettes.

In the spirit of full disclosure, I always thought the Apache Belles were better, mainly because I was in the Apache Band—and I ended up marrying one of the Apache Belles.

Anyway, Pinky Fowler saw something in my playing and offered me a full scholarship to Tyler Junior College, including tuition, books, fees, and bus transportation to and from Tyler Junior College every day. I took him up on it. Had it not been for the trumpet, I never would have gotten that scholarship. In turn, I would not have been able to get any higher education at all. My parents didn't have the money to send me to college anywhere.

During the 1930s, Jacksonville, Texas had gained a reputation as the "Tomato Capital of the World," and the Fightin' Indians of Jacksonville High School played football while the band performed in a stadium they called the "Tomato Bowl." Not to be outdone, the City of Tyler calls itself the "Rose Capital of the World," and their Junior College team and the band with the Apache Belles played in Rose Stadium.

On Friday and Saturday nights, the local Methodist Church Youth Center in Tyler set up a little "canteen" area where kids could go dance and meet and have a soda. That's where I met Glendya. Glendya Lois Odom was in the senior play there at Tyler High School while I was a freshman at Tyler Junior College. Once again, I was in love.

I spent a great deal of time in the band hall there at Tyler Junior College practicing and rehearsing. One day, I came across a big bass violin, and was curious enough to pick it up and start teaching myself how to play it. I got to where I was pretty good playing that bass, and even played a couple of gigs with a country singer in Tyler. He and another man played guitar, while I was on bass. We weren't very good, but we had fun doing it.

Around that time I met Steve Wright, who made his own electric bass out of an old standard, hollow-body kay guitar. Steve stuffed it with cotton, put a ukulele pick-up on it, wired it with four cut-down bass strings, and—believe it or not—it made an excellent, outstanding, electric bass. It had a unique sound, more like a big stand-up bass violin, but it worked.

Steve eventually wrote a rockabilly song called "Wild, Wild Woman." We drove over to Dallas and recorded it in a recording studio that was up in the back of an old movie theatre. Glendya and I sang backup, and a guy named Mike Danbaum played guitar. If you search the internet, the song still comes up pretty quickly.

> *Can't stay in one place, can't settle down*
> *Always a-runnin', a-runnin' around*
> *Don't think you love me, don't think you care*
> *Always a-runnin' all over town*
> *Well-well-well, wild-wild woman*
> *Wild-wild woman, always runnin' 'round*
> *Wild-wild woman, wild-wild woman*
> *Never seen you touch the ground*
> *Well you're the meanest girl-girl*
> *That ever came to this town, this town*

Afterward, Steve got us a gig down in Houston for a dance at some school sponsored by KILT radio. We were driving down into Houston to go perform at that prom, and we heard our song on KILT radio; naturally, we were very excited. The song didn't sell very many copies, but I've got one and my daughter, Linda, has another. That's proof enough to me that it really happened!

I thoroughly enjoyed my two years at Tyler Junior College playing in the band, but clearly it did not contribute to my achievements as a scholar. In my excitement about making music with Glendya and my friends, I did not hit the books regularly enough. In fact, I flunked most of the courses I took except music and band.

I also joined a fraternity. In 1958, one of my fraternity brothers, Pat Hughes, started working as a disc jockey at radio station KGKB in Tyler, one of the oldest radio stations in Texas. In fact, KGKB went on the air in 1928, and was located in the same building as KLTV-Channel 7 on the east side of Tyler. Both the radio station and the television station were owned by the same family.

Pat worked in the early evenings from 5 to 7 p.m., and, being curious, I started accompanying him out to that radio station to sit and watch him do his thing. He taught me everything, including how to operate the "board" and the turntables, and queue up the records and audio tape. Those old turntables were probably the original ones in there. They ran at 16, 33 1/3, 45 and 78 rpm—"revolutions per minute" for you friends who did not grow up with the joys of vinyl records. Most of the music that we played was at 45 rpm, although we did do some 33 1/3 rpm long-play albums.

Pat dreamed of working in a union shop where he would only talk, and there would be an engineer to run the board and queue up the records. That's where I came in. He put the microphone up over the back of my head, and talked as I queued up the records. When it came time for the record to be played, he patted me on the shoulder. I would let the record go, and cut off his microphone. It sounds simple, but I enjoyed it very much. For a kid in junior college who was infatuated with machines of all sorts, being part of a team sending music out over the airwaves was exciting.

Eventually, Pat got a job at KBOX-AM radio in Dallas, and moved on. That left an opening for his evening slot. By then, I had caught the broadcasting bug, bad. I pestered the station manager, Ed Smith, to give me a job out there. He finally hired me as a disc jockey, on one condition.

He insisted that I change my name. He told me, "You can't go on the air as 'David.' It's too biblical. You need to shorten that to 'Dave.' It's more jaunty."

I didn't know what jaunty meant at that time, but I would have called myself "Pinocchio" if it would get me a job on the air! Starting out, I made $1.25 an hour, or $2.50 a day, for $12.50 a week. And I swear I think I had more money in my pocket back then than I do today. I got Pat's time slot, too, working from 5 to 7 p.m., Monday through Friday.

It was the first job I'd ever had where I could work inside. Not only that—I could sit down, and it was air-conditioned. That alone was like heaven. The job began connecting all the parts of me—my experiences and ideas and dreams—in ways that would, after several more twists and turns in the road, lead me to my career. But at the time, I was just happy to be in the cool air spinning records, thinking about my girlfriend, and not studying.

I opened my radio show every day using a track off an old Spike Jones album that sounded like he took a big washtub full of empty cans and jars and bottles and threw them down a staircase. It made a horrible din, but the idea was to get people's attention. At the bottom, I queued in where Spike Jones comes on and says, "And now, music lovers…" That's where I would hit my first record, and off I'd go for the next two hours. I did not realize it at the time, but that was working what we call "drive time" today. I had a lot of fun doing that.

In the fall, I also hosted a college football scoreboard show from 3 to 7 p.m. every Saturday, where I would give the scores from games all over the United States. It was a call-in show, and I had a telephone headset on one ear and a station earphone on the other ear. In front of me was a huge score sheet that had every game that weekend. I would get the scores off the Associated Press wire, and write down the scores during commercials. People would call in and ask for the score of their team or their favorite college team, including Slippery Rock. After wearing that headset and earphone, and answering calls for four straight hours, I would have a horrible headache every Saturday night, but that didn't slow me down.

In early 1959, a man named Harry O'Conner, who owned another radio station in Sherman, Texas, bought KGKB and brought a couple of disc jockeys with him. My first boss, Ed Smith, meanwhile, left KGKB and went to work for KTBB radio in downtown Tyler—as a competitor. Somehow, I survived the shakeup and transition.

Harry O'Conner was quite a showman. Almost immediately, he moved KGKB from out at the edge of town right into downtown Tyler, with a street-side studio on Broadway about a half a block from the city square. He also put the studio right behind a big plate glass window in the front where people could stop and watch the disc jockeys work. We had an audio speaker outside, and people would stand there and watch the disc jockeys queue up and spin the records. They could hear the music outside, and even talk to the disc jockey inside through a microphone that people used to request songs and so on. It was quite fun.

On the first day we were on the air downtown, as a publicity stunt we played the same record over and over and over for a full twenty-four hours. The record was a silly song called, "He Who." We would introduce the record: "Now here is the latest from Elvis Presley," and "He Who" would come on. Or we'd say, "Now, here's Frankie Avalon and Dede Dinah," only to re-rack and play "He Who" again. It got a lot of talk all around town, and after that first day O'Conner went on the KGKB air and announced the new KGKB would play nothing but Top 40 music. Really, more like Top 20.

We played the hottest records at that time. I remember distinctly when the singer, Marty Robbins, came out with a song called "El Paso." Disc jockeys loved it because it ran over four minutes long, but our managers and owner hated it because it cut into their commercial time. But, we played it.

The main competition to KGKB was KDOK radio, and their top disc jockey was a young man named Paul Williams. Shortly after we moved the station downtown, we had a Hooper rating book come in (Hooper was to radio ratings what Nielsen eventually became to TV ratings) and KGKB had actually beaten KDOK for the first time. Everybody at our station was just delighted, but Paul Williams at KDOK was definitely *not* happy—not at all. Paul had a 1957 Ford hardtop convertible, and late, late one night he came driving from the city square on South Broadway. He stopped in front of our radio station and threw a whiskey bottle right through that plate glass window. When the whiskey bottle didn't make a big enough hole, he threw a Dr. Pepper bottle through the window for good measure. Just as he was about to drive away, a Tyler police officer turned around the corner of the Square, saw what Paul had done, and arrested him.

The next day, the local paper reported the news under a headline: "Warfare Breaks Out in Tyler Radio." KDOK immediately fired Paul Williams, but our owner Harry O'Conner, ever the showman, hired Paul immediately and went on the air with a commentary saying, "We hold no animosity toward this young man. We admire his enthusiasm and from now on the 'Paul Williams Show' will be here on KGKB."

After Paul Williams joined KGKB, we were pretty much unstoppable. Our ratings continued to grow. It was during this exciting and fruitful period that I got my first taste of broadcasting the news. All the DJs at KGKB took turns reading newscasts for the other disc jockeys' radio programs. My very first tip on how to give a newscast came from Paul. He said, "David, if you ever lose your copy, or drop your copy or anything, just come on with the line, 'President Dwight Eisenhower today declared the farm veto bill null and void.'" It sounded like an odd thing to do, but Paul reasoned that Eisenhower was always declaring some veto—and a throwaway line like that would give me enough time to find my script, or wire copy, and continue with the newscast.

In a speech years later, I told an audience in Houston, "If you ever see me on television and I say something stupid, like 'President Eisenhower today declared the farm veto bill null and void,' you'll know I am totally lost and don't have any idea where I'm going." Fortunately, I never once had to use that phrase on the air.

That's not to suggest every show or newscast went smoothly— far from it.

Having the KGKB studios in downtown Tyler in full view of the public was a great publicity stunt, but I discovered there were also a few drawbacks. One day while I was on the air at KGKB in the middle of my show, I got a call from a man who asked, "Are you the disc jockey on the air right now?"

I said, "Yes sir, what can I do for you?"

The voice said, "A 30-06 rifle bullet with your name on it is going to come through that plate glass window in about five minutes," and then he hung up.

Well, excuse me! We called the police, who came immediately, but there was not much of anything they could do. As for me, I did the only thing I could do. I pulled the microphone down to the floor and would queue the records with my hands on the turntable up above me, never once lifting my head up over the turntables where anybody could shoot me. It turned out to be a prank call. There was nobody with a gun, and no 30-06 bullet ever came through the window, thank heavens!

Of course, radio is an audio medium, so sound is absolutely critical. Looking back, the fact that I got that job was unbelievable. I had a high-pitched voice and a thick east Texas accent. When Harry O'Conner took over, he brought in a consultant for the announcers and disc jockeys, and he told me, "David, your voice is too high and tinny. When you're driving your car, just take a deep breath and exhale as hard as you can through your vocal chords, and it'll stretch them out." I did that for months, and gradually it gave me a much deeper voice, which I still have to this day—thanks to that technique I learned in radio in Tyler. I would sit in the production room at the radio station and tape record myself reading newspapers, news clippings, Associated Press wire copy—whatever—and then listen back to it. It really took me quite a while to get that east Texas twang out.

In 1959, I came up with a new concept to put into my show called the "Gossip Column." The idea was kids could mail me their written comments—whatever they wanted to get on the air—and I would read them every day at 4:15 p.m. No last names, though. I'd put a soft music bed on under me and read whatever silly comments I received: "Susie and Johnny are lovers," or "Billy Bob sure does love Sally," or whatever. It was a hit with our primary audience, which were teenagers and especially teenage girls. Most importantly, Mr. O'Conner, the station owner, loved it. Because it was so popular with listeners and advertisers, he gave me a twenty-five dollar bonus. I'll never forget him saying, "David, I wish it could be more."

That same year, the "Big Bopper," J.P. Richardson, came to Tyler. Jayp Richardson was his real name. He was the disc jockey from Beaumont who came up with the hit record, "Chantilly Lace." I interviewed Jayp in our studio just off the city square. Just a few months later, on February 3, 1959, he died tragically with Buddy Holly and Richie Valens in a plane crash near Clear Lake, Iowa.

The actress, Martha Heyer, also came to Tyler promoting her new movie, *Some Came Running*, which also starred Frank Sinatra, Dean Martin and Shirley MacLaine. Before she arrived, I told the driver who was picking her up at the airport to tune into KGKB, which he did. When I knew Martha was in that car, based on what time her airplane was to arrive and what time they were driving towards downtown, I played the song "Mostly Martha" and dedicated it to our special guest in Tyler that day. She heard it and later thanked me profusely.

The movie theater in Tyler was right across the street from our radio station, and as part of Martha's visit, she stood in the lobby and greeted every boy who came with a movie ticket with a kiss. I went to see the movie, but I did not want to kiss Martha Heyer. I was very much in love with my sweetheart, Glendya—who I married just a short time later with my father officiating.

On August 20, 1960, when Glendya went into labor with our first baby, she called me at the radio station for help. Frantically, I immediately jumped into the car I was driving at that time, a little two-door, four-cylinder 1958 Austin Healy Sprite, and drove home as fast as I could. Well, being nine months pregnant, Glendya simply could not get into that little car. What was already a stressful time just got worse.

So, I raced back to the radio station, and borrowed a car from one of the other disc jockeys who called himself "Charlie Brown." He gave me the keys and said his black and white, two-door 1956 Chevrolet was parallel-parked just around the corner and about a half a block up. Mildly panicked, I tore around the corner and ran about half a block up to find a 1956 black and white Chevrolet—just as Charlie had described it.

I jumped in, cranked the car up and remembered thinking the things I found in the car looked a little odd. But, I had to get to my wife. I drove off, and hadn't gotten but about two blocks when a dump truck pulled up right beside me when I stopped at a red light. The driver hollered down, "Where are you going with my car?"

"What?" I shot back, stunned.

He said, "You're stealing my car!"

I assured him I would take it right back to where it was. As I hadn't been gone two minutes, the same spot was still open. So I parked, and the dump truck driver came over. I showed him the keys, and how it unlocked the door and started the engine. Then, he and I both looked down the street, and on the other side of the street about six spaces further west, there was another black and white, two-door 1956 Chevrolet—exactly like the one that belonged to that dump truck driver.

Finally, I had the right car. So I raced back to the house, picked up Glendya—who happily could fit in that vehicle—and got her to the hospital in time. A short time later, our daughter was born. We originally named her Sherry. But, for whatever reason, neither Glendya nor I thought that was too good a name, and within about a day, we decided to call her Linda. We had the hospital change the birth certificate, and six decades later—happily—my daughter still likes being Linda rather than Sherry!

I had a job, a wife, and a baby daughter. It was time to settle down and be a family man. I loved my little family dearly, but I was very young. The music was still calling me, and my love of fast machines was strong as ever.

On my first day of high school in Cisco, they made all incoming freshmen wear ties with an "F" on them. I hated it.

*Standing outside the KGKB studios in Tyler, Texas, in 1958 after making
my first break into broadcasting—not news, but hit records.*

Sporting the popular hair style of the day in the late 1950s — the flat top.
Once I went into TV news, the short haircuts I preferred
as a younger man went by the wayside.

8

CLEARED FOR TAKEOFF

After two years as an on-air personality at KGKB, I got an opportunity to move to WACO 1460-AM radio in Waco, Texas—which is, incidentally, one of only three radio stations where the call letters spell out the name of the city it is in. By then, I had gotten rid of my small, totally impractical Austin Healy sports car in favor of a proper family car, a four-door Pontiac Tempest. We rented a U-Haul trailer and put it on the back of that Tempest. I put everything we owned in that trailer, and my little family set out from Tyler to Waco.

About forty miles outside of Waco, however, we ran out of gas. I'd never driven a car pulling a trailer before, and I had no idea how that U-Haul trailer would knock down the gas mileage of that little car. Fortunately, a farmer or somebody came by, and Glendya stayed in the car with little Linda while I went to a gas station. We finally made it to Waco.

There, we rented a furnished, two-bedroom house with all bills paid for $85 a month. (Can you believe that? I am not sure even the Waco specialists on that "Fixer Upper" show could beat that.) In our case, the owner and his wife lived in a house right next to the little house that we rented, and became very good friends of ours.

The station manager at WACO was Lee Glascow. He had a long-time disc jockey on the air named Goodson McKee, whose program ran from 6:00 a.m. in the morning to 1:00 p.m. in the afternoon. That was one of the longest radio shows I ever heard of anywhere. Well, not long after I started at WACO, McKee retired—and Lee

Glascow put me on that same 6:00 a.m. to 1:00 p.m slot. To this day, it's the longest continuous radio shift I ever had.

In the middle of that show everyday, we had an hour-long show from 11:00 a.m. to noon that we did live from WACO. It was called the "Mary Holiday Show." This woman would come on and talk recipes and interview people. Her theme song was Vaughan Monroe's "Racing With the Moon." I had to play that every day when the program stated, and again when it ended. To this day, I cannot listen to "Racing with the Moon." If it comes on my radio, I am compelled to switch stations. I heard that song far too many times, and I was not a big fan of "The Mary Holiday Show" in general.

Early in 1962, on February 20th, the famous radio commentator Paul Harvey came to Waco. He usually did his programs out of Chicago, which aired on affiliate stations like WACO all across the country. That February, however, he came to Waco to speak at a Chamber of Commerce banquet. As a result, his team had arranged for Mr. Harvey to do all of his daily broadcasts that day from WACO. I was assigned to be his assistant. I was to do anything he wanted, get him anything he needed—coffee, more wire copy, more paper to write on, anything.

At 4:00 a.m., Paul Harvey arrived in a chauffeur-driven car at the back of the radio station. He stepped out wearing a black suit and black hat, carrying a black cane and a black briefcase. I was standing on the steps when he got out of the car. I introduced myself and said, "Come in, Mr. Harvey." His first five-minute broadcast was set to go on the air at 5:00 a.m., so I took him directly to the studio. Later in the day, at noon, he was to do a fifteen-minute newscast.

It just so happened that, on that day in 1962, John Glenn was launched into orbit aboard the Mercury 7 "Friendship" mission from Cape Canaveral, Florida, becoming the first American ever to orbit the earth. It was one of the most important flights in American history, and as a result, Paul Harvey's noon newscast was pre-empted. There was a small TV set there in the newsroom, and I was in there along with Paul Harvey and the news director, Bob Vandiventer, watching the coverage of Glenn's historic mission.

As the rocket went out of sight, I turned to Paul Harvey wondering what the great announcer would say. He was standing there with his arms crossed: "Well, I dunno." As if to say, "Where are we going with this space thing?" I think he was mostly angry that his newscast had been pre-empted. I was so excited by any machine that moved fast, and here was a man being launched into space. Surely, Paul Harvey had something to say that would reflect the deep impact the launch had made on me. I couldn't believe his lack of commentary.

Twenty-five years later, on the anniversary of John Glenn's flight into orbit, I wrote Mr. Harvey a letter. I reminded him of where he was and what he said in that newsroom. Two weeks later, I got a letter back that said, "Dear Dave. Very well written letter. Sincerely, Paul Harvey." That was it. Not one word about the space program, or Waco, or anything else. I still don't understand his inability or unwillingness to put words on this historic experience.

I had always wanted to learn how to fly an airplane, and when we moved to Waco I was making $250 a month—which was almost enough money to justify taking some flying lessons. Howard Basinger ran the flying school at Waco Municipal Airport. He charged twelve dollars an hour for dual flight instruction, and nine dollars an hour if you flew the plane solo. I took lessons in a 65-horsepower Aeronca Champ, which is like a Piper Cub with tandem seating—one seat in the front, one in the back. Both the front and back seats had maneuvering sticks and rudder pedals, but all of the instruments were in the front. As the instructor, Howard sat in the back seat while I, the student, sat up front.

Howard taught me how to taxi using the rudder pedals, how to get to the runway and how to get clearance from the control tower to take off. This little airplane had no radio, so at the end of the runway, we would turn the airplane to face the control tower, and then wait for the operator to flash a green light. A red light, as you might expect, meant "wait."

Once cleared to take off, Howard would advance the throttle to full power, push the stick forward to raise the tail wheel off the runway, and when we achieved flying speed, he pulled back on the stick to lift off. Just over the runway, he would level off at around ten feet, and wait until the little plane reached a climbing speed of fifty miles an hour. Then, he would pull back on the stick and set up a normal rate of climb. At about a thousand feet, just past the end of the runway, we would turn forty-five degrees to the left to clear the pattern and to exit the airport.

Once in the clear, and well away from other traffic, I would follow through on the controls as Howard taught me how to fly, using both stick and rudder to turn the plane, to climb and to descend. Of course, the most difficult part of flying is getting back on the ground— learning how to land. There was a small auxiliary field about fifteen miles northwest of Waco Municipal, where we would practice our landings and takeoffs. We would also circle that runway as Howard taught me how to circle a point on the ground, maintaining the same distance away from that point for a full 360-degree circle. To do so, I would have to adjust the bank angle to compensate for the wind direction and velocity.

Setting up for a landing was pretty simple in that little Aeronca. It had a fixed landing gear and no flaps, so you just had to fly the thing down to the ground. Howard showed me how to approach the runway and set up a glide rate that would put us over the end of the runway, about fifty feet above ground. At that point, you cut the throttle, pull back on the stick and let the plane stall just above the runway. It was very tricky, requiring a very light touch to do it just right.

After six hours of dual instruction, Howard got out of the plane. He told me he wanted to check the tail wheel, which was just a ruse. Once out, he told me, "Take it around yourself." I was shocked. I didn't really think I was ready to solo in that airplane, but it was time to do it. So, I lined up on the runway, advanced the throttle, lifted the tail wheel off the ground and gained speed. When I pulled back on the stick, that little airplane just leapt into the air.

At first, I thought I had done something wrong, but then it hit me that my instructor, Howard, weighed about 350 pounds. Without him in that back seat, the airplane flew like it should. I had not realized how much difference that amount of weight would make. I kept climbing to about 1,500 feet, made a left turn and then another left to enter the downwind leg parallel to the runway. Just past to the end of the runway, another left turn on the base leg, then a final left to line up with the runway. I had set up a gradual rate of descent, came over the runway at about fifty feet, cut the throttle and held back on the stick as the little plane settled on to the runway. I made a perfect three-point landing. It was the only perfect landing I ever made, and it was on my very first solo flight.

Just because I had soloed, did not mean it was the end of my instruction. I still had to make some solo cross-country flights where I would land at an airport and have someone there sign my logbook to prove I had made the flight. On one return from the Bryan/College Station Airport, I ran into a strong headwind and entered some severe turbulence. At one point it was so severe, I had to throttle back the engine and slow-fly the airplane. Well, that headwind was so strong that I wasn't making any progress. I looked down at the ground and the headwind had me actually going backwards! That was a unique experience. To make any progress at all, I had to advance the throttle and just fight through the turbulence.

I finally made it back to Waco, relieved to be on the ground again. The flight had taken much longer than I had expected, and Howard was getting a little worried. I explained the headwinds and the turbulence, and he understood.

I also made a few dual cross-country flights with Howard in the back seat. On one flight, I filed a flight plan that took us south to the Bryan area, east to the Lufkin area, and then back northwest to Waco. All nonstop, without landing. When I arrived at the Waco airport that morning, Howard said he would pre-flight the airplane while I filed the flight plan. Well, I thought that since he owned the plane, he ought to know how to check it out. So we took off, flew to Bryan, then east to Lufkin, all the time checking our flight path over the ground with known objects, structures or certain checkpoints on the ground to make sure we were on the right track.

When we turned to the northwest from Lufkin, I noticed that the fuel gauge was getting a little low and I asked Howard about it. He said we had enough fuel and to just keep going. Well, the closer that we got to Waco, the lower that fuel gauge read. When we were about fifteen miles from the Waco airport, the engine sputtered. Well, I about lost it. Howard said to retard the throttle a bit and continue to fly the plane. It ran smoothly, but when I tried to advance the throttle it sputtered again. I, again, cut the throttle a bit and it ran okay, but when I tried more power again, it sputtered.

By that point, we were over James Connally Air Force Base, just to the east of Waco. I hollered at Howard, "I'm going to land at the air base." As I was saying that, I glanced over my left shoulder to see if Howard heard me—and I saw his big, chunky left hand on the fuel lever that controlled the rate of fuel to the engine. He had purposely been cutting the fuel flow just to see what I would do. He laughed and turned the fuel on to full flow. We made it back to Waco without any more problems, although when we landed that fuel gauge really was on empty.

When I got out of that plane, I was covered with sweat and ready to punch Howard in the face. That's when he told me I had just learned an important lesson. "Never let anyone pre-flight your airplane for you," he instructed. It was a hard way to learn that lesson, but I never forgot it—and I would never let anyone check out an airplane for me again. Not even the guy who owned the plane.

I eventually completed my flight training with just a little over forty hours of actual flight time, took the written test, and then a check ride with an FAA instructor. Howard had also checked me out in a Cessna 172, a bigger and much nicer four-place airplane. On the day I got my license, I raced home, picked up Glendya, and drove back to the airport to take her up in that plane. Understandably, she was a bit nervous. When we rolled down the runway and lifted off, Glendya went "Oh, Oh, OH!" She was terrified!

I flew the Cessna as smoothly as I could, went down over Waco for a few minutes, and then went back and landed. She felt a little bit better about the whole thing. Sometime later, I rented that Cessna to fly her and our little daughter, Linda, over to Tyler to see Glendya's parents. Linda says she still remembers that flight, standing up in her mother's lap, and looking out the passenger side window. I still remember it, too. And I always will.

On the return flight to Waco, we didn't get back until just before sunset. Complicating matters, I had to land on the runway that was facing the setting sun. As I came in on the end of that runway, the sun was right in my eyes and it made the landing very difficult. I flared out a little too high, eased the throttle back and stalled the airplane about six feet over the runway, resulting in a very heavy landing. My instructor, Howard, had heard my radio clearance from the tower, and he saw my sloppy landing. The aircraft wasn't damaged, but he didn't think much of my landing abilities—at least not in that airplane.

I really didn't fly very much after I got my license. It was the thrill of the chase—just learning how to fly, and the achievement of getting the license—that was exciting. And, after I got my license, I really didn't have any excuse to go rent a plane just to fly around.

Despite my lack of opportunity to fly, our trip to Tyler was not the end of exciting experiences in the air for me. Later that year, I flew in the back seat of a T33 jet trainer with a commander of an F89 Squadron at Connally Air Force Base in Waco as the planes practiced for an upcoming air show. Those F89s were called "Scorpions" because with their high tails they looked like scorpions when they were rolling along on the ground. They were twin-engine monsters and made a lot of noise. During that flight, we tucked under the wing of one of his F89s as it was approaching three others coming from three different directions. The one I was in was the lowest to the ground, which meant we were only fifteen feet above the ground. It was so bumpy, my helmet kept hitting the canopy. But, we got through it okay.

One day, a flight of those F89s came flying over our house at a very low altitude. Linda was playing in our backyard, and when they flew over she just rolled into a ball on the ground as they roared overhead. Well, Glendya ran out to comfort her and let her know it was all right.

Later, while in Houston, I flew twice with the Navy's high-performance team, the Blue Angels—once in a F4 Phantom jet, and once in an A4 Skyhawk. I also flew with the commander of a F101 Squadron at Ellington Air Force Base. We flew out over the Gulf of Mexico and actually went faster than sound. He also let me fly the thing from the back seat, and I was all over the sky with it. It was very hard to keep that airplane straight and level.

Those were very exciting times, but I was not invited along because of my skills as a pilot. I would not have been invited to take any of those flights if I had not been a news reporter. And, friends, that brings us back to Waco.

The news director at WACO Radio was Bob Vandiventer. He was an old network announcer from Kansas City, and while working at the station, he also taught a radio news-writing course at Baylor University nearby. As a result, all of his students ended up coming out to the radio station to learn about, and practice, writing radio news scripts. If there was a fire, or a bad car wreck, they would take off, going to the scene of whatever incident to report on it.

Sitting in the disc jockey studio and watching those students come in excited about breaking news, it occurred to me they were having much more fun than I was sitting in there playing those same old records over and over. They were in the middle of the action, and that really started to appeal to me. I sat in on Bob's radio news writing course, and that is when my interest in becoming a news reporter took root.

I had finally found a subject I was excited to study, and I dug in. I learned the basics of writing news copy for radio, which is a lot different from television. People say it can't be that different, but it is. When you're writing a script to go with TV pictures instead of having to write for a radio audience that will not see pictures, it makes a huge difference. Just ask my friend and former colleague, Shara Fryer. She was a superb news anchor at KTRK-TV for over two decades before she became a fantastic radio news anchor and reporter at KTRH-AM 740 in Houston.

I wasn't thinking about the differences then. I was just glad to be learning more about reporting the news. I would have plenty of opportunity to discover the nuances of what made good copy in the years to come. For a little while longer, my day job would still be spinning records.

*My arrival at KNUZ-AM in Houston in 1962 also marked my first foray
into news reporting—a craft I would work at for the next 55 years
as a broadcaster in the Bayou City.*

A familiar sight for me, especially early in my career.
A late-night edit session, with a strong cup of coffee in hand.

CITY OF THE FUTURE

In 1962, I started moving closer to the excitement. My old radio friend at KGKB in Tyler, Paul Williams, called me from Houston to tell me about a job I should consider. KNUZ-AM 1230 had lured Paul there two years before as a disc jockey after they switched to a Top 40 music format. They were trying to take a run at KILT-AM 610, which today is a leading sports talk station, but back then it was the local King of the Hill in Top 40. Station owner Gordon McLendon had dubbed it the "Big 6-10 KILT," and with good reason. In January of 1962, they registered a very impressive 30 share in the Hooper Radio Audience Index compared to KNUZ's respectable, but still-distant, 20 share.

Anyway, Paul was calling to let me know KNUZ had an opening for a news reporter. By then, I really had caught the news "bug," so I called the news director, Bill Jay, and set up an appointment for an audition.

In the end, I got the job, and in the latter part of 1962 moved to Houston to join the KNUZ team that included DJs Paul Williams, Paul Berlin, Chuck Adams, Joe Ford and Arch Yancey; news reporters Fred Jones, Jim Carroll and Jay Oliver; and Bill Jay.

Driving into Houston, the city made quite the first impression. Four or five big construction cranes loomed over downtown, and they had just topped out the Humble Building at forty-four stories tall—making it the tallest building west of the Mississippi at that time. As I write this book, you can barely see that same building surrounded by all the huge skyscrapers. Between 1958 and 1963, the city added twenty-three major new office buildings. What's more, the city was experiencing a major growth spurt. In the preceding decade, Houston's population had grown by sixty percent—seven times the national average. And perhaps most exciting, certainly as it worked out for me and my career, this once sleepy frontier town was in the process of becoming the American headquarters for our space program.

So, there was a buzz—an energy—about Houston even back then. The city looked really progressive, upbeat—like the city of the future.

When I first arrived in Houston, I was alone. Glendya was pregnant with our second child. She and Linda went to her parents' home in Tyler to get ready for the baby to be born as I settled into the new job. On January 1, 1963, our second bundle of joy, David Jr., arrived. David was born a few days after the doctors had expected, and the fact that I had lost an income tax deduction from the previous year did nothing to diminish my joy at his birth. We were a family of four now, and I had to work to support us.

Shortly after I arrived in Houston, KNUZ got a great Hooper rating and beat out the "Big 6-10 KILT" for the very first time. To celebrate this newfound success, the general manager, Dave Morris, took all seven disc jockeys and five newsmen to Glen McCarthy's Cork Club near downtown Houston for dinner, drinks and a show. The entertainer that night was a very young Wayne Newton, along with his brother Jerry.

As the son of a devout Baptist preacher, I had never ordered a mixed drink anywhere. When the waitress came to take our drink orders, it was a new experience for me. I watched nervously as the other guys around the table ordered things like "scotch and soda," "bourbon and coke" and "vodka and water." When the waitress got to me, I awkwardly said, "I'll have a scotch and coke, please."

Hearing my ridiculous order, the other guys hooted. "Ward, you really are from the sticks, aren't you?" they crowed. The kind waitress, seeing my embarrassment, said, "Yes sir, that is a very popular drink in Canada."

A scotch and coke wasn't popular anywhere. It was the worst tasting drink ever. In fact, I couldn't drink it. After dinner and that show, I left—warm from embarrassment, but still stone cold sober.

My new job provided me with a steady stream of new experiences. One of the first assignments I had at KNUZ radio was interviewing Texas Governor John Connally as he reviewed the "Honorary" Texas

Navy, which had been reactivated in 1958 by Governor Price Daniel together with an annual Admiral's Ball at the Houston Yacht Club. As part of the revelry, the Governor was also expected to "review the fleet" near the San Jacinto Monument in the Houston Ship Channel. The truth is, this was no fighting navy. As they themselves describe it, the modern Texas Navy "consisted of every conceivable type of vessel from a luxury cruiser to a canoe." They would come parading by the reviewing boat, and the captain would stand on the side to dip the flag out of respect for the Governor.

At the time, KNUZ Radio kept a small cabin cruiser down at Clear Lake that they called "Big Mike Mobile Unit Number 1." During the fleet parade that day, we took a transmitter with us and a sixty-foot long cable cord for a microphone. Bill Jay pulled that boat right beside the Governor's boat. I climbed up over the rim with the microphone, while Bill kept "Big Mike" steady nearby so I could walk over and interview Governor Connally and his wife Nellie. We were watching the Texas Navy go by, and I asked him something profound like, "Isn't this great?" We had a fun conversation, and the Connallys were both very cordial and welcoming—not standoff-ish at all with a young kid reporter.

Not long after, the actor, Mickey Rooney, came through Houston for a theatrical performance. I don't recall which theater we were in, but I remember he welcomed me to his dressing room. He was in the process of removing his stage make-up, and he was the kindest, most outgoing, bubbly and enthusiastic guy I had ever met. Of course, Mickey Rooney was *the* biggest, number one box-office draw for Hollywood from the 1930s through the 1940s. He had been a huge star at one point and was an older man when I interviewed him in the early 1960s. But, he was very cordial as we talked about his remarkable career and the current project that brought him to Houston.

During my early KNUZ days, another mega-star, Bob Hope, came through town to help developer, Frank Sharp, break ground for the Sharpstown Shopping Center. This would have been right around the time they finished the Southwest Freeway to the Sharpstown area—which today doesn't seem very far at all. Anyway, being Bob Hope, he did not break ground using the standard shovel. He did it instead with a golf club, and afterward, he gathered with Sharp and others for a little press conference that I covered. In fact, I clipped a microphone on Mr. Hope while he was still holding his golf club. Afterward, he got up on a bulldozer and had a little more fun—ever the prankster.

But, early in my career, not every experience was so positive. In fact, there is one interview I would have like to have done that I regret to this day that I did not get. In late 1962 or early 1963, Lyndon Baines Johnson, who was then the Vice-President of the United States, came to Houston for an appearance. He was staying downtown at the Rice Hotel, and the station sent me to get a word from him. So, I went down, staked out a spot I thought might work, and was standing there with my handy-dandy tape recorder. Before long, the tall and imposing figure of LBJ comes striding down the hallway.

All of a sudden, I was totally intimidated. I hadn't been in Houston long, and here is the Vice-President of the United States walking right up to me. He looked at me, acknowledged me, and then I said, "Mr. Vice-President, may I ... ??" I could have gotten an interview had I been more assertive, but I froze. I have never told anyone that until now.

So, the Vice-President walked right on by me and disappeared into his waiting motorcade. I went to find a phone, because we didn't have cell phones back then, and called Bill Jay.

"Did you get Johnson?" he asked excitedly.

"No, he wouldn't talk to me." I couldn't bear to think that I had balked in a crucial moment, and I lied.

That is the one work incident I have regretted all of my life. All of my life.

Many other memories are more humorous than humiliating, however. On April 1, 1963, I was in the newsroom early in the morning, and Jim Carroll was about to do the 9 a.m. news. After he finished reading the headlines, he said, "I have a woman on the telephone here who says she is leaving her husband, is that right ma'am?"

"Yes," the caller said. "I'm taking my children and I'm going away today."

Well, all this time Paul Berlin was in the control room queuing up his records for his next segment. Jim asked the caller, "Can you tell us why?"

The woman replied, "Well, my husband works all the time. He never pays attention to me, or our kids, and I'm just fed up."

Jim said, "Would you give us your name, please, ma'am?"

"I'm Mrs. Berlin...Mrs. *Paul* Berlin," came the answer.

Well, at that, Paul jerked up. He looked at the newsroom, turned on his mike, and said, "What's going on here?" Paul's wife and Jim both shouted out, "April Fools'!" It was probably the most perfect April Fools' joke I ever witnessed anywhere, anytime.

A year or two later, some disc jockey on a Houston radio station, and I don't remember which one, came on the air on April 1st and said, "A Russian nuclear attack submarine has been spotted in Lake Houston. The authorities are investigating."

Anybody who knows anything about Lake Houston knows that no submarine of any kind could get in there, much less a Russian nuclear attack submarine. Nevertheless, in short order, all of the roads to Lake Houston were packed with people rushing out there to see this Soviet sub. After about twenty minutes, the Sheriff's Department started calling all the radio stations in the area to tell us, "Please tell your listeners this report of a submarine in Lake Houston is an April Fools' joke!" Which, we all did.

I never knew who the disc jockey was that pulled off that little stunt. Had it backfired, it could have had tragic results. The power of the media to cause chaos, soothe fears, or influence beliefs was increasing rapidly. Pranks like this were just a foretaste of the social and political hype we see created by manipulative media figures so often today.

In the hands of responsible practitioners, the reach of the media also served to share the news rapidly and broadly in even the most remote places, in ways that often impacted outcomes. On September 12, 1962, President John F. Kennedy came to Rice Stadium in Houston and asserted, "We choose to go to the moon," in one of his most famous speeches. That simple—but bold—declaration captured the imagination of the world, but it positively shocked everybody at NASA. They were just really getting into orbital flights and wrapping up the Mercury program. There had been no rendezvous in space; no plans made for a lunar orbital mission; no plans for a moon landing mission. At the time, NASA was only beginning the Gemini program, which sent two men up in a spacecraft.

Kennedy's speech at Rice changed everything, and tucked away in that same speech was a passage that meant big things for Houston and the surrounding community:

Houston, your City of Houston, with its Manned Spacecraft Center, will become the heart of a large scientific and engineering community. During the next five years, the National Aeronautics and Space Administration expects to double the number of scientists and engineers in this area, to increase its outlays for salaries and expenses to $60 million a year; to invest some $200 million in plant and laboratory facilities; and to direct or contract for new space efforts over $1 billion from this Center in this City.

Another regret I have about my early reporting days is that I was not there at Rice University when Kennedy made that speech. I talked to a number of the people at the Johnson Space Center afterward. I think it was Dr. Christopher Kraft Jr. who told me later in 1962, "We were just barely in orbit. Nobody had even talked about, or thought about, going to the moon until the President of the United States there at Rice Stadium made that statement. That caught everybody out here totally by surprise. We were still working on orbital, just finishing up the Mercury program and had not even started to work to get to the moon."

The race to the moon meant the spending and building "boom" in the Houston area was on. As it was, NASA already had offices spread all around Houston, while down near the Webster/Clear Lake area they were working to build the huge, new Manned Spacecraft Center (MSC), which would be re-named the Lyndon B. Johnson Space Center in 1973.

A few months later, the final mission of the Mercury program, Mercury-Atlas 9, launched on May 15, 1963. I had hoped that the KNUZ news director would send me to Cape Canaveral for that final, historic mission piloted by astronaut, Gordon Cooper, but that was not to be. He went and covered that one himself. Fifty-five years later, I have to say I am still a little sore I missed that.

On November 21, 1963, President Kennedy returned to Houston with Mrs. Kennedy to re-visit the subject of the space program. That night, he spoke in the old Sam Houston Coliseum about NASA, and at one point he said, "Next week, NASA will launch the biggest *payroll* ever into orbit."

Hearing his error, he stopped and said, "Really, that should be biggest *payload*."

Everybody chuckled.

Then the President wryly observed, "Actually, that will be the biggest payroll ever launched into orbit." The crowd broke up.

He and First Lady Jacqueline Kennedy spent their last night together in the Rice Hotel. The next morning, Air Force One flew them to Fort Worth and then over to Dallas, where, we all soon discovered to our horror, Lee Harvey Oswald was waiting.

As the President's motorcade moved through downtown Dallas, I was on duty at the newsroom at KNUZ—which was about fifteen feet wide, and twenty feet deep. The reporter faced the disc jockey through double-paned glass. The glass was about five feet high, and about eight feet wide. I was there at the board, with my feet propped on top of it, when a reporter, Fred Jones, walked in. He said, "What's going on, Dave?"

"Nothing, absolutely nothing," I replied, visibly irritated. "Since President Kennedy left this morning, it's been a very dull day."

As I was saying that, I heard the bells on the Associated Press wire machine ringing. *Ding, Ding, Ding, Ding, Ding, Ding!* Fred walked over to the machine and he said, "Dave! The President's been shot!"

"Oh yeah, sure," I snickered in reply.

"No, I'm serious," he said, turning white. "Look at this."

He ripped off the wire copy and handed it to me. "*Shots have been fired at the presidential motorcade in Dallas,*" it read.

I immediately banged on the window and showed the bulletin card, which is how we interrupted the KNUZ music programming for breaking news. The disc jockey on that morning was Arch Yancey. He immediately put on the bulletin intro and turned on my microphone, whereupon I reported, "Associated Press bulletin from Dallas saying that shots have been fired at President Kennedy's motorcade in downtown Dallas."

When I looked up, Yancey had the deepest expression of shock and horror that I had ever seen. These dreadful feelings filled me, but I didn't have time to stop and process them. As the AP bells continued to ring, Fred kept passing me copy. One reported: "*Texas Governor John Connally appeared to have been wounded.*" Another: "*The Kennedys' motorcade is proceeding to Parkland Hospital...Dallas police are searching for the gunman.*" Other grim updates followed.

Finally, over the Associated Press wire came a "news flash." I had never before seen a news flash coming off the wire, and soon it was clear why. I hit the bulletin glass; Arch turned on my mic; and I reported on the air, "From the Associated Press this news flash, President Kennedy is dead."

Once again, I saw that ashen look of total dread and disbelief wash across Arch's face.

Dr. "Red" Duke, who later became very well known in Houston and across the country, was the trauma surgeon on call at Parkland Hospital in Dallas that fateful day. Red and I were close friends, and he told me in an interview many years later that when they brought the presidential motorcade into Parkland, he got the alert and immediately went down to the emergency room. When they wheeled President Kennedy in, he told me, "There was nothing I could do, David. I could tell this man was dead. Half his head was missing."

So, Red walked across the hallway into the other treatment room, where he found Governor Connally. Red recalled, "He had been shot through the back, the right side of the back, and the bullet came out and hit his right wrist. Governor Connally was seriously wounded, but I could tell this man could be saved—and I worked on him to get him and his wounds stabilized."

As the search continued for the gunman who had killed President Kennedy, word came across the wires that a Dallas police officer had been shot and killed in Oak Cliff, which is a suburb right across the Trinity River from downtown Dallas. They chased the gunman into the Texas Theater at the corner of West Jefferson Boulevard and South Zang Boulevard. He was watching the movie *War is Hell*, about the Korean War. That's where they arrested Lee Harvey Oswald.

As I read these bulletins on the air, my shock and dismay were heightened by my memories of Zang Boulevard in Oak Cliff, where my grandfather, Jesse Warren, had driven his streetcar, right where that movie theater still is. How could something so unfathomably tragic happen in a place that I remembered so fondly? A peaceful place? Dealing respectfully with this disconnect is one of the hardest aspects of broadcasting the news when tragedies occur. Like the rest of America, I continued to reel with the aftershock and questions.

After his recovery, Governor Connally disputed the finding in the Warren Commission Report that said he was hit by the first bullet that went through President Kennedy's neck. Connally said he heard that first shot and was turning around to see what had happened when he was hit by the second shot. He maintained he was slumped over on the limousine seat when he heard the third shot that hit the President in the head. Governor Connally was very firm on that.

We all remember the scene on Air Force One, later in the day, after they had loaded President John Kennedy's casket onto the plane. Lyndon Johnson took the oath of office with Mrs. Kennedy to his left side, and Lady Bird Johnson on his right. Aides had asked Mrs. Kennedy if she wanted to change out of her blood-stained clothes, but she refused, saying, "Let them see what they've done."

There has been speculation that Lyndon Johnson may have been involved in the assassination. I believe that's pure nonsense, but what is undeniable is the fact that Lyndon Johnson becoming President of the United States changed everything for the state of Texas, and everything for us in Houston. It was the reason why KNUZ sent Bill Jay and me to cover both national political conventions the following year.

When Air Force One arrived back in Washington with the slain President's body, the Johnson family returned to their residence until after the Kennedy funeral. Back in Dallas, Jack Ruby, who owned a couple of strip clubs in Dallas, forever silenced Lee Harvey Oswald when he shot him at point blank range on the morning of November 24, 1963, in the basement of the Dallas Police Headquarters as Oswald was being transferred. Oswald was rushed to Parkland Hospital, the very same place his victim, John Fitzgerald Kennedy, had been pronounced dead less than forty-eight hours before.

In Houston, our attention naturally turned to the recovery of Governor Connally, the drama of the new presidency of Lyndon Johnson, and, eventually, the national political conventions that would be coming up in 1964. KNUZ decided we had to cover both of those conventions. The Republicans were meeting that year in San Francisco, and the Democrats in Atlantic City, New Jersey. Bill Jay chose me to accompany him, so in July of 1964, he and I flew to San Francisco. We checked into a hotel and then went out to the Cow Palace, in Daly City south of town.

An FDR-era Works Progress Administration project finished in 1941, the Cow Palace was used extensively to support the World

War II effort before reverting to its intended use as host of the Grand National Livestock Expo, Horse Show and Rodeo. It had already hosted the 1956 GOP convention—the first such Republican gathering on the west coast. But in 1964, a conservative insurgency led by firebrand Barry Goldwater of Arizona roiled the party and establishment moderates, promising quite the firestorm in what proved to be the first political convention to play out in front of the media and TV cameras.

This was the first political convention since several of the network TV newscasts expanded from fifteen to thirty minutes. It was also the first major political gathering since President Kennedy's assassination, so not-surprisingly members of the media outnumbered the delegates by a two-to-one margin. Excitement and anticipation buzzed as what everyone knew would be a hotly contested—or at least hotly debated—convention neared. After receiving our media credentials, Bill and I set up our KNUZ audio feed point inside the arena, and I immediately started looking for delegates from Texas—especially from Houston.

On the second day of the convention, a large group of counter-culture hippies blocked the turnstiles—preventing anyone from entering or leaving the Cow Palace. I was standing outside this protest with my tape recorder when I met an alternate delegate from Houston. His name was George H. W. Bush, and I had never met him before.

I asked this tall, thin, very affable delegate about the Republican platform, the presumptive nominee Barry Goldwater and various other issues, before finally asking about the protestors who blocked the turnstiles. I will never forget his answer.

"Dave," Mr. Bush said, "if they would go home and take a bath and put on some decent clothes and come back out here, we would sit down and talk with them. But they stink!"

He was right. You could smell them from thirty feet away. I don't remember if I used much of Mr. Bush's comments about the platform or Barry Goldwater, but I sure used his comments about the hippies. And Mr. Bush said he remembered that interview forever after.

Meanwhile, Barry Goldwater secured the GOP nomination as expected, with little-known Congressman William Miller of New York easily confirmed as his running mate. In Senator Goldwater's acceptance speech, I heard him state: "Extremism in the defense of liberty is no vice, and moderation in pursuit of justice is no virtue." The line drew a huge cheer from Goldwater's conservative base inside the Cow Palace, but the speech and convention as a whole were widely panned in the mainstream media as appealing to extreme elements.

The next month, at the Democratic National Convention in Atlantic City, the Republicans erected a billboard right over the boardwalk. It showed a picture of Barry Goldwater, and the cutline on the billboard said: "In your heart, you know he's right."

The next day, the Democrats added a line right below the Goldwater billboard that said, "Yes. Extreme right."

The Democrats nominated Lyndon Johnson as their presidential candidate. With Hubert Humphrey as his running mate, he won a landslide victory that November. Barry Goldwater only carried six states—five in the deep South, and his home state of Arizona. Now elected in his own right, President Johnson began instituting the policies of what he called "The Great Society" even as he faced the growing escalation of the war in Vietnam.

What was going on at home while I was involved with all this excitement at work? During the 1960s, Glendya, Linda, David and I lived in southwest Houston in the Loch Lohman Apartments, off Chimney Rock near Braes Bayou. I had a long drive to go to work at KNUZ radio, at the corner of Caroline and Blodgett just south of downtown. At that time, what is known as the Southwest Freeway ended at Chimney Rock; there was no West Loop; and what is now the Galleria area was still cattle-grazing land. I can picture it vividly in my mind, but it's still hard to imagine Houston before the Galleria was the same city we live in today.

The Loch Lohman Apartments consisted of twenty units surrounding a swimming pool. Eventually, Glendya became the manager of our building, and as a result, we got our rent for free. There was another twenty-unit apartment building right next to ours, and she became manager of that one too—earning a small monthly check as a result. My job was to clean the swimming pools at both properties, which I did once a week. I must have pulled everything out of those swimming pools except a dead body: lawn furniture, dead rats—I think I even pulled a dead cat out once. But, it was my job to keep those swimming pools clean, and I did the best I could.

During this time, I got a toothache and had to find a dentist. I never liked going to the dentist, and I hadn't been in several years. So, we looked in the Yellow Pages, and found Dr. Kenneth Horwitz, right across Braes Bayou, south of the Loch Lohman apartments. He put me in that dentist chair, took one look at my mouth, and said, "Don't move. Don't go anywhere."

My teeth were horrible—just rotten. To this day, I do not like looking at pictures of myself taken during that period. Dr. Horwitz quickly came back with an apparatus that opened my lips up wide so he could take pictures of my mouth and teeth. Then, he proceeded to clean my teeth, pull some of them, and replace and repair others with implants and crowns. Dr. Horowitz rebuilt my mouth with the caps that I still have on my teeth today. If I hadn't gotten that toothache and visited Dr. Horowitz, would I ever have had the opportunity to move to television?

Dr. Horowitz also took a series of pictures of my mouth as he was doing this work. Those pictures, I found out, later went into a dental school textbook where he was teaching dentistry. You've heard of "textbook cases"—well, my mouth literally was one.

In March of 1965, I was sent to cover my first space launch—which also was the first manned launch of a Gemini Titan. To get from Houston to the launch site in southern Florida, National Airlines had a daily flight to Melbourne, Florida, the closest airport. There, I rented a car, took my gear and checked into a motel near Cape Canaveral.

Arriving at the NASA Media Center, at what later became known as the Kennedy Launch Center, one of the first things I encountered was a pencil drawing of a rocket hanging up on the wall. It was the most rickety looking thing you ever saw, and the caption underneath it said: "Built by the lowest bidder." It obviously was a joke, but as a first impression it didn't instill great confidence in NASA or their rockets.

The Titan generation of rockets used during the Gemini program featured "hypergolic" fuels, in which there is no ignition source. When the countdown hit "zero," the combustion caused by combining two highly specialized chemicals provided the tremendous amount of energy needed to propel a large rocket into space at never-before-seen speeds.

During the launches I covered for KNUZ, I always had a microphone and an amp with wires hooked up to a telephone line so I could report live from the scene. The radio, television and print media were all kept together in an area about three miles from the launch site. But, we had an unobstructed view and could see those rockets as they took off.

What a miraculous sight! It was like watching the Humble Building take off and fly into orbit. At the moment of lift off, you could see the blue-hot flame and sparks, followed by the angry billowing smoke as the boosters released their incredible energy—but it would take maybe thirty seconds, when it got high enough, before you could hear it. And when it got about forty-five degrees up, that's when you not only heard it, but you felt it in your chest: *BOOM BA BOOM BOOM BOOM BA BOOM.*

It never got old, I can tell you. Watching a rocket launch is an awesome sight.

On one occasion, we were there for a Gemini flight, and as the countdown hit zero, one of the rocket motors gimbaled too far—and the system automatically shut itself off, so the rocket did not leave the ground. There was no roar of the engines; and certainly no chorus of reporters shouting in their microphones trying to be heard.

In the unusual silence that followed the aborted takeoff, a young reporter covering that Gemini launch for a Florida radio station caught everyone's attention. He had written out in advance what he was going to say, and as the countdown ensued, we could hear him saying, "3, 2, 1…Ignition! Lift off! And the beautiful Gemini Titan spacecraft roars into the blue sky over Florida waters…"

At that moment, he looked up and saw that the rocket hadn't gone anywhere. We were all holding our breath, wondering what this guy was going to say next.

"Oh, oh!" he excitedly exclaimed into his live microphone. "Two giant hands just reached up and pulled the rocket back down to the launch pad!"

Well, of course, that broke everybody up. I never saw that reporter at any future launches for the Gemini, Apollo, or Shuttle programs that followed. As far as I know, that was the one and only launch he covered.

In 1966, I went to Chicago to attend the Radio and Television News Directors Association convention. The highlight of that trip, without question, was the chance I had to interview former President Dwight Eisenhower. He was there to give a speech, and it being a news convention, at one point, they allowed ten or fifteen of us reporters to gather at a table with Ike—and ask him questions.

This time, I did not freeze.

"Mr. President," I asked when I sensed an opening, "could you give us one outstanding memory you have when you were the Supreme Allied Commander in Europe?"

"I can tell you that very quickly," the former president said. "The D-Day invasion was set for June 5, 1944. There were reporters all over England, and speculation was running rampant as to when we were going to launch our mission, where the troops were going to land, where they were going to go from there and what they were going to do."

"We were *very* conscious of maintaining secrecy," Ike continued. "This just had to be kept secret from the Germans, but there was so much rampant speculation that, on June 4th, I called all those reporters together in the briefing room in London and pulled back the drapes on the invasion map of Normandy with the five landing beaches named: Juno, Gold, Omaha, Utah and Sword. I told them when the ships would be loaded, and when they would leave early in the morning of the next day, June 5th. Then, I told them, 'Now, if any of you leaks this information, you will be tried before a military tribunal; you be found guilty; and you will be shot. End of briefing.'"

As we now know, heavy seas in the English Channel the next day postponed the invasion for a full twenty-four hours. Operation Overlord finally commenced on June 6th, and wouldn't you know no one had leaked that information!

"Dave," President Eisenhower said, concluding his answer to me, "over the years almost all of those reporters have come up to me, to a man, and said, 'General, I wish you hadn't done that. I was sweating blood for two days thinking somebody else was going to spill the beans, and you'd blame me.'"

That was one of the most fantastic answers I ever got in any interview. I felt so close to the WWII history that had fascinated me since I was a kid, and I could distinctly imagine what it must have been like in the briefing room, and how those reporters must have felt sitting on news that would impact the world in such a major way. Getting a valuable answer depends on asking the right question, and so often you don't even know which one will unlock the vault.

I will always remember interviewing Ike, and I'll always be glad I asked that question. But, politics was not the only thing I was getting the chance to report on those days.

Covering entertainer and mega-star Bob Hope (third from the left) and businessman Frank Sharp (to his right) at the dedication of the Sharpstown Center in April, 1965.

*With KNUZ radio covering the Gemini 3 Mission in March, 1965—
only the ninth manned spaceflight in U.S. history.*

ASTROS AND "STARS"

On April 9, 1965, the much-anticipated, eighteen-story tall Harris County Domed Stadium opened after three years of construction. It cost $35 million (nearly $300 million today). The first game was an exhibition game between the newly re-named Houston Astros and the New York Yankees. Nearly 48,000 fans including dignitaries such as President and Mrs. Johnson, Governor and Mrs. John Connally and Houston Mayor Louie Welch were on hand to experience the first domed sports stadium in modern history.

And what a stadium it was! In addition to the Lucite skylight roof over their heads, fans were treated to a number of other firsts: the first stadium luxury suites, five restaurants, cushioned seats, and a truly novel $2 million, 474 foot-long multi-display scoreboard.

To this day, it stands as perhaps the greatest monument to the innovation and audacity of the Houston spirit.

The Astrodome, quickly dubbed the "eighth wonder of the world," was the brainchild of Judge Roy Mark Hofheinz—one of the most fascinating men you could ever hope to meet. Born in Beaumont in 1912, Roy's father died in a truck accident when he was fifteen. Roy had to start hustling to support his family. He worked as a paper boy, music promoter and disc jockey. In high school, he printed programs that featured the team lineups with local advertising that he sold for a dime.

After moving to Houston, he won the election for the Texas Legislature at age twenty-two and won countywide election as Harris County Judge just two years later. When he lost his 1944 re-election bid, Hofheinz, known ever after as "The Judge," went into a variety of businesses—including gaining partial ownership of several radio stations and KTRK-TV—that made him a millionaire several times over. During this time, he also reconnected with another rising young politician named Lyndon Baines Johnson, and helped manage several of LBJ's campaigns for Congress. These iconic Texans would remain friends and allies for the rest of their lives.

In 1952, at the age of forty, Hofheinz was elected as Mayor of Houston, cementing his reputation as the "Boy Wonder of Houston Politics." City council was not so impressed, however, and a few years of acrimonious relations with the young new mayor ensued. Relations got so bad, that Hofheinz felt compelled to push through an amendment to the city charter in 1955 that effectively ended the terms of the mayor and the council a year early. It also called for a special election, during which Hofheinz urged voters to give the city a fresh start by electing a new council. They did for the most part but, tired of the bitter infighting, they also turned the mayor out of office. That gambit, a rare miscalculation for Hofheinz, is the reason why Houston's city elections are held on odd-numbered years to this day.

His political days behind him, The Judge banded together with several other businessmen for the purpose of luring a new major league baseball franchise to Houston. He simultaneously pushed for building an air-conditioned, indoor stadium to be the home of the new team. Legend has it that Hofheinz conceived of the concept for a domed stadium in the early 1950s when he attended a baseball game featuring the local minor league team, the Houston Buffs, which was rained out at Buffalo Stadium (also called Busch Stadium since it was part of the St. Louis Cardinals farm system). The idea may have also been inspired by Hofheinz's trip to the ancient coliseum in Rome.

Whatever influences came together in Judge Hofhienz's active mind, packaging the pitch for a new team with a state-of-the-art facility succeeded. On October 17, 1960, Houston was awarded a new franchise, initially called the Houston Colt .45s. After Houston voters approved an $18 million bond, construction on the Harris County Domed Stadium began on January 3, 1962.

KNUZ did progress reports from that construction site once a week. I remember seeing a huge hole in the ground where the playing field would be. I wasn't sure why they were digging so deep, but about half the Astrodome is built below ground level. The Judge thought seats had more perceived value if you had to walk down to them.

On one occasion, I interviewed Judge Hofheinz at City Hall. He had just come out of making an appearance before the City Council, talking about the Astrodome. What exactly he was telling them, I don't recall. But I do remember that his breath was terrible that day, so I had to do the interview at arm's length with my tape machine down at my side.

True to his signature flamboyance, Hofheinz built a three-story office and personal suite in the outfield near the big scoreboard complete with an artificial golf putting green, a shooting gallery, and one room built tilted on an angle—but with the furniture correctly oriented straight up. It really messed with your mind just looking at it. When you walked in, you'd almost get vertigo. (The apartment was demolished in favor of more seating when the Astrodome was renovated in 1988, six years after Hofheinz's death.)

Before moving into the Astrodome, a legal dispute with the Colt 45 firearms company forced Hofheinz to re-name the Houston Colt .45s to something else. When he announced he was re-naming the franchise the "Astros," Judge Hofheinz explained at the news conference that it was short for astronaut. Originally, everybody thought that was the worst name he could have chosen. But it stuck, and soon everything related to the facility had an "astro" prefix to it. The cute female ushers, for example, were dubbed the Astro-ettes. When the Lucite panels prevented the natural grass to grow inside the dome, the artificial playing surface Hofheinz helped create became AstroTurf, and in time, the hundred-acre amusement park that opened in 1968 just across the 610 freeway from the Dome became Astroworld.

Meanwhile, when the Astros got on a losing streak, we would go on the radio and say, "We're calling them the -*Tros* now, which gives you an idea of what they lost." Back then, we couldn't have said "ass" on the radio. But, win or lose, I enjoyed going to a whole lot of Houston Astros ball games in the Astrodome, and before that I even attended a few games at Colt .45 Stadium—the temporary structure hastily erected next to the Astrodome site while the eighth wonder of the world was going up.

One baseball memory stands out in particular. I was seated between third base and home plate, about fifteen rows up behind the visiting team's dugout. At one point, a left-handed batter hit a screaming foul ball straight at the first row of seats. The ball hit the guardrail and went straight up in the air. The man who was sitting in that seat, who would have been hit by that ball if it had been two inches higher, pulled out a white handkerchief and waved it over his head as if to say, "I surrender, I give up." That got the crowd chuckling.

Then that guy stood up and turned around. When the crowd realized it was the world-famous comedian Milton Berle, they just *roared*. After the game, I happened to be walking out of the stands right next to Milton Berle. He had a cigar in his mouth, and he was flanked by two beautiful women—one on each side. I said something like, "It's nice to see you here, Uncle Miltie."

At that he just nodded and said, "Thank you, kid, thanks a lot."

Uncle Milton Berle had actually spoken to me!

As Houston grew and prospered, the radio and television scene was also growing and changing. People moved around, sometimes jockeying for better jobs and getting them, and sometimes being passed over for them. In late 1964, our news director at KNUZ, Bill Jay, went to work for a radio station in Florida. After his departure, General Manager Dave Morris appointed me the news director. That seemed to upset my fellow reporter Fred Jones very much. He and I had both come to work at KNUZ at about the same time, and I was promoted over him. When he didn't show up for work one day, I traced him to a pool hall not too far from KNUZ. I went down and confronted him. "Fred, you need to go to work," I told him.

He said, "No, I'm not. I'm through there." He never did come back to KNUZ.

Late in 1964, the KNUZ disc jockeys formed a band and started playing sock hops and proms around the area. As an opening act, however, they were more than a little jealous that the headlining band got paid a lot more than they did. In short order, I was recruited to join. "Come on, Dave, get your trumpet," they urged. I soon joined a lineup that included Joe Ford trying to play guitar; Arch Yancey trying to play bass; and one of the other disc jockeys trying to play drums. The first time we got together to rehearse, you never heard anything that sounded so bad. I told them, "Guys, this sounds like hammered crap! If we hire ourselves out as a band from KNUZ and play like this, wherever we go, those kids are going to run us out of there. They'll probably throw rotten tomatoes at us."

I think it was Joe Ford who finally spoke up. "Listen," he said, "I know this kid named Steve Tyrell. He's got a band, and maybe he could help us."

So Steve Tyrell, whose real surname was Baleo, came over with a couple of guitar players and a drummer. With him and his group, we actually sounded like a real band. So much so, that we decided to have some blue outfits made. We settled on some blue spangly pants and matching tuxedo jackets, and thusly adorned we actually played a number of gigs—and had great fun doing it.

Steve Tyrell later moved to New York and worked for Scepter Records as an A&R man scouting talent. He eventually brought the recording star Dionne Warwick to Houston. Ever smooth, when he checked her into the Warwick Hotel, he told her they had re-named the hotel in her honor. Later, he moved to Los Angeles where he ran his own recording studio on Sunset Boulevard. There, he recorded and produced records for a number of big name artists, including Elvis Presley's "Suspicious Minds," a classic.

In 1991, they were filming the re-make of the old movie "Father of the Bride," with the new version starring Steve Martin. The producers picked Tyrell to do the music for the soundtrack, which included the song "The Way You Look Tonight"—which was played during the wedding scene as Steve Martin's character looks at his daughter. After Steve recorded the soundtrack, he took it out to the location where they were filming the movie. Steve Martin, the producer, and the director of the film all climbed in Steve's car, so he could play the instrument track he had on a cassette for them.

They had not yet picked anyone to sing that song, so Steve had added what they call a "scratch" vocal track to the recording, which is basically a placeholder track so you could appreciate the relationship of the lyrics to the music. After the assembled audience heard the recording, they said, "We love the instrument track, Steve, but who is that singing the song?"

"That's me," Steve said. "I just went in the booth and recorded the words so you would see where your singer comes in to sing that part."

Well, the producer, director and Steve Martin all said, "You sound so good, we want you to do it." They ended up re-shooting the wedding scene to include Tyrell with his group actually in the movie, and it made a tremendous film.

Many years later, in 2007, I did a thirty-minute program on Steve that the Channel 13 managers called "Steve Tyrell, a Houston Standard." I had wanted to call it "Steve Tyrell, the Accidental Singer," but they overruled me on that. The program won me an emmy.

One final note on my friend Steve Tyrell. He played a concert here in Houston several years ago, and between newscasts I drove down to see him at the Hobby Center. Before I went there, however, I took that old blue sequined outfit that we had made for our KNUZ band back in the mid-1960s and changed into it in a dressing room. When I walked out there on stage, Steve Tyrell was there; Joe Ford was there; Arch Yancey was there; Paul Berlin was there. They all erupted. "Dave I'm surprised you can still fit into it!" Tyrell said.

Frankly, I was more than a bit surprised too.

The fun I had with the band didn't distract me from my interest in the space program. As I had with information about WWII, I eagerly read everything I could about the space race. In the mid-1960s, during the Gemini space program, the astronauts had to learn how to rendezvous and dock in orbit. That was of paramount importance because they would have to do that going to, and returning from, the moon in future missions. They would have to separate from the lunar excursion module, and then the command module would come around and dock with that.

At this point, I was increasingly interested in the ways that news was presented. Even though I was still in radio, I remember how one of the TV networks worked out an ingenious way of showing the viewers what they were talking about using model trains—as primitive as that sounds now. They laid down a rail in a big circle, and they started this train going out into the circle. Later, they started another train, a model made to look like spacecraft—and while it kept "orbiting," they launched the other one and showed it coming in and coupling up to that other car, like spacecraft would do in orbit.

I thought that was a simple, great way to explain a very complicated process to the American people. This demonstration made a real impression on me.

As a reporter, you have to approach each story objectively—looking for, and sharing, the facts as best you can determine them. But I have to confess that covering the space program gave me a special joy throughout my career, especially in those early days. And perhaps one reason the space program holds so many important memories for me is that it is where I finally made the leap to television. Just as so many important milestones had been for me before, this one just seemed to happen: a natural result of following my interests and being in the right place at the right time. I think today the social scientists call that flow—when your work is such a natural part of who you are that it does not seem like work.

Here's how it unfolded: During the course of covering the many Gemini launches in Florida, I met a man named John Gehbauer, who was the science reporter and chief photographer with Channel 13. He carried both a sound camera and a silent camera with him, which was a challenge to manage. So we helped each other.

For example, John arranged for an interview with NASA official Kenneth Kleinknecht, who had been manager of the Mercury project and was serving as technical assistant to the Director of the Manned Spacecraft Center. Before the interview, John taught me how to operate his sound camera. He set it up on a tripod, showed me how to turn it on and off, how to focus, and how to operate the zoom lens. When it came time for the interview, John would hold the microphone and stand out in front of the camera, and I would operate the sound camera. After his TV interview was over, I interviewed Kleinknecht for radio.

A little while later, I was still at KNUZ covering another space shot. After checking into a hotel down near the manned spacecraft Center, I got a call from Jim Whisenant, who was the assistant news director at Channel 13. "Dave, I'm leaving Channel 13," he said. "I'm going to work for ABC in Atlanta, and my position will be open." Then he told me to call the news director and anchor, Ray Conaway, if I was interested in joining the small KTRK team.

I was, so I called Ray, went to meet with him, and we talked. Things progressed to the point that Ray wanted me to meet some of the other key people at the TV station. "Tomorrow, be at the Le Cue Billiard Parlor in Rice Village around noon," he instructed.

I materialized at the appointed hour, and found Ray together with Willard Walbridge, the station manager at Channel 13; Wayne Thomas, the production manager; and Howard Finch, the program director. We played a round of pool, and I don't remember if I let them beat me—or if I wasn't very good at it anyway. I was definitely nowhere near the pool shark my father was. The key thing is: I got a job. Not as the assistant news director, but as an on-the-street news reporter.

Thrilled, I called my father to tell him the good news. But when I shared my excitement with him, he was very uncertain and apprehensive. "David, you have had a very successful career now for nearly nine years in radio," he said. "You don't know anything about this television."

I always respected my father's wisdom, but I realized that there comes a time when a man knows in his heart what is best for him. I knew instinctually that my experiences to date had been leading up to this moment. I hadn't known that along the way, but I had followed my true interests and I had worked hard. Where would this new job lead? I couldn't know that any more than I could have imagined a man flying to the moon. "Dad, trust me," I assured him. "I really feel good about this."

On November 9, 1966, I walked through the back door of KTRK-TV Channel 13, and opened the door to a fascinating fifty-year adventure.

As newscasters, we can never forget that getting the facts right is where it all begins.

*One of the early KTRK-TV promotional shots after I teamed up with
another radio reporter-turned-TV anchor, Dan Ammerman (to my left).
We were TV news' version of "The Odd Couple."*

11

LUCKY BLACK CAT

Dr. Walter William Kemmerer had a dream.

An accomplished educator by training and the second president of the University of Houston, the diminutive, driven, bespectacled Kemmerer had a vision in the earliest days of television to build a Texas Television Center on his campus that would service all of the TV stations in the city. His idea was for the other stations to lease space from the university within this new center and share the same transmitting tower. The revenue the university would gain from this relationship would help fund the centerpiece of Kemmerer's dream: the country's first educational or public television station, run by the University of Houston. Today, we know it as KUHT-TV Channel 8.

With Dr. Kemmerer's support, the university had already taken a serious plunge spending some $400,000 starting in 1948 to develop a first-class FM (frequency modulation) radio station, which today we know as—you guessed it—KUHF-FM. It went live on the air on November 10, 1950, broadcasting programming from noon until 6 p.m. The Federal Communications Commissioner at the time, Paul Walker, declared at the dedication: "These are the finest radio facilities in the country, commercial or otherwise."[6] Capping things off in true Texas style, the station's first FM transmitter was put atop a 285-foot oil derrick that wildcatter extraordinaire Hugh Roy Cullen donated to the university—one of his many acts of generosity towards UH.

---

[6] https://books.google.com/books?id=trFBm32BxQMC&pg=PA16&lpg=PA16&dq=Dr.+
Walter+William+Kemmerer&source=bl&ots=6C0p4ibXKz&sig=59RT3b2rEZ2LDIONU-
OSzmkvZkHg&hl=en&sa=X&ved=2ahUKEwi1sI2rk_TcAhUPWq0KHQc4AicQ6AEwA-
noECAgQAQ#v=onepage&q=Paul%20Walker&f=false

With the university's lush, state-of-the-art radio station off and running, Dr. Kemmerer turned his full attention to the Texas Television Center. In the spring of 1953, the university's board of regents set aside thirty acres of land south of Wheeler Road and gave Kemmerer authority to start negotiating leases. The first group to buy into the ambitious concept was KNUZ-TV, when station president Max Jacobs and general manager Dave Morris—my boss at KNUZ radio when I later came to Houston—sank $2 million into building out a space and putting up a tower. They went live on air on October 22, 1953.

KNUZ-TV operated on Channel 39 and, as envisioned by Dr. Kemmerer, shared the transmitter tower with the university's Channel 8. Unfortunately for KNUZ-TV, the Houston television landscape was in a state of flux in those early days, especially after the FCC ended its four-year freeze on granting broadcasting licenses to a host of eager, well-funded applicants. In short order, the FCC allowed KGUL-TV in Galveston to acquire studio space in Houston and relocate its transmitter here. KGUL also became the local CBS affiliate, and a few years later changed its call letters to KHOU—as it has remained.

Meanwhile, KNUZ-TV struggled from the start with technical problems. It also was hampered by virtue of the fact it lost out on the CBS affiliation to KGUL and was left to partner instead with the troubled Dumont Network. Unable to overcome such early hurdles, KNUZ-TV went "dark" (or off the air) on June 25, 1954, and sold its assets to KTRK-TV Channel 13, the new ABC affiliate in town. The ill-fated Dumont Network, incidentally, was also dissolved just two years later in 1956.

KTRK was owned by the newly formed Houston Consolidated Television Company—which is a story in itself. The original "consolidated" ownership team was actually comprised of four groups who had previously been competing against one another to get the Channel 13 license for themselves. Negotiations started in November of 1953 and resulted two months later in an arrangement where Jesse Jones' KTRH Broadcasting Co., Houston Area TV Co., Houston TV Co., and Judge Roy Hofheinz's TV Broadcasting Co. of Houston divided ownership of the station among themselves. Had the competing interests failed to reach some sort of agreement, the competitive process could have delayed the granting of the Channel

13 license by another two years. Mr. Jones, a legendary Houston politician, entrepreneur and philanthropist, called the innovative, collaborative resolution to the impasse reached on January 8, 1954 "one of the greatest civic achievements in Houston in many years."[7]

The first general manager of the station was Willard "Bill" Walbridge, a Silver and Bronze Star winning war hero who was lured to Houston from Michigan by Jesse Jones' nephew, John T. Jones Jr. The Jones family was the largest shareholder in the ownership group, and John promised Walbridge total autonomy to run KTRK as he saw fit. To make a go of things at the new station, Walbridge brought Howard Finch, one of his Lansing associates, with him to serve as program manager, news director, news anchor and staff announcer. I think Howard did everything but the windows in those early days.

And so KTRK-TV signed on the air on November 20, 1954, adopting a black cat as its mascot owing to its "unlucky 13" spot on the dial. "We made everything that was unlucky, lucky," Walbridge later explained. "The black cat became our symbol."

The following year, Jesse Jones' *Houston Chronicle* company bought out the other partners, and "the Chronicle Station," as it was known for a time, continued adding operating space to its fledgling operation in the old KNUZ building. KTRK also launched a number of popular new shows including "Kitirik," a very popular children's show in the afternoon featuring my friend Bunny Orsak in a black leotard done up so she would look like our black cat mascot. They actually ran a contest to name the show, but I think management finally got the name Kitirik by simply inserting an "I" between each of the station's call letters, KTRK. Another early show was "Cadet Don" together with his space creature sidekick "Seymour," and eventually the "Larry Kane Show" aired on Saturday afternoons—a Dick Clark "American Bandstand" type of dance show that was a very big hit with younger audiences.

In 1961, KTRK moved to its current location on Bissonnet Street near Rice Village, a departure from Dr. Kemmerer's Texas Television Center that eventually spelled doom for the idea of a hub of resources on the UH campus. In hindsight, Kemmerer gambled on his vision, and lost. Despite his wide popularity, he was asked to resign as president of the university in 1953—possibly owing to the large sums of money

---

[7]   http://houstonradiohistory.blogspot.com/2007/06/this-is-test.html

he spent on what was then "new" media, and not on athletics. Of course, universities and their large backers are having the same tug-of-war today, aren't they? Still, out of the ashes of the Texas Television Center, today Kemmerer's twin legacies, KUHF-FM and KUHT-TV, are still operating, still doing great work, and still contributing to our community in a myriad of ways.

The new Channel 13 building, meanwhile, was designed by the same architect, Herman Lloyd, who a few years later gave life to Roy Hofheinz's vision for the Astrodome. I mention this because the KTRK building had a miniature version of the dome housing its studios—making it Houston's first domed structure—a few years before the "eighth wonder of the world!"

A 1961 promotional video giving viewers a tour of the new KTRK building waxed eloquent about its attributes: "A new landmark on Houston's streets...the great white dome, the rotunda of the new KTRK studios, our new home...The graceful fluted entranceway frames a delightful view to the visitor. The lovely garden patio with its gaily splashing fountain and shimmering pool. This beautifully landscaped area is surrounded by the glass walls of the reception lobby and the executive offices, providing a source of inspiration..." And it went on.

With due respect, I have to say that that was a load of high-falutin' bull. For the most part, the space served its functions well, but it was not the lush pleasure garden of the PR video. Even Walt Hawver, who served as KTRK's news director from 1970 to 1985, observed in his book *Capital Cities/ABC: How the Minnow Came to Swallow the Whale*, "the newsroom was an afterthought to the station architects who had allocated twice as much space to a circular swimming pool out front and to the entrance area."

While the criticism of the lack of original space devoted to the news operation was fair, the newsroom was not without other bells and whistles. When I walked into the studio in November, 1966, the station had just taken delivery of seven brand new, state-of-the-art, black-and-white cameras. I thought then it would be several years before we finally broadcast in color, and it was.

In the news department, Ray Conaway served as our news director and anchor on the 6 and 10 o'clock newscast. Ray had cut his teeth in print journalism and was in the first generational wave of TV news anchors. The rest of the news team consisted of weatherman Troy Dungan, who had started at KTRK in 1964, and a longtime sports broadcaster Guy Savage on sports—Guy Savage, what a name for a sports reporter! My friend from our days covering space launches in Florida, John Gehbauer, got the job as assistant news director. And Ben Perlman and Joe Gaston were the photographers. I remember Gaston always chomping on a little cigar butt.

As KTRK's first on-the-street reporter and photographer, I was given a Bell & Howell hand-wound silent camera. It shot 16-millimeter black-and-white film. They also gave me a little eight-page booklet titled *How to Shoot News Film*. Gehbauer, still generously sharing his knowledge with me, told me to read that booklet, go home and take some shots and tell a story in the camera without editing. *How to Shoot Film News* had some interesting instruction in it. One instruction still makes me chuckle: "Never shoot a parade from both sides of the street. You want to keep your parade going in the same direction." Very logical.

I went home with that Bell & Howell camera and looked around for a worthy subject. We had a little beagle that my daughter Linda had named Blackie, and I thought he would be perfect. I loaded the camera, shot film of Blackie looking up anticipating, and about three seconds of a can of dog food. Then I filmed Glendya opening the can, filling up his dish, putting it down on the floor, and Blackie eating. My last shot was his tail wagging.

I took that back into the television station the next day and developed the film. John Gehbauer looked at it and said, "Dave, you're a natural at this." I knew it didn't hurt that I had a very cute subject, but I was pleased and encouraged by his response.

Starting out, my primary job was shooting news film and writing scripts for some of the stories on the 6 and 10 o'clock newscasts. Each newscast was only fifteen minutes long—and with two minutes for weather, about three minutes for sports, and another five minutes of commercials, that only left about five minutes for actual news content. That meant that the stories had to be *very* condensed, as short as you could make them. Over the years I've had many opportunities to do longer reports, but I always stay as close as possible to the heart of the story. Those early time limits taught me to trim the fat, right down to the bone. Today, when we talk about what it was like writing those early scripts, my wife Laura often says, "Dave took a gallon and put it in a quart jar."

When I had only been at KTRK three weeks, I wrote up a story at the last minute to go in the 6 o'clock news. I don't remember what the story was about, a wreck, or a fire. Anyway, I rushed into Ray Conaway's office and handed him this script. He was waiting and looked it over proof-reading it. Then he put it in his scripts in the proper place, and he was ready to go on the air. Before he left his office, though, he opened the bottom right-hand drawer of his desk and pulled out a pint bottle of vodka. It was about half-full. He opened it and took a long swig. I may have been living in the big city, but I was still the son of a Baptist preacher, and I was shocked. When he offered it to me, I was flustered. I thought, *Is this a test?* I said the only thing I could think to say: "Ray, what are you doing? You go on the air in ten minutes."

He looked at me with a little grin and said, "What, kid? You don't think I go out there all by myself, do you?"

Every night, at ten minutes to 6 p.m., and then again at ten minutes to 10 p.m., Ray would bolster himself with a strong shot of vodka. When he went on the air, he never flubbed a single word. How he was able to maintain his composure, I have no earthly idea. I do know, however, that everyone who steps in front of a news camera has to find ways to deal with stress and leave nerves behind. Many of us in this business have learned the hard way that the short-term peace that alcohol may offer isn't worth the long-term price. But even when my own drinking was causing me the most problems, I knew I could never present the news clearly when I was intoxicated so I was always sober on air.

But I'm getting ahead of the story. Let's go back to my early film editing duties. In those days, we would run the film between two reels through a "viewer" so you could see exactly what you shot. When you saw the scene you wanted, you would tear the film and pull it out. We had a tool on the editing table that measured film clips in seconds. A certain length would be three seconds, for example, and you would stick the clip on the wall with a piece of tape. Once you got the scenes in order, you then put them through the splicer, and glued them all together. It was laborious, like putting together a puzzle, but we managed to get stuff on the air pretty quick in some cases. Today, this same process is all done digitally with no tape or film. I would have thought it was science fiction if you had explained today's editing to me back then.

To help our news team communicate and track stories, we had two-way radios, police radios, sheriff radios and other gadgets so we knew what was going on and where. We also had Key Maps—no GPS or smart phones in those days—and I got pretty good at using that Key Map. If my camera guy Rick Hartley was driving, I'd take the book with all its pages keyed to each other. I'd quickly flip through the connections to look up where we needed to go and could get us there pretty quick. But when I was driving, and Rick had to look up an address on the Key Map, it was a real challenge for him. While I'm still not sure that Siri is the best way to find an address, people who didn't ever get the Key Map concept must find her a delight.

One night, around 2:00 in the morning, Rick and I were prowling through downtown. This was back when Union Station, where the Astros' ballpark is now, was still an active train station. On the side of one street, maybe Harrisburg, there was a railroad track where freight cars pulled in and out. There were some warehouses along there as well, and the street ended not far from the train station. While the street ended, however, the railroad track kept going. Those tracks called to me, just like they always do. Just to see if I could do it, before we got to the end of the street, I drove up on those tracks and just kept going on. Sitting in the passenger seat, Rick pretty much lost his mind. "What in the hell...what are you doing...??!!" he exclaimed clearly exasperated. Another great friend from those early KTRK days, David Glodt, who went on to have his own very successful career with big jobs in Los Angeles, London and Washington, D.C., recently reminded me he was in the backseat that night. He was just as unnerved by our cruise on the tracks as Rick.

What I knew that night that Rick and David obviously didn't was that the wheelbase of most cars, which is 4'8" or around there, is basically the same width as a standard train track. I am pretty sure it is still true today. So we went on down the track, actually turned a little bit, and on the other side of the Union Station I turned off onto a cross street. It's safe to say I enjoyed the ride more than my friends did that night!

Jim Priest was another photographer with whom I made a number of night runs. There was a shooting just north of downtown about 1:00 in the morning. Since we were just three or four blocks away when we got the news, we arrived before the police. We pull up and here's this guy lying in the street. He looked like he was dead. We had to do something to help. I tried to shove his chest but didn't really know CPR. Lucky for him, about that time, he gasped and a police car showed up and called for an ambulance. This was back when ambulances were privately owned, mostly by funeral homes. When the ambulance finally showed up, the attendants looked at that guy in the street and told the police officer, "This guy is dead. He ain't going to make it."

About that time, the shooting victim gasped again, loudly. The police officer said, "Load him up and take him to the hospital."

They loaded him up, probably to take him to Ben Taub, the charity hospital that had opened in 1963, and we don't know if that guy lived or died. That incident and reporting on how long it took to get an ambulance there was one of the key cogs that led the city to take over the emergency ambulance service from funeral homes and run them through the fire department.

While we were having some wild times out on the streets, back at the station, things were getting interesting as well. As the news director *and* anchor, Ray Conaway had regular commentary at the end of every 10 p.m. newscast that aired just before the station signed-off every night. Called "Conaway Comments," it gave Ray the chance to talk about whatever he wanted for about five minutes. Then the station played the "Star Spangled Banner," and then signed off for the night.

At one point, Ray was scheduled to be out of town for a whole week, so he went into the studio to record five of his "Conaway Comments" segments. He got through Monday's and Tuesday's just fine and was about a minute into his Wednesday commentary piece when George Ishee, our carpenter, cranked up a buzz saw back in the shop—which was right next to the studio. Of course, you could hear that buzz saw all throughout the studio. Well, that annoying sound stopped Conaway cold in the middle of his comments. He looked up straight in the camera and said, "Would somebody go turn off that goddamn, motherf-ing buzz saw?"

Well, a lot of mistakes were made right there.

First, Ray should have never said that with a microphone on, and even worse on camera—even though it was being taped, and not live. Second, the director should have stopped the taping immediately, and instructed the videotape operator to make sure that first take for Wednesday's commentary was cut and re-queued. What happened instead was the videotape operator, thinking the taping session was going to last about thirty minutes, had gone off on a coffee break and wasn't even near the video tape machine. I later learned that Ray labeled the videotape reel "needs to be edited" or some such, but no one heeded his warming.

As a result, nobody caught his profanity-laced outburst.

The next week, while Ray was out of town, Monday's and Tuesday's "Conaway Comments" went just fine. But on Wednesday night, sure enough, a minute into his commentary viewers heard that buzz saw followed by Conaway's tirade. Immediately, the station went to black then quickly put up its "Technical Difficulties" slide. "One moment please, we are experiencing technical difficulties," it read.

Well, the tape operator could not find where they picked up the "Conaway's Comments" again, so after about a minute or minute and a half—which can seem like an eternity in live TV—the operator made the decision to just play the Star-Spangled Banner and sign off.

This was not an era when popular music filled the airwaves with profanity. There were laws about propriety on air, and respectful language and content was demanded in every form of media. The next day, it was in the *Houston Chronicle* and *The Houston Post*: "Houston anchorman turns the airwaves blue!" Many people were understandably very upset by what had happened. And of course, the 60s were a time of transitioning moral standards, and some others thought it was funny. Willard Walbridge, the station manager, had a buzz saw blade painted blue and he mounted it in a frame, like a plaque, and presented it to Ray for the night he turned the airwaves blue. I don't think Ray ever really got over that.

When I started working at KTRK, there were two beautiful young women working at the station: the aforementioned Bunny Orsak who starred as our own "Kitirik"—and Kitty Bora, who also hosted a children's program on the weekends. Every day, when it was a sunshiny and warm, around noontime they would go into the restroom, change into their bikinis, and go out and lay around that much-ballyhooed swimming pool in the middle of the station. In no time at all, every guy in the building would make some excuse to walk down the hall just to look through the windows and see our two beautiful young ladies out there in their bikinis.

While today I recognize that we were objectifying our colleagues, at the time, we just thought we were very appropriately appreciating their loveliness. And we certainly respected their talents on air. Whatever our motivations were, however, there was one drawback we were aware of even back then: I feel certain that the architects and ownership team did not consider how much productivity would be lost when they proudly installed their "lovely garden patio with its gaily splashing fountain and shimmering pool!"

TOP: *I was fortunate to be KTRK's first on-the-street reporter when they expanded the news department in 1966. Here I am in my first week on the job.*
BOTTOM: *Here I am reporting from the Bat Mobile.*

*While on the news set, it seems I have always had a habit of spinning
a ball point pen to help pass the time between commercials.*

12

ANCHORMAN

On January 4, 1967, barely two months after I started at KTRK, the station announced that a company out of Albany, New York, called Capital Cities Communications had bought Channel 13 for $22.5 million dollars—a record sales price for a local station at the time. By 1966, as Walt Hawver later recalled in *How the Minnow Came to Swallow the Whale*, "the (KTRK) ownership was splintered; even the Houston Symphony held a minority interest. Eleven of the original investors were dead with their stock in estates. No one could remotely claim control." Jesse Jones died in 1956, leaving his nephew John the largest stockholder. The other investors were pressuring John Jones Jr. to sell, and general manager Bill Walbridge persuaded him to go with Capital Cities.

My first thought on hearing this news was, "Maybe my dad was right. Maybe I did make a mistake coming to this television station if there's going to be new ownership."

My second thought was, "My Lord, they must be crazy to pay that much money."

Capital Cities made that original investment back in two years, and every year after that they made twice that.

Immediately following the Capital Cities announcement, Walbridge called us all into the conference room to announce some changes. He was taking Ray Conaway off the anchor desk and assigned a young booth announcer, Bob Lowry, to be the anchor on the 6 and 10 o'clock newscast. It surprised that kid completely. He seemed as nervous as a cat and didn't last very long.

As for Conaway, someone asked him, "Ray, how do you want to be remembered?" He said, "I don't care how I'm remembered...or even *if.*" It was an oddly ungrammatical sentence for him. Ray never would have done anything remotely like that on the air. He was a stickler for the correct use of the English language in everything he did.

I was still nervous about the ownership change and bracing for potential bad news when Mr. Walbridge then announced, "Dave Ward will be the new anchorman on our 7 a.m. news." I didn't even know we had a 7 a.m. newscast. I'd been working for the 6 and 10 o'clock at night. So I asked Mr. Walbridge, "Sir, what do we do at 7 a.m.? Is that a five-minute news cast? A ten-minute newscast?"

Walbridge bristled and shot back, "No, Dave, that is a full thirty-minute newscast, as you would know if you watched the television station where you work."

I'm still naïve enough to think that, when it comes to television news, getting your facts right is by far the most important thing we can do. But I will concede it is also a visual medium; and, as such, appearances matter. When I first got to Channel 13, even though I was starting as a beat reporter, they took me on the anchor set to read some copy, to see what I would look like on camera. We had no teleprompter in those days, which meant your head was constantly bobbing up and down as you read your script. Watching my little screen test, John Gehbauer observed, "Ward, you need to let your hair grow out. We broadcast in black-and-white, and on camera your blonde, flat top haircut makes you look bald when you look down."

So, I let my hair grow out, and I've been fighting it ever since.

Taking over that anchor desk for the 7 a.m. newscast meant I had to be there by 5 o'clock in the morning. I had to write the whole thirty-minute program, re-edit the film from the ten o'clock news the night before, pull the wire copy and put that in order, and have everything ready to go by 6:45 a.m.

Our morning weatherman was a wonderful guy named Ted Bennett. One day, we had a cold front moving through Houston. Ted went on the air, and what he wanted to say was "There's a cold air mass headed for Houston." Only, on the air, he said, "There's a cold mare's ass headed for Houston."

Hearing that, the floor crew giggled. Ted stopped and said, "Well, of course, I meant to say cold mare's ass."

Now the crew was laughing.

Finally, Ted said, "Of course, you know I mean it is a cold mare's ass."

I was not far away from making my own faux pas on the 7 a.m. news. I had to report on the results of a PGA golf tournament over the weekend. The line in my script read: "He won the tournament with a 72 hole total of 272." But it came out of my mouth that morning as "72 toe hotal, I mean a toe hotal, I mean…well he won the tournament with 272 strokes," and got out of that.

In addition to anchoring the 7 a.m. news, I was still an on-the-street-reporter and filming for the news department. I ran a lot of film through that old Bell & Howell camera: fires, wrecks, shootings, drownings—you name it—all over the city.

A call came in late one night around 1:00 in the morning. "Fire in the Pink Pussycat Nightclub down there on Market Square." I took off, and by the time I got there it was a two-alarm fire, which very quickly became a three-alarm fire. The whole building was a mass of flames. From the outside, all I could see was flames through a couple of small windows. The rest of it was all above me. So I went down the street about a half a block, where there was a fire escape on the outside of a building. I pulled that fire escape ladder down, climbed up about four floors, and suddenly I could see the entire inside of that old nightclub. It was just a cauldron of flames.

I shot a ton of film of that fire and the firefighters running around, all the while wishing I was shooting color film—not black-and-white. Just then, the wind changed and the smoke from that fire came right across the street and right up the side of that building into my face. It was a choking, horrible disaster. I stumbled down that fire escape, not sure if I was going to survive. Well, I did, and KTRK was the only station that had film of the Pink Pussycat Strip Club fire that night, especially from that angle.

Just recently, a retired police sergeant approached me at a local restaurant and reminded me of another early story I covered. A report came in that a car had crashed into a house at the corner of Richmond and Kirby. "My partner and I headed that way and I thought, 'There are no houses there, that's all businesses,'" the officer recalled. I remember it too. What had happened was, in the middle of the night, they were moving a house and were coming down Richmond headed east. They were going to turn north on Kirby, when a drunk driver crashed his car into that house. I shot film of the car and the house out in the middle of the street.

Another time, there was a plane crash at 3 a.m. close to Houston Intercontinental Airport long before it was named for President George Bush. The incident involved a twin-engine private plane with fifteen passengers, so it probably was a chartered flight. My camera man Jimmy Priest and I had been riding all night—again—when the news came over the police radio: "Airplane down, not far from the airport."

Well, we went zipping out the North Freeway in the Channel 13 mobile unit and came up behind a marked Houston police unit with his red lights and siren going. This police officer was only driving about sixty miles an hour, so Jimmy passed him. We arrived at the address and stumbled through the bushes and trees to the accident scene. There was no fire, but someone from the airport or another police officer was there and had a flashlight. Well, Jimmy had his big Frezzy light so he could light up everything in the area, and we helped find the wreckage of this airplane. Everybody in it was dead. We were shocked and still shooting film when that police officer, who was a sergeant, came up to Priest and read him the riot act. "Jimmy, I ought to throw you in jail," he shouted. "If you ever do that again, if you ever pass up me or any other marked unit with red light and siren going you're going to go to jail."

Trust me, we never did that again.

In the middle of 1967, the station's programming director at the time, Howard Finch, called me into his office and he told me, "David, we're putting a new program on the air called 'Dialing for Dollars.' We want you to host it."

Whoever dreamed this show concept up, it must have come to them in a nightmare. For starters, it was an hour-long, pseudo game show running from 9 to 10 o'clock in the morning. The way it worked was we took phone books from Houston and all around our viewing area and cut each page into little strips. There would be ten or fifteen names and numbers on each strip. At the beginning of the show, I would announce what we called "the count" as well as the amount. For example, the count would be "fourth from the top" or "sixth from the bottom" on those little strips from the phone book. Then I would dial that number, and if the person who answered the phone knew the count *and* the amount of the jackpot, they would win the money.

We started the show off with a $5,000 jackpot, which back then was *really* a lot of money. Every time I called someone and they did not know the count or the amount—or it was a wrong number or whatever—we would add $100 to that jackpot. I made six phone calls in each one-hour show, which meant that if no one had the count *and* the amount, the jackpot would go up by $600 each day. I did those phone calls live on the air, and also in front of a live studio audience. We called so many wrong numbers, people who were not home, and "this number is no longer in service" messages, that those $100 increases to the jackpot started to add up.

It was at least three weeks, maybe a month, before we had our first winner. A woman knew both the count and the amount, and the studio audience went ballistic. I'll never forget it. And then, of course, the same woman had to come to the station the next day and accept the check from me, live on the air. With that, the show was really off and running, and started to get people's attention. Even my daughter Linda, very young at the time, asked me one day why we never called her. I had to explain why that would definitely not be okay!

During my "Dialing for Dollars" run, I had a co-host named Betty Rogers, who would talk about recipes and all kinds of women's things. Every Thursday, she would also have a fashion show, live, there in the studio with the Ben Shaw agency fashion models. Every Thursday, five or six of these models would come out wearing dresses and the like. Then, they would go off camera to the side and change into the next outfit.

While changing that first week, however, the models stripped down to their underwear and sometimes they had no brassiere. Well, as you might expect, the studio audience just went crazy—and not in a good way—because those models, just off camera, were still in front of them in plain sight. Seeing that, I told the studio people, "Look, we can't do this. You've got to put up a screen or something over there where these models can walk behind to change their clothes." Which we did, for every show thereafter.

When Howard Finch first called me into his office and told me I would be doing "Dialing for Dollars," he said they would pay me $25 per show, which meant another $125 a week in my paycheck. "You're in the big money now, right?" Finch told me.

After a week or so, though, the assistant news director, my friend John Gehbauer, called me into *his* office and said, "David, you work for the news department here at Channel 13. You're hired to put in at least eight hours a day, but this game show takes you out of the news department for two hours. You have to be in the studio by about 8:30 to warm up the audience, and you don't get out of there until around 10:30 after everybody is gone. So, from now on, you're going to work an extra two hours in the afternoon for the news department."

I had been getting to the station at 5 a.m. and leaving about 1 p.m., but Gehbauer's new edict meant I had to work until 3 p.m. I probably shouldn't have, but I put a pencil to it a little later and figured that, if they had just paid me the time and a half overtime instead of that $25 a show talent fee, I would have ended up making more money.

"Dialing for Dollars" continued on the air for quite some time with a string of hosts. When I left the 7 a.m. news, Troy Dungan did it, I believe, then eventually Howard Finch, and my friend Don Nelson had a turn dialing. It eventually made way for the very popular "Good Morning Houston" hosted at the time by Don and Jan Glenn.

In April of 1968, Bill Walbridge called me down to his office. When I walked in another man was already in there, and Walbridge said, "At one point somebody had to introduce David Brinkley to Chet Huntley, so Dave Ward meet Dan Ammerman. You two will now be co-anchoring the 6 and 10 o'clock newscasts Monday through Friday."

I was flabbergasted. I had no idea anything like this was in the works. After I left Mr. Walbridge's office, I immediately went to Charlie Harrison, who at that time was the sole anchor on our 6 o'clock and 10 o'clock newscasts. I told Charlie, "I had absolutely nothing to do with this."

I think he believed me. Anyway, I hope he did, because it was the truth. Even though I had never experienced anything like it at the time, I could imagine what it must have felt like to be in his shoes.

But with all respect to Charlie's disappointment, the news was also very exciting for me.

Ammerman and I became the first co-anchors on any Houston television station. The two of us wrote our own scripts on manual typewriters, edited film, and otherwise produced each newscast. We hit the air with our first co-anchor newscast, I believe, sometime in May. Rounding out the news team, we still had Troy Dungan forecasting the weather and Guy Savage covering sports.

When Dan Ammerman and I first started co-anchoring, KTRK was a very poor, distant number three in the market—and sometimes number four, even behind KUHT Channel 8. As Walt Hawver put it, in the late 1960s "the station was better known for its domed architecture than for its ratings." Swanky, nice offices were great, of course; but as a practical matter, a TV station lives and dies by its ratings. That's our bread and butter.

Despite our meager standing in the Houston market at the time, I'll never forget Ammerman, an extremely confident guy, who boldy declared, "We're going to be number one in the next ratings book. Just you watch." I cautioned him to manage his expectations. We were, after all, the new kids on the block, and we were going up against some serious competition: Ron Stone and Sid Lasher and sports reporter Johnny Temple on Channel 11; and Larry Rascoe and a good team over on Channel 2.

In the next ratings book, we had made a very small move upward, but were still cellar dwellers. "Just hang in there, and we'll get there," I reassured Dan. Ratings don't just change overnight. To make an impact, you do the best you can, and stay consistent. In the news business, you have to be believable—and it takes a long time to build trust. It can take a few years for a television news anchor team or person to build confidence among the viewers that they're going to give them the right information and give them the truth about it.

Not long after we started, Dan came to me with a complaint. He felt that I was giving myself all the lead stories, and all the good stories. He also told me that I had more lines than he did. When I asked him why he felt this way, it turned out that he had actually counted the lines in each script. I thought I had just been doing my share of the work but perhaps in my enthusiasm, I had gone overboard. From then on I consciously tried to let Dan have the lead stories, or the best stories, or longest stories.

Looking back, my pairing with Dan was no doubt like watching "The Odd Couple," a popular TV show airing around that time. Like Oscar and Felix, Dan and I were different in almost every way. Walt Hawver described Dan as "the quintessential urbanite—perfectly tailored, prepared, proper and poised on the set," while I was, in Walt's view, "pure country—not in the least fashion-conscious, more comfortable riding in police cars and chasing fires than reading copy."

When I joined the news department of KTRK-TV, there were seven men working there. Make that seven white men. I know, for a fact, had I been an African American male, or a Hispanic male, or a woman of any race, they would not have even let me in the door, much less given me a job at that time. That's just the way it was back in 1966. Happily, we've seen a lot of progress in terms of diversity since then—but it did not come quickly at first.

In fact, it wasn't until late December 1970 when KTRK became the first station in town to integrate its newsroom when they hired former radio newsman Charles Porter, who was African American. A few months later, Greg Dumas (whose real surname was Guerrero) joined the team. In due course, we added Diana Fallis, the city's first Black female reporter and anchor; and Elma Barrera, the city's first Latina woman on air. We were moving—and in terms of the other TV stations in town, we were actually leading the way—but the criticism that we and other stations were moving too slowly in hiring and promoting minorities was absolutely fair.

During the civil rights movement, meanwhile, I remember some sit-ins, like the Sears lunch counter on South Main, where Black students would go in and sit down even though they would not be served. They would sit there and, inevitably, the owner of the restaurant or coffee shop would call the police and have them evicted. But there were never any full-blown race riots in Houston.

The closest we came to a riot at the time occurred at Texas Southern University on May 17, 1967—while I was still anchoring the 7 a.m. newscast. I came in at 5 a.m. to find all the other news guys there.

"What the hell is everyone doing here?!" I asked, sensing something big was clearly going on.

"We had a riot at Texas Southern University in the middle of the night," someone explained.

"Why didn't you call me?" I shot back, upset that I had missed the story.

"Because you've got to be here to anchor the 7 a.m. news, that's why."

Apparently, a rumor had spread that a six year-old Black child had been killed by police, and TSU students had started to gather and chant. They were reportedly loud and angry, but none of them had guns. The only gunshots fired were by the police, and one of those police officer's bullets hit another officer and tragically killed him.

One of the reasons Houston fared better than almost all other cities in terms of race relations during what was otherwise a very tense and difficult time was due to the remarkable efforts of, and leadership by, the Reverend William Lawson—who was still in the early days of establishing his influential Wheeler Avenue Baptist Church. Now, right here I need to disclose, in the spirit of transparency, that the good Reverend's daughter, Melanie, has been my friend and respected colleague at KTRK for over thirty years. So, I am hardly objective where the Lawson family is concerned.

And, I could also be accused of a certain bias where Baptist preachers are concerned.

At the time of this near-riot at TSU, Reverend Lawson was serving as the director of the Baptist student union and teaching as a professor of Bible studies there. That devout man, great family man, and great leader in Houston had a calming effect on our entire community. People have always respected Bill Lawson, it seems, and they listen when he speaks. On more than one occasion, I remember him saying, "We are not like other cities. We are not going to riot, and tear things up. Yes, we have a right to protest. Yes, we want voting rights, and basic fairness and equality in society. But no one has a right to riot, or loot, or commit a crime to achieve these worthy goals."

It was a powerful, and effective, message.

In a relatively short time, I had moved from radio to television anchor. I went from crusing the dark streets for breaking news, to being on the scene at emotionally-packed events, to searching for words to convey the experiences, and finally to being in front of the camera, calm and collected, to report them to our viewers. I was no longer floating from interest to interest learning new skills; my early experiences had come together and solidified into a career, and by all measures, it was going well.

But for all the success I was finding at work, the adrenaline rush created during these times was beginning to create challenges in my personal life. It would be quite some time before I was willing to recognize the price my family, and my body, were paying.

In 1967, the powers that be at KTRK asked me to host a daytime game show called "Dialing for Dollars." Here I am with one of our early winners.

My one and only foray into serious acting, playing a wrong-headed sheriff in the very first made-for-TV movie "My Sweet Charlie."

DAMN GOOD SHOTS

$\mathbf{S}$hortly after I started anchoring the 6 and 10 o'clock newscasts, our news team discovered Kay's Lounge just a few blocks down the street from the station on Bissonnet Street. It was originally named for the wife of Gordon Edge, the man who built it back in 1939. The single-story building actually won an architectural award for its art deco, futuristic design. One of the guys on our floor crew, Bobby Jewel, found it. He had been going to a bar just down the street from Channel 13, but one night, for some reason, it was closed—so he just went further east on Bissonnet. On the other side of Kirby, before you came to Shepherd Drive, he found Kay's Lounge. It was owned at the time by Janelle Black, a lovely woman, and the bartender was Eldon Creech, a former Merchant Marine who stumbled in one night and asked for a job.

When you walked in, the first thing greeting you was usually the wafting aroma of stale beer and the seductive glow of neon beer signs. It had a bar down one side of the building with stools. There were pinball machines and a coin-operated pool table in the back room, and near the end of the bar there was a coin-operated bowling machine. On the two other walls there were booths and then some tables scattered around the interior of the place—the most famous of which was the "Texas table." As the name suggests, it was a big table crafted in the shape of the state of Texas. *Texas Monthly* magazine back in the 1970s named it the best table in the entire state two years in a row.

Kay's was a dive bar without equal. In all the time I spent going there, which was more than is advisable, I never once saw anyone get into any arguments or fights over games—or anything else for that matter. I do remember distinctly, though, one night I was walking out of the back room after a visit to the restroom. By the juke box, there was a single step—and as I stepped down, a woman grabbed me by my necktie and yanked me around. I ended up going over a table and crashing to the floor. I never knew what her problem was, but I never wore a necktie in there ever again.

Kay's Lounge sold only beer, wine and set-ups. You could bring your own alcohol in a brown paper bag, and they would sell you ice and water, soda, or whatever you wanted. Our Channel 13 crew ended up going down there almost every night right after the 10 o'clock news. As in, right after. We'd be down there by about 10:45 at the latest. One night we walked in, and it was empty. Eldon was leaning up against the bar, and he straightened up and said, "Ah, customers! Come right in!"

Eldon looked and sounded like the old vaudeville actor W.C. Fields. He was quite a guy. When the city health inspectors said he had to erect a sign on the wall advising his patrons that the wines he served contained sulfites, Eldon devised a sign that read: "Our wines contain sulfites, at no extra charge to you, our valued customer." He also had a sign put in the men's room: "Please do not throw cigarettes into the urinal. It makes them soggy and hard to light."

Eldon and Janelle later got married and bought a beautiful home out on the west side of Houston with a nice big swimming pool. I spent a lot of time with them both in the bar and at their home. In the 1980s Janelle died, and Eldon became the sole owner. He let me run a tab there, and I would pay it every six or eight weeks. I always paid in cash, but would also always leave ten or twenty bucks on it, so there would be an ongoing, running tab.

It was at Kay's Lounge where I first met the one and only Dr. Red Duke. He liked to go in the kitchen and make his own pizza, but he would use so much garlic it would just about run everybody out of the place. Part of the folklore around Kay's maintains that Red and I were occasionally seen dancing together on the tables at Kay's. I can't confirm that…but then again, I cannot deny it either.

By any account, I was a regular at Kay's, but my drinking wasn't interfering with my ability to do my work. And my work continued to be exciting, introducing me to more people in more walks of life than I could have imagined when I was growing up in small-town Texas.

Houston was a big city—getting bigger fast—and I was living for the news it generated.

The rodeo plays a big part in Houston's civic and social life. In 1967, I was assigned for the first time to co-anchor our coverage of the Houston Livestock Show and Rodeo parade through downtown Houston. They set us up on the second-floor balcony of the old Rice Hotel. My co-commentator was a *Houston Chronicle* columnist named Morris Frank. The balcony where we were sitting that day was surrounded with high shrubbery, so as a result we could not physically see the parade. We had to call the parade off of television monitors set up right in front of us. As the parade proceeded, Morris kept commenting on the short skirts worn by the majorettes of the high school bands that were parading down there in the street. He kept saying things like, "These skirts are even shorter than the band in front of them!"

After we went to a commercial break, I told Morris, "You've got to stop talking about those little girls' short skirts. Everybody is going to think you're a dirty old man!"

Morris looked me straight in the eye and said, "What's wrong with that?" Different times, for sure.

I anchored forty-nine consecutive Rodeo parades, most of them from the steps of the Alley Theatre near the parade route. Along the way, I had many wonderful co-anchors, including Jan Carson, Shara Fryer, and Don Nelson. And of course, helping us behind the scenes to get the parade on the air was a Herculean task which, for so many years, was beautifully managed by one of the most capable production and programming executives with whom I've had the pleasure of working—Kim Nordt-Jackson. Kim started working at KTRK in 1981 and quickly rose through the ranks owing to her talent and unmatched work ethic.

One year, there were a few glitches during the course of our three hours of parade coverage, which, believe me, is a long time to be on the air. Basically, we got out of sync at one point, and the parade elements our lineup sheet indicated were coming up did not match with the pictures being aired. That's the way it goes on live TV sometimes, but for some reason it really got to me that day. When we came off the air, and after I had taken off my earpiece, Kim came bounding up the Alley Theater stairs and enthusiastically asked, "What did you think?"

Well, I lit into her—complaining rather childishly about how some of the shots did not match what we were saying. That really upset Kim, who turned and quickly walked in the other direction. Realizing my screw up, I rushed after her to apologize. Being the gracious professional that she is, Kim quickly got over it—but all these years later, it remains one of the biggest regrets of my career.

The Rodeo started back in 1932, and as of the time I write this, they've given over $475 million to support Texas youth. Sharing the Go Texan Day parade with the proud city was an honor, and always high-energy with all the cowboys, cowgirls, trail riders and fans ready to rodeo.

Thinking of those early parade newscasts reminds me of another Morris Frank story, which illustrates how carefully we always had to watch our language on air back then. Morris also did a nightly pre-recorded segment on Channel 13 called "From the Morris Chair." They were about five minutes long, on any topic Morris chose. The rest of the news staff had orders that no one was to be in the studio when Morris taped these pieces, because if Morris could see you he would talk to you instead of into the camera.

One day, I was standing behind the camera operator when Morris recorded his commentary. He started off on the singer Engelbert Humperdinck. Only Morris said, "What is with this singer named Engelbert Humpingdick? How does he get away with using that name on the radio?" I had to step out from behind the camera and tell him, "No, Morris, his name is Humperdinck." So they re-racked the tape, and he went on and talked about something else. It was funny, but it would not have been funny had it slipped onto the air.

While we were still in our first year of the Ammerman-Ward era, there was one 10 p.m. newscast on a Monday where the substitute weatherman who was supposed to fill in for Troy Dungan did not show up for work. We found out from him later that he thought 10 o'clock news was a tape of the 6 o'clock news. In the meantime, when we came to the commercial before the weather report, the floor crew chief came out from behind the camera and said, "Troy Dungan's substitute is not here. You and Dan are going to have to do the weather."

I said, "Hold on, wait just a minute…"

It was too late. "Stand by, cue," said the floor chief. We were back live.

Having no choice, I gestured to the map of the United States and said, "Let's take a look now at the weather forecast. As you can see, there are Hs and Ls on the map and they are moving, generally, from left to right. And now the forecast…"

In those days, the weather team used abbreviations on a sandwich board and filled in the numbers and letters by hand. That night, the board read 1-2 sct (scattered) thshr (thundershowers). Dan Ammerman gave the forecast and based on that sandwich board info said, "The forecast for tomorrow will be 1-2 inches of rain in scattered thunderstorms."

I hated to do it but knew that was not the right way to read it. I jumped in. "No, Dan," I said, "I think it means just one or two scattered thundershowers."

A little flustered, Dan shot back, "That's so insignificant we shouldn't even mention it."

Simply put, it was a disaster. That was the last time they had Dan Ammerman and I do the weather on any newscast.

Though I wasn't cut out to be a weatherman, there were still so many aspects of the news business that continued to interest me more and more. Politics in particular, with the constantly shifting landscape, always provided good stories. And, as in any line of work, there was always some comic relief. In 1967, Lyndon Johnson visited Houston. My photographer, Wayne Zerr, and I were sent out to Hobby Airport to film the President's arrival. Wayne shot film of Air Force One circling over the airport, then landing, then taxiing over to where the President was going to get off the plane. Then he shot film of the Air Force officers taking the stairs up to the airplane, going up those stairs, opening the door, and entering the plane.

Quite a crowd was on hand that day. They had positioned the media on risers about six feet high so we had a clear view. Usually, several minutes elapsed before the President would come out—so Wayne turned his camera and began shooting film of the crowd. Well, apparently LBJ was in a hurry that day because, within a few seconds, he came out the door of Air Force 1 and started down the stairs. Wayne was still shooting the crowd, and I hollered at him, "Wayne, there he is, shoot him! Shoot him!"

That was a very poor choice of words. Immediately, I saw the heads of Secret Service agents snapping around, looking very alarmed. So immediately I re-phrased it and said, "I mean take his picture! Take his picture!"

Well, Wayne did. We got our film and left.

Inevitably, some days we got the shot, and others, we didn't. In 1969, the Apollo 11 astronauts went to the moon. I was very disappointed my television station did not send me to the Cape for the launch of Apollo 11. I had covered Apollo 7, 8, 9 and 10, but when it came time for the Apollo 11 shot, news director Red Cook held firm. "This will be all over the networks," Red said. "There is no reason for us to be there." So, much to my chagrin, I was not there when NASA launched the first manned mission to land on the moon.

Despite missing the launch, I did get my Apollo 11 moment. After the astronauts returned from the moon, Neil Armstrong, Buzz Aldrin and the command module captain, Michael Collins, were all in isolation for two or three weeks just in case some kind of microbe from the moon had come back with them. After they got out of isolation, the city threw a big parade through downtown Houston to honor the first men on the moon.

Red came up with a great idea to put Dan Ammerman and me in the back seat of a convertible with thousands of little American flags. Then, we somehow broke into the front of that parade. We were about a block ahead of the actual parade with Channel 13 banners on both sides and a sign that read "Channel 13 Welcomes Our Moon Astronauts." We drove down the parade route handing out little American flags to thousands of people who had lined the sides of the streets. Where Red got all of those flags, I will never know. But we were quite a hit, and when the Apollo astronauts finally followed along behind us, everyone in the crowd was waving a small American flag. That was one of Red Cook's best ideas.

Astronauts were the big excitement in those days, but on the ground the trains were still running, and occasionally making news. In 1969, a wealthy Englishman named Adam Pegler brought an iconic British train called the "Flying Scotsman," which he had refurbished at no small cost, to tour the United States—starting on the East Coast. With support from the British government, at least for that first year of this unique U.S. tour, the train was really a traveling trade mission for British goods—"boosting British exports" as Pegler described it. The Scotsman was a big, single-chimney steam engine painted in the customary "apple green" livery of the London and North Eastern Railway, and it was pulling a nine-coach train; two sleeper cars for staff; and an observation car that Mr. Pegler had converted into a rolling pub. Accompanying Pegler on the trip was one of Winston Churchill's nephews—who looked, drank whiskey and smoked cigars like his uncle—as well as the pipe major who played at Churchill's funeral, and ten mini-skirted sales girls.

In November, Pegler's tour with the Scotsman made it to Dallas for the final leg of their 1969 campaign, which would take them to Houston by way of Fort Worth. Our photographer Ben Pearlman was as much of a train freak as I am, if not more so, so we went to Dallas together and chased it out to Fort Worth. One of the very best reports I ever did, like something out of a movie, took place during this assignment. Ben had the camera set down on kind of a low angle, and I was standing in front of Scotsman about fifteen feet behind me. When the bell rang and it was time for them to leave, Ben started rolling and I said something like: "We're about to see the Flying Scotsman depart Dallas, eventually making its way to Houston." Just then, the engineer blew steam out of the engine, and it completely covered the whole front of the train. When the engine started moving, it re-emerged coming out of the steam. It was an unbelievable shot— again, like something out of Hollywood.

Flushed with that first success, we jumped in our rental station wagon and chased the Flying Scotsman to Fort Worth. I knew that rail line well, and also Highway 80 that ran parallel to it. I drove while Ben hung on the tailgate with the door down as he was filming the train. After a good bit, Ben told me, "Dave, the carbon monoxide is getting to me!"

I knew we were getting such great material that I told him, "Just keep shooting, just keep shooting." Meanwhile, I had a microphone and had prepared a script with facts about the Scotsman, which I recorded while driving. Somehow, it worked. When we got to Fort Worth, we were invited to ride the train into Houston—which also was the very last stop on the 1969 U.S. tour. Along the way, I saw more than a few panicked cattle that had obviously never seen a big steam engine.

Pegler's butler told me that, when we pulled into Union Station, his boss was going up into the cab with the engineer and the fireman where they would drink a champagne toast together and smash their glasses on the fire box. He asked if we might like to film that. Yes, we did! I took my 16mm silent camera up into that cab to film that very proper, very British closing ceremony.

But in England, just as we were experiencing in the U.S., times were rapidly changing, and with them social values. After that very elegant closing ceremony, one of the mini-skirted lasses on Pegler's crew got off the train in very see-through skirt. As we were exiting Union Station, a few people commented on her risqué outfit. She said, "I don't know what the fuss is all about. We wear clothes like this in London all the time."

"Well, you ain't in London now, dear," a proper Texas lady near her responded dryly.

That first year, which ended in Houston, Pegler's tour broke even. But his financial support from the U.K. government evaporated and further sponsorships failed to materialize, so his second U.S. tour the following year eventually forced Pegler into bankruptcy. The Scotsman was actually stranded in America for a few years—impounded on the docks of San Francisco. It was finally repatriated to the United Kingdom in 1973, after railway preservationist Sir William McAlpine put together the funds for a rescue plan.

Even if Texas wasn't changing its definition of appropriate dress codes as quickly as the youth of London, the world was changing around us in more important ways. Race relations continued to simmer and sometimes boil over. We covered those stories on the news, but the changing landscape was also making its way into entertainment. Additionally, as film and television evolved, more ways to share stories of all kinds developed.

On January 20, 1970, the first ever made-for-television movie "My Sweet Charlie" aired nationwide on NBC. The story depicted a young black attorney from New York named Charlie Roberts, who was falsely accused of killing a police officer during a civil rights protest in rural Texas. After escaping the police, Charlie meets a southern, pregnant teen runaway named Marlene Chambers while both are hiding out along the Texas coast in an abandoned house. At first, the two characters are suspicious of and prejudiced against each other, but soon realize they need each other to survive. In the end, they become friends.

The main stars of this groundbreaking project were Patty Duke, Al Freeman Jr., and an older character actor named Ford Rainey. Duke was the biggest name, having won an Academy Award in 1962 at age sixteen for her portrayal of Hellen Keller in "The Miracle Worker." Freeman, meanwhile, had just started a twenty-year run on the soap opera *One Life to Live* playing Police Captain Ed Hall. Freeman would go on to have an impressive list of other TV, Broadway, and movie credits as well.

There were also a few local folks cast for supporting roles, including yours truly. Fred Smith, who worked in the Channel 13 newsroom, was a member of Screen Actors Guild and had acted in a few other productions. He was contacted by Universal Studios to help find some local talent, and Fred told Dan Ammerman and me to go audition for the role of the deputy sheriff. So, we both read for the producers, and in the end, I got the part. Dan was a little bit upset at that, but a few years later, he was chosen to play a doctor in six episodes of the long-running TV series, "Dallas," in which he was very good. Another local actor, Bill Hardy, was picked to play the role of the sheriff, but at the last minute discovered he had a contractual conflict—so I inherited the role of the sheriff.

I got to know Ford Rainey, who played Treadwell, the owner of the general store down near the beach, very well. He was a genuinely nice man and told me a little about his film career, including his first role playing a steam locomotive engineer in the 1949 James Cagney movie "White Heat." Ford's character, Zuckie Hommell, was shot and killed by Cagney in the very first scene, but Rainey was still getting residual payments from that movie twenty years later. Hearing that, I thought this movie-making stuff must be rather lucrative.

I did not get to know Al Freeman Jr. or Patty Duke very well during filming. They seemed to remain in character through the entire project, and since I played the part of their nemesis, they kept their distance and didn't socialize with me.

We filmed most of the project in two big beach houses on the Bolivar Peninsula near a lighthouse on the north side of the highway—

just down from the ferry landing. Universal Television Studios brought three huge eighteen-wheelers loaded down with cameras, lights, even a portable air conditioning system to put in that beach house where the lead characters filmed their parts. The film was shot in July but set around Christmas, so during my scenes I had to wear a Galveston County Sheriff's uniform with a heavy jacket. I was melting during most of the shoot, but they did a great job concealing that in the final edit.

I originally read for the part with a cigar in my mouth, and since that seemed to work I showed up on my first day of shooting with another cigar. However, the director of the film, Lamont Johnson, told me, "Lose the cigar, Dave. There may be cigarette sponsors when this airs."

In my first scene, my character and the deputy sheriff drive up in a sheriff's vehicle to check those two beach houses. Exiting the car, I told the deputy, "You check that one over there, and I'll check this one." The house I checked was the one in which Charlie and Marlene were hiding inside, in the kitchen. I walked up the stairs, and on screen you saw me peering through a window, take off my sunglasses, then go to the door. Then I rattled the doorknob, but it was locked.

Eventually, I said something like, "Let's get out of here. Obviously he's not here. He's probably miles away by now." The director then cuts to Charlie, lying down on the floor just inside the door, clearly terrified. This leads to a very tender scene between Charlie and Marlene where they get to know a little bit about each other.

Later in the movie, when Marlene goes into labor, Charlie runs down to Treadwell's store to get help. Well, Treadwell messes around and picks up the phone and calls the sheriff's department. When Charlie finds out about it, he says, "You need to get an ambulance. It's a white woman!"

Treadwell said, "Well, why didn't you tell me that?"

At that point, I come driving up in a sheriff's car with lights flashing, and Charlie runs out the back door. Treadwell runs out the front door and shouted, "Get him Sheriff! He's getting away!" The script called for me to just fire one shot at Charlie as he's running away, but I told the director that any law enforcement officer would first fire a warning shot up in the air and then shoot to kill. Johnson said, "Okay, we'll do it that way."

On my first take, I ran by the camera, which was on a dolly going down a track on my left. I pulled out the gun and hollered, "Stop! Or I'll shoot you!" Then I held the pistol straight up at arms-length and fired.

The director and the photographer yelled "Cut! Cut! Stop!" Then the photographer told me, "Dave, this is a tight shot on you, a head-and-shoulder shot, but when you hold the gun at arms-length it is up out of the camera frame. You've got to hold it closer, lower to you." On the second take, I held the pistol just to the right of me, about head-high, and fired. In an instant, I heard a deafening ringing in my right ear, but I completed the scene. I still have that ringing in my right ear to this day. After I fired, Al Freeman fell on a mattress in the scrub brushes near the beach, and that ended the scene.

In the last scene of the movie, we're looking up the staircase at this beach house as Patty Duke is being escorted by a doctor played by Fred Smith. She's about to have a baby, and the doctor puts her in the sheriff's car. Ford Rainey turns to me, and I have the last line in the film: "I thought he was robbing your store." Then I get in the car and drive away. The last scene shows Marlene looking forlornly out of the car window towards that beach house where she and Charlie had found each other and discovered a unique friendship.

Fade to black; roll credits; end of film.

I recall being paid about $650 a week, and filming took two weeks—so all in I made $1,300, bucks which was pretty good money back then. When it aired, it was on Channel 2 from 8 to 10 p.m. When I came on Channel 13 that same night for the 10 o'clock news, it was just a weird feeling to have been on one channel acting in a controversial and sinister role, and then to be a news reporter on my usual channel. More checks came in every three or four months for about the next three years. If I remember right, the last check was for only about $15.

"My Sweet Charlie" won three Emmy Awards including Patty Duke for Outstanding Single Performance by an Actress in a Leading Role—and Outstanding Writing Achievement in Drama. The movie was also nominated for five other Emmys, including Al Freeman Jr. for Outstanding Single Performance by an Actor in a Leading Role.

I still suspect this might have been some kind of hoax, but about two weeks after the initial airing of the film, I got a hand-scrawled letter that read, "Dave Ward, I seen you shoot that feller on TV. You are mean. You are so mean. You should not be allowed to be on TV. But I has to admit, you a damn good shot!"

*"There's good news and bad news. Bad News—it's hot—
good news—there's lots of beer!"*

*This caricature of me captures the way many Houstonians
got through a hot summer back in the day.*

*Getting ready to film a report from the streets of Managua, Nicaragua in 1972—
the scene of so much devastation after a horrific earthquake
reduced much of the city to rubble.*

THE HORSEMEN
FROM ALBANY

In late 1969, I was on an assignment with news director, Red Cook, and photographer, Ben Pearlman, in Laredo when the devastating news reached us that KTRK's sports director, Guy Savage, had died of a heart attack between the 6 and 10 o'clock newscasts. Guy was a broadcasting institution unto himself, having debuted as a radio sports announcer in 1932 with the Beaumont Exporters baseball club. Later in the 1930s, he made the move to KTRH-AM in Houston, and then became part of the Houston Buffs' broadcast team starting in 1949 on KLEE-TV Channel 2. Guy also called Colt .45 games in the 1960s and had been KTRK's terrific sports director since 1960.

And, he had the best name any sportscaster ever had.

When we returned to Houston, Red Cook put Dan Lovett, who had been doing the weekend sports, on the weekday news team Monday through Friday. "A weird way to get a promotion," Dan later wrote.

Dan and I first met during my radio days. He was at KNUZ's main competitor, "the Big 6-10 KILT," and over time we became great friends and running buddies—all the more so after he joined KTRK in 1968. We got so close, we even bought homes on the same cul-de-sac in Spring, a suburb just north of Houston. My house was in the back; our friend Ben Bedner's two-story home was right next to mine; and Dan's single-level home was next to his.

Ben had a swimming pool in his backyard, and so did Dan. I did not, but my back lot was shaped like a pie so the backyard stretched very wide and went right into a thicket of woods. As a result, we had a lot of visiting raccoons and squirrels around that house for quite some time. For Dan and I, the drive time from our homes to the television station was thirty-six miles. Many times, Lovett and I would just ride in one car.

It was through Dan that I met Anthony Joseph Foyt, who is—not just in my mind, but based on all the racing record books—the greatest racecar driver in the history of the sport. He was the first to win the Indy 500 four times, as well as win 24 Hours of Le Mans, 24 Hours of Daytona, and the Daytona 500. If it has wheels and a motor, chances are A.J. Foyt has won it—probably more than once. He started on the racetrack off South Main Street in Houston. His father, Anthony Joseph Foyt Sr., started him on go-karts and then midget cars (a class of very small race cars with a high power-to-weight ratio).

Lovett and I went to the Indianapolis 500 in 1967, the year A.J. won it for the third time. I will never forget that experience as long as I live. After the race, his entire crew jumped on the back of a pick-up truck and took a lap around the racetrack—and Lovett jumped up there and rode around with them.

Later, in 1972, Lovett and I bought cars from A.J. He had a Chevrolet dealership on South Post Oak, so he arranged for us to get matching Chevrolet Monte Carlos. They were different colors, but both were two-door cars—and the engines and drive trains were identical. But, A.J. didn't stop there; he took them to his racing garage and tweaked those engines.

Some nights, Lovett and I would get off at 10:30, go down to Kay's and have more than a few beers, and—after they closed Kay's at midnight—we'd get in our cars and head up I-45 to Spring. Looking back, I recognize it was very irresponsible for us to be driving after drinking, but attitudes and accepted norms were very different at the time. That's a weak excuse, but it's also the truth.

And, I am afraid in terms of local road safety, it gets a worse. On I-45 heading north from downtown, a little past the cutoff to Bush Airport, there is a stretch of straight road three miles long with no entrances or exits. Just three lanes of asphalt. When we hit that stretch, we would get side-by-side and just run those Monte Carlos as fast as they would go. Thanks to A.J., those cars could hit 130 mph.

One night around 1:00 a.m., we hit that three-mile straight stretch on I-45, and there in the center lane ahead was this big eighteen-wheeler. Lovett got in the right lane, and I got in the left. After we passed that eighteen-wheeler at about 130 miles an hour, we crisscrossed in front of that trucker. I didn't hear a horn, but he blinked his lights like crazy.

I am thankful to this day that we didn't kill ourselves—or worse, someone else.

In 1972, Lovett and I went to the Ontario Motor Speedway in California to watch A.J. try to repeat as champion in that NASCAR race. At that time, he was driving the number 21 car, the Wood Brothers Mercury, in which he had a whale of a record. I had just gotten a new digital watch with a timer and was still learning how to work that thing. We had fun sitting in the stands taking lap times and stuff like that. A.J. took the lead, and somehow I calculated on my watch and told Lovett that our buddy was going to win. Sure enough, he did.

A few years later, they had a midget car race in the Astrodome, and to help put on a show for his hometown fans, A.J. agreed to race on that dirt track with the rest of the field. Again, not surprisingly, it wasn't long after the race started before A.J. was leading the pack. I was down there on the infield watching, and it was clear to me he had the race won. But, as A.J. came into turn three on one of the last laps, his car hit a rut—and instead of rolling over to the outside, it flipped towards the inside and landed upside down.

I was the first one to get to A.J., who was, thankfully, uhnurt. They pushed his car over, and he climbed out. Though unscathed, he was hopping mad. "I can't believe out here in front of my hometown crowd, I done flipped that damn thing!" he told me, still disgusted with himself.

A.J. Foyt has been such a huge attribute for the City of Houston. He was one of the many sports superstars who play and live in Houston and has brought so much recognition to the city. Lovett and I enjoyed living the race-car driver life vicariously through him.

Lovett and I did much more together than drag race home. During our 6 o'clock newscast on July 4th in the early 1970s, we covered all of the obligatory patriotic speeches, parades, fireworks—everything. At one point, we did a pre-taped report from Galveston, and I wrote the lead-in to it that said: "In Galveston today, the beaches were busy as thousands of people flocked to sun and surf." Then, we rolled the film.

We did another report on Galveston that night at 10 o'clock, only this time leading into the piece I said, "In Galveston today, the bitches were beezy as thousands of people flocked to sun and surf." As I was saying that, I could hear Lovett next to me snickering. Then they rolled the film, and he turned to me: "Do you know what you just said?"

I said, "Yeah, in Galveston today the beaches were busy."

He said, "No you didn't. You said the 'bitches were beezy.'"

"No, I did not."

About that time, the camera operator poked his head out from behind the camera saying, "Oh, yes you did!"

Hearing that, I shrugged and said, "Well, I did it on purpose."

Now everyone was really hoorahing me: "Right, Ward! Ha, ha, ha."

Finishing the newscast, the crew was still laughing it off when I beckoned Lovett to come with me. We walked out of the studio, down the hall, and over to my desk. Once there, I told Lovett, "Open the lap drawer of my desk." He opened the drawer. An envelope was there with his name on it. I said, "Open it." He opened it up, and inside the envelope there was a single strip of paper. Typewritten on it: "In Galveston today, the bitches were beezy."

Dan Lovett turned to me in shock and said, "You really did do that on purpose!"

The shock on his face gave me a great laugh.

For the record, that was the only time I ever intentionally misspoke on television. Later on, I got to thinking I really shouldn't have done that. But, it wasn't a critical story of any kind, just a light July 4th piece, so why not have just a *little* fun?

I believe that having fun when we could was one way that we dealt with the intensity of the news business. Yes, some of the stories we covered were parades and holiday celebrations, but the nature of the news is that so many more were devastating events.

Just after midnight on December 23, 1972, a catastrophic 6.3 magnitude earthquake rocked Managua, Nicaragua and surrounding areas for some fifteen seconds, crumbling tens of thousands of older, poorly-built homes and inflicting severe damage on most of the buildings in and around the town. Two massive aftershocks hit within the next two hours. When the shaking stopped and the dust had cleared, as many as 10,000 people were dead, another 20,000 were injured and an estimated 300,000 Nicaraguans were homeless. By Christmas Day, the rampant food and water shortages made it clear this was a humanitarian disaster of epic proportions.

Houston has long been home to tens of thousands of Nicaraguan immigrants and expatriates, so we covered this story very closely. The instant response we got from our viewers was that our station, our city—all of us—had to do something to help. And fast. It would have caught everybody's attention no matter when it happened, but the fact that it occurred right before Christmas no doubt heightened everyone's desire to help those in need.

Immediately, Houston fire stations opened to receive canned goods, other non-perishable food items, medical supplies and clothes. Appeals went out for anything you can think of—and Texans responded. Then, the day after Christmas, organizers loaded it all up and took it to Hobby Airport for a relief flight to Managua. This was a big deal to Houstonians—a really big story—so, the station sent me along to cover this so our viewers could get a sense of what was happening.

Unfortunately, the flight organizers hired some fly-by-night charter airline out of Miami, which sent an old four-engine, propeller-driven Lockheed Constellation. They loaded the Constellation with all of that food and medical supplies. If memory serves, the Nicaraguan Consul General's wife and children were also going to occupy four or five of the seats in the front. Once they loaded that airplane up, however, an FAA inspector declared, "This airplane is overloaded. You cannot take that and a full fuel load. You will have to stop in Mexico City and re-fuel before you can fly on to Managua."

After the FAA inspector left, the pilot told the organizers to continue filling the plane, so they did. Then, against FAA instruction, they topped off the fuel tank. When my photographer, Greg Moore, and I walked out to board around 1:30 a.m., the plane's tires looked flat—it was that loaded down. Nevertheless, the pilot taxied down to the end of the longest runway at Hobby. There, he cut the engine and sat for several minutes waiting for the temperature to go down another degree—which would help get the plane off the ground. Finally, the pilot fired up those engines, and we started rolling.

I have two vivid memories of that particular takeoff. First, as we were lumbering down the runway, the stacks of canned goods started cascading down all around us. Greg and I were frantically grabbing at the cans, trying to hold all this stuff up. Second, I have never, before or since, rolled on the ground in an airplane as long as we did that night. We were taking off from the southeast headed toward the northwest, and I watched the airport going by, then the terminal building going by—and still we were on the ground. I knew we were nearly out of runway when we finally lifted off. As a pilot, I knew enough to be worried.

When we flew over the intersection at Airport Boulevard and Telephone Road, we were maybe fifty feet in the air, barely clearing the red light signals. We were still so low I could see houses and trees flying past. Shortly after takeoff, I went up to the cockpit as I like to do and watched the pilots in action. I noticed they had set a very slow climb rate of maybe fifty feet or so. That's because if you pushed this old plane too hard, the cylinders on those engines overheated. When the did, the pilots leveled off for a while until the engines cooled down. Then they set up another rate of climb, very gradual.

When we passed over the Texas shore headed out over the Gulf of Mexico, we were still only 600 feet off the ground. "My God, I don't know if we're going to make it," I remember thinking. But we did—non-stop.

When we landed, Greg and I got off the plane and headed straight to downtown Managua. I have never seen such utter destruction in my life. To me, the whole city seemed destroyed. Every building and house I saw was structurally cracked or toppled. The streets were deserted. Turning the corner onto a hard-hit street, I saw an arm sticking up out of the rubble. The palm of that person's hand was wide open. It was devastating. On another street, I found a broken Styrofoam *Feliz Navidad* sign and stuck it in my backpack to bring home.

We spent a few more hours in downtown Managua shooting film of all this gut-wrenching, mind-numbing destruction before catching a flight on a U.S. Air Force C-130 that had delivered more relief supplies and was bound for Panama. Arriving exhausted in Panama, we checked into a hotel and collapsed into bed. We were so tired, we overslept our alarm the next morning and had to race to the airport. We just barely made our flight back to Houston. After such an emotionally draining experience, I was so thankful to get home.

Following that first mission of mercy, the outpouring of Houstonians wanting to send more help to Managua only intensified. The fire stations kept their doors open, and people were bringing more supplies and food. The relief coordinators flew a couple more flights to Managua, but eventually that got too expensive.

Finally, around March I think, they decided to take trucks. Five eighteen-wheelers in fact. A couple of them were donated by Rose Trucking Lines, and they were full of relief supplies. One of our go-to photographers, Jim Priest, got on one of those trucks along with a representative of the Nicaraguan government. Then they drove from Houston, through Mexico and Guatemala, and into Nicaragua and Managua.

Even with a Nicaraguan official with them, though, it took them two weeks.

When they finally arrived in Managua, I flew down and met them on the highway just outside the city. As they came over the hill, they were honking their horns and going crazy. They pulled over, and we discovered that all of them, the drivers and Jimmy Priest included, were ready to kill this Nicaraguan government official. I mean, literally. They had been on a long, hard trip, and this guy had pushed them beyond reason. They were all talking at once, telling me how the official had been so terrible. They were so mad they were saying crazy things, like they wanted to kill the guy and throw his body in a ditch. Having not endured the long trip or the frustrations that they had, I was able to calm them down and convince them not to do anything stupid. They didn't, and we continued driving into Managua.

Eventually, we were allowed to take a few of the supplies and borrow some kind of truck, so we could go out into a neighborhood and film relief workers delivering food and supplies to these people who were actually starving. At one point, I met a young child who had been orphaned by the disaster, and I did my best to console her—to show her that her friends in America cared. It was one of the hardest things I ever had to do, but I felt compelled to try to let her know how we were all feeling.

From the outset of the crisis, the Nicaraguan dictator, President Anastasio Somoza, had been roundly criticized for his government's ineptitude at handling basic relief and recovery efforts and helping the starving people. In fact, early reports of government inefficiency led baseball star Roberto Clemente to arrange relief flights to Managua, and he was killed on December 30, 1972, when one of the planes he was on crashed. And we found out later that Somoza and his cronies confiscated those five truckloads of goods we brought from Houston, and put them in stores to re-sell them. He turned Houston's kindness and relief efforts into money in his pocket.

I am not alone in my belief that these brazen, singular acts of corruption by Somoza, whose family had ruled the country since 1937, emboldened the leftist Sandanista forces and led to Somoza's violent overthrow in 1979. (I later interviewed Daniel Ortega, the communist head of the Sandanistas, who did what all communists do—which is, namely, deny they are communists.)

When we returned from Nicaragua that second time, we put together a thirty-minute television special called "Managua: An Odyssey of Mercy." The report outlined all of the amazing efforts by Houstonians and others to provide emergency supplies and food for the people of Managua. It covered our first flights down there, the grueling truck drive that took them so long to get down there. After it aired, I got a call from the Mayor's office asking me and my photographer, Jim Priest, who made that long truck odyssey, to visit with him in his office at City Hall. Jim and I went down there, and Mayor Louie Welch presented us with a plaque from the City of Houston with the official seal of the City. Of all the plaques and awards that I've received over the years, I appreciate that one most of all because it was the first big recognition that our team at KTRK was making a difference.

Though Capital Cities had bought KTRK in 1967, it was not until 1970 that the "four horsemen from Albany" landed in Houston. WTEN-TV in Albany, New York had been a part of Cap Cities' expanding empire since 1957, but in early 1970 Cap Cities acquired two stations in bigger, more lucrative markets. FCC rules at the time precluded Cap Cities from owning more than five VHF (very high frequency) stations. That forced Cap Cities to put WTEN on the market which, in turn, freed up a quartet of their talented, proven leaders to come to Houston. These four Albany transplants would help jump-start our station, which to that point had done little to improve its fortunes in its first three years in the Cap Cities family.

In April of 1970, Ken Johnson, our new general manager, arrived along with program manager Jim Masucci—followed later in 1970 by news director Walt Hawver and a superb reporter, David Glodt. "The slim news staff of 12 was sorely undersupplied, underpaid and undertrained," Hawver later wrote of the situation they first encountered here. "Previous management had contributed to the disarray by experimenting with no fewer than five news directors in as many years."

The new management team would soon make their presence felt. One of their first decisions was to go with me over Ammerman as a solo news anchor, which Hawver wrote was owing to my popularity with the blue-collar families that formed KTRK's core audience at the time. In 1971, Dan left Channel 13 to take a lucrative offer as the news anchor at KULF-AM radio in Houston. He later formed a very successful communications consulting company called the Ammerman Experience.

Other important changes followed. In 1972, weatherman Troy Dungan took a job at a WCAU-TV in Philadelphia and was replaced by Ed Brandon—most recently of KHFI-TV in Austin. Ed was both an easy on-air conversationalist and an instant hit with our news team and viewers. His arrival started a thirty-five-year run with KTRK— and what was more than a forty-five-year friendship with yours truly. Sadly, Ed died in August of 2018, and I miss him dearly. The relationships like this that I was so lucky to find in the news business are powerfully important to me, and each dear friend had such unique gifts. There was only one person besides Ed, however, that I had the opportunity to work with for so long.

In 1974, my buddy Dan Lovett left Channel 13 to work for WABC-TV Channel 7 in New York City, after being offered the incredible opportunity to replace sports icon Frank Gifford—who was moving over to ABC's top sports perch at "Monday Night Football." A few months after Lovett left, Robert Alan Egalnick—better known, and widely admired, as "Bob Allen"—took over as the sports director, and he would be by my side on that news set for the next thirty-eight years.

Just as a house is only as good as the foundation on which it stands, it was in the early 1970s that some key pieces fell into place for KTRK. These early moves coming under the "horsemen from Albany" brought together the nucleus of a news team that would lead to great success in the years and decades ahead. Just looking at how long we were together still amazes me—the stability and camaraderie of it all.

Of course, there was one more critical piece to add to this puzzle. And as controversial as that unique man would prove to be, he was perhaps the biggest piece. I am happy to say I had a hand in getting him into place.

A happier moment from my trip to Managua in 1972, making a new friend.

*With a true Texas legend and my wonderful friend, Red Adair.
One of the most original, generous and capable men I ever knew. One of the great
honors of my life was eulogizing this good man after he died in 2004.*

*For some 35 years, I never went on the Channel 13 news set without the one—
and certainly the only—Marvin Zindler sitting to my right.*

THE ROVING MIKE
OF MARVIN ZINDLER

Sometime after I moved to Houston in 1962 to work in radio, a call came in over the police radios that a man wanted for murder in eight states had been captured and arrested over in southeast Houston. Hearing that, I took one of the KNUZ big mic mobile news units, drove over there, and walked up to the scene. There were a number of sheriffs' cars, police units, and a bunch of uniformed officers already assembled. And in the middle of this chaotic setting, there was one guy standing out there in front of the house where this fugitive had been captured. He was in a white suit with a white shirt, and white tie. That was unusual enough. But he also had an unnatural-looking wig on his head and was wearing full facial make-up.

As usual in Houston during the summer months, it was hot and humid. So this character who was capturing my attention was sweating, and sweat and make-up ran down his starched high white collar.

I turned to a *Houston Chronicle* photographer next to me and asked, "Who in the world is that guy in the white suit?"

He said, "That's Marvin Zindler. He's the deputy sheriff who captured this guy."

When I heard that, I thought *if that guy is a sheriff's deputy loose on the street with a badge and a gun, then I have moved to a very colorful place.*

Marvin's father was Abe Zindler, one of the founders of the town of Bellaire inside the Houston city limits. At one time, I think Abe owned most of Bellaire. Anyway, Abe Zindler also had a bunch of clothing stores around the Houston area called Zindler's Fashions. As a younger man, Marvin hated working in that store. His father once sent him to New York on a buying trip. Marvin came back with a whole carload of women's fashions—but they were all out of style. They were too short. Women's dresses and skirts that next year went much longer. So Abe Zindler was stuck with a whole carload of dresses that I don't think he ever was able to sell. But, thankfully, Marvin was not destined to go into the family business.

Starting in March of 1951, Marvin debuted on the Houston airwaves with a thirty-minute radio program on the now-defunct KATL. The show was called "The Roving Mike," and he did it using old wire recorders in the back seat of his car and a police radio. Marvin covered shootings and all manner of seedy crime scenes around the city, and then he interviewed people, or made a statement. I do remember hearing one of those shows where Marvin said, "This is Marvin Zindler. We're at the scene of a shooting, and one of the injured, wounded victims is lying on the sidewalk here."

Next, you heard Marvin walking up to the victim. "Talk to me, this is Marvin Zindler with KATL radio, Marvin Zindler's 'Roving Mike,' tell me what happened? How did you get shot?"

You could not really hear the person, so Marvin said, "Here, let me take that cigarette out of your mouth first so the audience can understand you." So the guy was lying probably in a pool of his own blood, trying to enjoy a cigarette, and Marvin reached down and takes it out and interviews him. I have actually heard that tape.

From there, Marvin started his migration towards television. First, he became a freelance photographer for the old *Houston Press*. He was still doing his radio "Roving Mike" show, but he would also shoot freelance pictures of a domestic disturbance, or a fire, or whatever—and the *Houston Press* would use his pictures. Though it was on a freelance basis, it still got to where Marvin had more pictures published in the paper than any of the *Press* staff photographers. As a result, he was making more money than the staff photographers. When they protested, they all got a pay raise.

Long before he ever came to KTRK, or before he worked for the *Press*, Marvin also was photographer for our rival station KPRC-TV Channel 2—the local NBC affiliate. Once again, Marvin would shoot fires and police calls. He filled the back seat of his car with batteries so he could run a sound camera. Marvin also learned how to put his sound camera up on the hood of his car and focus it to about fifteen feet out in front of the headlights where he would interview a police officer or whoever. He covered one fire where he interviewed the district fire chief in front of his car and it went on the air on Channel 2. The next day at 6 p.m., after that newscast, the KPRC station manager Jack Harris called the news director, Ray Miller, and asked: "Who is that guy we just put on our air?"

"Oh, that was the district fire chief," Miller said.

"No, I don't mean him," Harris shot back. "I mean that kid who was interviewing him?"

"That was Marvin Zindler," Miller answered. "He's one of our photographers."

The manager said, "Listen, that kid is too ugly. I don't ever want to see his face on this television station ever again."

Well, that spurred Marvin into beginning a whole series of facial reconstructive surgeries. Enter Dr. Joe Agras, Marvin's plastic surgeon, who created a chin for Marvin, straightened out his nose, built him some cheek bones. This happened over a series of surgeries that took a while, but it changed his whole facial appearance.

Still, Marvin was never again on KPRC Channel 2.

I suppose as a favor to his father Abe Zindler, the old sheriff, C. V. Buster Kern, gave Marvin his job as a deputy sheriff and Marvin made quite a name for himself. A couple of years later, in 1964, I became the news director at KNUZ radio. One day Marvin called me and said, "Dave, I've got a warrant for the arrest of someone in the Fugitive Warrant Division." It was a well-known name, somebody that people knew.

He continued, "I'm going to go out here and arrest him at 11:00 this morning."

I said, "Marvin, I don't have a reporter at 11:00, so I won't have anybody to send."

"When would you have a reporter?" he asked.

"I can have one by 1:00 this afternoon."

"Okay, I'll go arrest him at 1:00," he said, relenting. Given his media background, Marvin never let the long arm of the law get in the way of a microphone or a camera.

Later, Marvin established the consumer fraud division with the approval of the county sheriff within the district attorney's office, whereupon he proceeded to step on a lot of toes. A lot of big toes, it turns out—a lot of business people who, maybe as a result, donated money to the campaign of the sheriff's opponent, Jack Heard.

Well Jack Heard won the election for county sheriff and the very first thing he did on January 1, 1973, was to fire Marvin. That made everybody's news that day, because even back then Marvin was a well-known character.

After we did our 6 p.m. newscast at Channel 13, I was walking back into the newsroom, and the assistant news director, Gene Burke, was standing there at the door. "Gene, you know that story that we had on Marvin Zindler?" I asked. "We ought to hire him and make him our consumer reporter."

"Dave, that sounds like a great idea," Burke replied. "You know him, don't you? Why don't you call him?"

I immediately went in the newsroom and called Marvin at home. When he got on the phone, I said, "Marvin, this is Dave Ward at Channel 13. How would you like to continue doing what you have been doing, only instead of preparing consumer fraud cases to go to court, you would prepare consumer fraud cases to go on television, on Channel 13?"

Marvin told me the absolute truth. He said, "David, there is nothing I would rather do."

There really was nothing Marvin would rather do than come on the air every day and tell you what kind of dirt he dug up, or where he found slime in the ice machine, or all of those colorful things. Marvin Zindler became the very first television news consumer reporter anywhere in the United States—called "Action 13." Of course, now they are everywhere.

After he was hired by Channel 13, but before it was announced publicly, Marvin called a news conference to talk to the media, and everybody showed up. The *Chronicle* and *The Houston Post*, all the TV stations, radio—they were all there. Marvin got up and started into this long-winded thing about his career and about the fact that he got fired.

And then he said, "But I'm going to continue my work in consumer fraud, and I will be working on KTRK-TV, Channel 13 in…"

Well, as soon as Marvin said that, the guys from Channel 2 and Channel 11 said, "Aw, drat." They packed up their cameras and didn't even carry the story.

But it was our lead story on KTRK.

When Marvin came to work with us, we had promoted his "Action 13" consumer reporting by asking anyone with a complaint to write us. Well, they did. For one of his first stories, he took a crew and drove all the way down to Clear Lake, where a little boy twelve years-old had been in a store or restaurant where they had a pinball machine. He put a quarter in the pinball machine, and it didn't work. And the owner there refused to give the kid his quarter back. Marvin raced down there to the rescue, cameraman in tow. I don't know if he did interviews or what, but he gave the kid a couple of quarters out of his own pocket.

At the start of Marvin's thirty-four-year run with KTRK, the management insisted that his reports always be pre-taped or recorded. Back then, Marvin never went on the air live. I was in the studio the day he was recording his very first report. This was, again, in the days before we had teleprompters. So you were constantly looking up and down at your script.

Marvin launched into the story, but he kept flubbing lines and messing up. He must have gone through twenty-five or thirty takes, and it just seemed to go on and on. But each time he got a little closer to making it.

This had been going on for quite a while, to the point to where Marvin finally had his entire script memorized. In his last take, he's getting down toward the very end of his script, and you could see it come over his face: *my God I'm going to make it!* And he gets to the last line: "So, the situation was resolved…" and he's so hyped now it just explodes out of his mouth: "MARVIN ZINDLER, EYEWITNESS NEWS!!"

And it stuck. That became his trademark.

Several years later, Marvin came on the set one evening and did his report. When he finished, he said in a low-key, unexcited tone: "Marvin Zindler, Eyewitness News."

After we went to commercial, I asked him, "Marvin, are you okay?"

He said, "Yeah, the boss told me I need to just sign off like any normal, regular reporter."

Well, it didn't matter what the boss wanted, the phones at the station exploded with concerned viewers. "What's the matter? Is

Marvin sick? What's going on? He didn't scream like usual. There must be something wrong with the man."

So many phone calls came in, with so much visceral reaction, that management told Marvin the next day to go back to using his trademark sign-off. And he did, from there on.

It wasn't too long after he started with Channel 13 that he established his weekly restaurant report, featuring his favorite phrase "Slime in the Ice Machine!" Marvin brought a special passion to this feature as he was a genuine germ-o-phobe all his life. In fact, he refused to use the school lavatory as a boy, so the family chauffeur had to take him home to use the bathroom. Still, he did more to clean up restaurant kitchens around the Houston area than all the health inspectors combined. Nobody wanted to be on his rat and roach report. He did, later on, establish a clean kitchen award, that he would present to restaurants that were particularly nice and places where he liked to eat. The station ran a promo: "Marvin Zindler on places where he likes to eat."

On the way back from one of his reports, Marvin, his producer Lori Reingold and photographer Bob Dows stopped at a restaurant on Houston's South Loop to get lunch. Marvin ordered something and a glass of iced tea. Well, when the waitress brought his glass of iced tea it had a dead roach in it! Probably on purpose. That incensed Marvin. He insisted, "Bob, go get your camera." They came in there and shot video of the roach, and Marvin was ranting and raving like crazy.

Incidentally, Marvin used to carry a little plastic roach in his pocket, just as a joke, but this was a real roach. A real, dead roach. And it sent Marvin into a tizzy.

I'm sure that waitress eventually regretted that, and the owner of the restaurant did too. I don't think that restaurant stayed open too much longer. At any rate, the original story he shot that day got pushed back so Marvin could put that thing on the air that night about the roach he got in his iced tea.

Those of you who remember Marvin Zindler know that he fractured the English language. He misused and abused almost every cliché in the book. On one particular broadcast at night, he wound up his report by saying, "It's time for somebody to grab the bull by the tail and do something about this. MARVIN ZINDLER EYEWITNESS NEWS." Hearing that, I thanked Marvin and turned to the camera saying: "Now friends, having a bull by the tail is not to be confused with having a tiger by the horns. Those are two totally different situations."

I got a lot of reaction to that.

Another time, Marvin was taping a promo that was to run sometime later that week and it had the word in it, "voila!" As if something great had just happened. Well, Marvin kept pronouncing it as "VI-O-LA." When he did, the camera operator came from behind the camera and pointed it out to him, "No, Marvin. It's pronounced "vwalla." It still took him another couple of takes before he finally got that right.

Of course, Marvin will always be best-known for taking down the "Chicken Ranch"—that infamous, bawdy, whorehouse right outside of La Grange. According to the *Handbook of Texas*, the brothel that became the Chicken Ranch was reportedly first established at a hotel in La Grange in 1844 and run by a woman named "Miss Swine." It closed during the Civil War, but in 1905 another enterprising woman named "Miss Jessie" Williams opened another house of ill repute on the lower Colorado River, which she relocated to the eventual, final location just outside town a few years later. Williams got her staff and operation through the Great Depression by allowing customers to barter one chicken for services rendered, and the moniker "Chicken Ranch" stuck.

Marvin originally maintained he had received "an anonymous complaint" about the Chicken Ranch. He later divulged it was actually a man named Herb Hancock, who worked for Texas Attorney General John Hill, who tipped Marvin off during a meeting at Houston's Rice Hotel in April of 1973. Hancock said they were concerned that there might be organized crime involved not only at the Chicken Ranch, but also at the second-most infamous whorehouse in Texas, "The Wagon Wheel," outside of Sealy. This information was presented to the district attorney who oversaw both jurisdictions, Oliver Kitzman, who had brushed it off saying it was "a local problem."

The previous November, Texas state officials had set up surveillance on the Chicken Ranch, with a couple of agents sitting out there on the road just to get an idea of how many men went in—and how much money was involved. Turns out, it was a lot of money, but only two days after these officials started that surveillance, they got orders from the Governor, Dolph Briscoe, to stop and leave the Chicken Ranch alone. That made John Hill even more suspicious, so that's when his man Hancock brought his story to us at Channel 13. Marvin got a hold of it and took off on a series of reports that eventually led to the Chicken Ranch being closed down.

There was one incident when Marvin and a photographer were in downtown La Grange, and the Fayette County Sheriff, T.J. "Jim" Flournoy, confronted Marvin while he was still sitting in his car. Flournoy punched Marvin in the face, grabbed Marvin's wig, threw it on the street, and stomped on it. Marvin's photographer was sitting in the front seat with a 16mm sound camera and started rolling film. He didn't get any pictures of the sheriff's assault on Marvin, but the sheriff's office still confiscated that camera. The station demanded its return, which they did—but only after the sheriff's team had exposed all the film to the light and ruined it.

What the sheriff's office didn't realize, however, was that the audio track was still on that film—and as a result, when that audio hit the air on Channel 13, there was really hell to pay. The "Chicken Ranch" was closed. The Old Wagon Wheel in Sealy was also closed, but this also led to the *Texas Monthly* magazine article which resulted in the play, "The Best Little Whorehouse in Texas." Marvin's character's name in the play was "Melvin P. Thorpe, Watchdog News."

Marvin loved the play. As a matter of fact, Marvin, Sheriff Flournoy, and the Chicken Ranch madam, Edna Milton, all went to Broadway for the opening of that play. That led later to a movie by the same name starring Dolly Parton and Bert Reynolds. Marvin just assumed that Burt Reynolds would be playing him. I was the one who had to go to Marvin and tell him, "No, Marvin, Burt Reynolds is playing the part of the sheriff. You're being played by an actor named Dom DeLuise."

Marvin was crushed. He and his wife Gertrude went to the opening of the film in Houston, but at the point where Dom DeLuise stuffed a sock in his pants, Marvin and Gertrude got up and left the theatre. He never saw the rest of that film.

One of Marvin's most memorable reports, at least to me, involved an old Houston restaurant called Vargo's out on the west side of Houston in a fairly wooded neighborhood with a scenic lake. Al Vargo, the owner of the restaurant, was keeping peacocks on the property, but neighbors were complaining because the peacocks were squawking and making a horrible noise.

Well, Marvin went out there and interviewed the neighbors, talked to a bunch of folks, came back, and he did his report that evening. He wrapped it up saying: "So the peacocks are there, and they're alive and well! *Squawk!!* MARVIN ZINDLER, EYEWITNESS NEWS!"

Over the years, I have had a lot of people have accused me of having a smirk on my face after Marvin finished one of his reports. And I always told them: "If you were sitting there next to this wonderful but crazy guy, you'd have a smirk on your face, too!"

Anyway, that night when Marvin squawked like a peacock and threw it back to me, I simply said, "Thank you…thank you, Marvin. Sometimes you make us so proud."

Marvin Zindler will always be remembered as a remarkable addition to the lore of Houston. No matter how big and sophisticated this city gets, we seem to maintain a fondness for our most colorful characters. And we keep producing them. While Marvin was keeping the folks at home entertained with his reports, Houston was falling hard for a colorful coach and his surprising, almost-winning team.

*Just a couple of Texas boys here. With one helluva coach—
and the nicest guy too—Coach Oail Andrew "Bum" Phillips.*

16

LUV YA BLUE

In 1972, the Houston Oilers played their regular season opening game against the Denver Broncos on the road in Denver. My buddy Dan Lovett, who was our sports director but also worked on the Oiler's radio crew, was heading to Denver for the game so I decided to tag along. Arriving at Mile High Stadium, I accompanied Lovett into the radio booth where he and Ron Franklin did the broadcast. Franklin was the play-by-play man, and Lovett was the color analyst. To try and "earn my keep," I sat next to them and kept a limited number of statistics on the game on a piece of paper—focusing on the number of first downs, rushing and passing yards, and basic stats like that.

After the game, both Franklin and Lovett turned to the general manager of the Oilers, Dan Downs, who had also been in the radio booth during the game, and said: "Dan, we would really like to have Dave with us at all the games, keeping statistics. It adds so much more to the broadcast."

Downs replied, "I'm sure we can arrange something on that." That evening, Lovett got me on the team's charter plane flying home, and by the time we got back to Houston, Downs had approved my joining the radio crew. I was very excited.

The next week, I created a full stat sheet to track the performance of both teams—including the number of each team's first downs, passes attempted and completed, passing yards, individual receiver's yardage, rushing yards, the number of penalties and the yardage, and so on.

The owner of the Oilers, Bud Adams, wasn't stingy. For my meager services rendered, he paid me a whopping $15 a game, home or away. Mr. Adams didn't know it, but I would have paid *him* $15 a game just to be on that crew—and make all those charter flights. As a result, I got to meet all of the players, and I got to see first-hand what their culture was like behind the scenes.

When I joined their traveling circus, the Oilers' coach was Coach Bill Peterson, who had a very successful career in the college ranks, including a stint in 1971 at Rice University. He was a colorful guy who tended to make some really Yogi Berra-type of statements.

Before the second game of the 1972 season, which was also a road game—this time in Miami—the team had its Saturday night meeting. Usually it was a chance for the players to relax, and Coach Peterson got up and announced, "Tonight's movie is going to be 'Two-Eyed Jacks.'"

One of the players piped up and said, "I think I've seen half of that one, Coach."

Another time, the Oilers had been criticized a little bit a for not being at attention during the performance of "The Star-Spangled Banner." Sound familiar? So before the next game I heard Coach Peterson tell the players, "When they play the national anthem, I want all of you lined up together, standing on your helmet with the sideline under your arm."

Later in the 1972 season, which the team ended with a 1-13 record, we flew to San Diego for a game against the Chargers. That Saturday night, the coaches hosted those of us on the radio crew at a restaurant run by one of the Chargers' owners. We were outside sitting at what would be like picnic tables waiting for our table when Dan Lovett sat down next to me and said, "Dave I just don't understand it. I'm starving to death, and it's only seven o'clock."

I told him, "Yeah, it's seven o'clock here, Dan, but back home it's nine o'clock. That's why you're so hungry."

At that, Coach Peterson piped up and said, "That time difference, that's ridiculous. I would not live out here for that reason."

All Lovett could do was chuckle and say, "Hadn't thought of it that way, Coach."

Coach Peterson could be just as colorful on the field too. NFL Films had a video clip of him on the sidelines reacting to a play where somebody had absolutely crushed one of the Oilers' players—leaving him limp on the sideline. Seeing the injury, Peterson went to the referee and said, "That boy, he's got a mother! His mother's watching! You've got to do better to take care of these players, ref!"

In 1975, O. A. "Bum" Phillips became the new head coach and general manager of the Houston Oilers. Bum had coached at Jacksonville High School in the 1950s, but by the time I moved there in 1956, he had gone to Beaumont. It was just as well, because, as I've mentioned, I wasn't into football in high school—at least not playing it. though I did have one lackluster season on the B team, my best performances on the football field had always been on my trumpet at the half-time show.

Still, I loved keeping the stats on the radio crew. The Oilers got off to a good start in the 1975 season by beating the Denver Broncos 21-14 at the Astrodome. The following week, we were on the road in Cleveland. That Sunday morning, I walked out of the hotel and headed for the team buses. I saw Coach Bum standing by the open door of the first bus, walked over to him, and jovially said, "Hey Coach! Tell me, how bad are we going to beat these Brownies today?"

Bum glared at me and said, "Oh, Dave, I wish you had not said that. Good Lord, I wish you had not said that."

I turned around and beat a hasty retreat to that third bus. I had the distinct feeling that Bum felt I had jinxed them, and maybe I did. They lost that game 20-7. When it came time to get on the charter back to Houston, I stayed as far away from Bum as I could.

Bum's trademark was that he always wore a cowboy hat, a Stetson, on the sidelines whenever they were playing anywhere—except in the Astrodome. He never wore his hat in the Astrodome. When somebody asked him why, he said, "My Momma told me you don't ever wear a hat indoors."

In 1975, after my buddy Dan Lovett moved to New York City, another buddy Ron Stone became the Oilers' color announcer. Ron Franklin was still the play-by-play man, so now we had Ron from Channel 11, Ron Stone from Channel 2, and me from Channel 13—all three of the major stations from Houston working on their radio crew.

On December 5, 1976, we were in Cleveland for the second-to-last game of a 5-9 season. Cleveland Municipal Stadium was a multi-purpose facility that also doubled as the home of the Cleveland Indians baseball team. There, the visiting radio booth was on the very top of the stadium overhang. We had to sit on bar stools, so we were looking straight down at the field. The low temperature that day was four degrees above zero, and this particular broadcast booth faced Lake Erie—so the north wind off Lake Erie ripped right into the booth. If you had a cup of coffee and didn't move or drink it within five minutes, it would be frozen solid.

Ron Stone read the disclaimer before every game: "The announcers for today's game are hired by, and paid by, the Houston Oilers." That was it. Well, that Sunday he went on the air and said: "The announcers for today's game are hired by and paid by the Houston Oilers...but not near enough to be up here in this freezer in Cleveland, Ohio!"

Incidentally, even if there had been a sliding glass window, Ron Franklin would not have closed it. He never liked broadcasting from behind glass. He wanted to hear the crowd and feel like he was really in touch with the energy of the game.

Of course, I just kept stats I never said a word on the air. Although at times in some games, you could hear me groan a little bit. In both of my first two years with the team, the Oilers went 1-13. Those early years especially were hard on all the fans.

There was one game in the Astrodome, we'll never forget this, when the Oilers on a fourth down had to kick the ball away. The kicker got off a terrific punt. Ron Franklin said, "Oh boy, that's a great one. That's a boomer." Ron Stone chimed in and said, "Yes, that's a great k-..." He started to say "kick," but in mid-sentence he realized technically it really was a punt. So, the way he finished saying the word sounded highly offensive.

Well, Franklin broke up, and I almost fell out of my chair. It was so funny because it was so completely out of character for a true gentleman like Ron Stone.

One time I took my father to an Oiler game. Being a Baptist preacher, he would never go to a game on Sunday, so this must have been a Saturday night game they had in the Astrodome. I wanted him to meet Bum Phillips and quarterback Dan Pastorini and some of the others. During the game, my dad sat with me up in the broadcast booth while I kept the full set of stats. Then after the game, we headed down to the locker room. To get there, you walked down a hall like a tunnel, then you turned 180 degrees and walked a little more—and there was the dressing room, wide open. So we made that turn and started walking in, and all of these players were walking around buck naked.

I had no idea how he would take this. Then my dad stopped and turned to me. He said, "Son, this reminds me of the war!" And not World War II, incidentally. He fought in World War I, and when he was in the infantry barracks the soldiers walked around buck naked after hitting the showers.

The team's charter flights were all arranged through Braniff Airlines. They were all on 727s, using the same crew on every flight, and usually the same flight attendants in the cabin of the airplane. The pilot was Dean Henry, and over the years I got to know him well. One day we were taking off on the team charter from Bush Intercontinental Airport and the engine, the middle engine in the tail of that aircraft, had what they call a compressor stall. On the tail of a 727 aircraft, there are three jet engines—one on each side, and the third in the middle with the air intake on the top of the fuselage right in front of the vertical stabilizer of the plane. Occasionally, when the wind is directly straight down the runway, as the pilot rotates to lift off, the center engine wouldn't get enough air—and it would have this compressor stall.

That happened to us taking off from Bush Intercontinental Airport that day. It sounded like the engine farted. It just went *brrrrdt!* And there was a slight loss of power, but then the airplane went on and got up off the ground. Quickly, Captain Henry came on the intercom and informed everybody, "That was just a compressor stall in the center engine. We were never in any danger at all."

I guess he just wanted to set us at ease, but it did not work on everyone. In fact, I looked back down the aisle and there was look of absolute terror on the faces of all of the players. And to tell you the truth, even knowing as much as I did about planes, I thought we were about to bite the bullet too.

In 1976, Braniff Airlines commissioned the American artist Alexander Calder to paint one of their 727s in a rippling red, white and blue effect in honor of the American bicentennial. That jet was subsequently dubbed the "Flying Colors of the United States." They also called it the "Calder Jet," and Braniff put it on routes all over the United States.

Later, the airline leased that plane to the Oilers for a charter flight to Oakland, California to play the Raiders on November 13, 1977. By that point, I always spent most of the flights up in the cockpit with the flight crew. From my own experiences learning to fly, I just liked sitting up there and watching them do their thing.

Landing in Oakland, Dean told me, "Dave, just stay on the plane. After we dump the players, we're going to fly over to San Francisco to return the Calder jet." After the team players and coaches exited the aircraft, as instructed, I stayed on the plane with the flight crew. In short order, we took off and flew to San Francisco's International Airport just across the San Francisco Bay, which only took about ten minutes; but instead of landing right away, the crew wanted first to do a "fly by" before landing.

As Dean crossed the bay and made his first approach to the runway in San Francisco, instead of slowing down his air speed to land he was coming in red hot. As the plane made its descent, the first officer was calling out altitudes: "500 feet—400—300—200—100." Then he said, "Fifty feet, that's it!" So Dean leveled the plane off.

In the meantime, the landing gear was not down. They also did not have the wing flaps down. And, they were still flying at air speed. As a result, all kinds of alarms started going off. It was the plane's way of telling the crew they were not flying properly. Landing gear not down! Flaps!

Finally, the automatic pull up warning sounded: "*Whoop Whoop* Pull Up! *Whoop Whoop* Pull Up!!"

Of course, Dean just disregarded that.

By this point, I was on my knees in the cockpit with Dean Henry on my left and the first officer on my right. We went roaring down that runway at 450 mph; and at the end of the runway, Dean pulled the airplane up into a climbing left turn. We pulled about 3.5 Gs on that pull-out. And as we were circling around to land, I looked back at the cabin and about two-thirds of the oxygen masks had dropped down from over the seats. That plane obviously was doing things it was not really designed to do.

Besides having thrilling flying adventures, I thoroughly enjoyed the regular aspects of those charter flights because they gave me such a good window on how the team worked. I saw their joking around, and I saw how the team came together during the course of a season. You could see lots of their chemistry when they were in close quarters on those flights.

TOP *It's amazing to look back at how basic our set and news gathering equipment were early in my career, especially compared to all the high-tech gadgets we have today.* | BOTTOM LEFT *You probably couldn't find two more different people than my first co-anchor Dan Ammerman and me.* BOTTOM RIGHT *It is a strange feeling to see your own face all over town. This is just one of many promo shots used over the years.*

TOP LEFT *It still fits! Donning my old blue sequin suit with my friend and former band mate—the talented Steve Tyrell.* | TOP RIGHT *The Eyewitness News team probably early 1990s. Call me "Captain Obvious," but I assume this was used to promote our Rodeo coverage.*
BOTTOM *The things you do for charity! Here I am as "Dame Edith," warbling not exactly like a thrush. Nobody knew who I was until I removed my wig.*

TOP *I cannot "Argggh-ue." I love a good costume!* | BOTTOM LEFT *More hi-jinx with my respected friend and peer Ron Stone, regaling the Press Club audience with some kind of nonsense.* BOTTOM RIGHT *Perhaps the crowning achievement of my cross-dressing adventures, this time as Carmen Miranda in the Hou-Dah Parade in Galveston..*

TOP *At City Hall with photographer Jimmy Priest, receiving a commendation from Mayor Louie Welch for our reporting in Nicaragua following the 1972 earthquake there. It was an honor to cover a story in which Houstonians really poured out their hearts to help those who were suffering.*
BOTTOM *My love of trains is just as strong today as it was when I was a very little boy. On this day, I was asked by Union Pacific Railroad to serve as the Honorary Locomotive Engineer as the 844 steam engine arrived in Houston.*

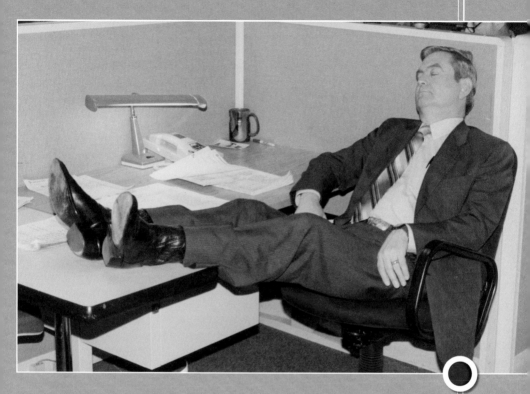

TOP *This photo did not help me win employee of the month, but in my defense you work long—and very odd—hours in this business.*   BOTTOM LEFT *One of the very happy byproducts of all the charity dinners I have emceed through the years was meeting, and befriending, the very funny and nice Rich Little.* BOTTOM RIGHT *Interviewing former First Lady Barbara Bush in her Houston home with son Neil, talking about their passionate devotion to the cause of family literacy.*

TOP LEFT *Accepting my Silver Circle Award in 2011 from the National Academy of Television, Arts and Sciences/Lone Star Chapter for my 25-plus years of "outstanding contribution to the television-broadcast community."* | TOP RIGHT *Actor Dom DeLuise with us on the news set. This was years after he portrayed Marvin Zindler in "The Best Little Whorehouse in Texas."* BOTTOM *Cutting the obligatory office birthday cake while my boss Jim Masucci and colleagues Marvin Zindler and Ed Brandon look on.*

Covering the news especially in a big, dynamic city like Houston requires constant effort to stay up-to-the-minute on the latest developments. Lord knows your competitors are! Here I am monitoring events as they come off the news wire.

BOTTOM LEFT *Outside of the time I spend with my family and friends, I am never happier than when I am on a train.* | BOTTOM RIGHT *Receiving Leon Goldstein Award from Crime Stoppers in 2002, which is that fantastic organization's highest civilian award. Pictured to the right of me is John Bales, former interim HPD Chief and Chairman of the Board of Crime Stoppers from 2003 – 2005, and to the left, Kim Ogg, who served as Executive Director from 1999 – 2006.*

TOP *I was honored to be one of only a handful of local news anchors around the country, and the only from Texas, who was invited to the White House to interview President Barack Obama as he was heading into a tough re-election campaign in 2012. Here we are in the historic Cabinet Room.* BOTTOM *Nov. 1, 2011 on the South Lawn of the White House with our great news director, Dave Strickland, and photographer Charles Fisher. If "Strick" (as I call him) looks cold, it's because I stole his overcoat.*

LEFT *Mineola, Texas probably late 1940. My parents both attended Baylor, so I was sporting a "Sic 'Em Bears" hat as soon as I could walk.* | RIGHT *Linda and David Jr.—my two children from my first wife, Glendya. They've been through it all with me, and as a result probably spent more time in the Channel 13 building, and that pool, than any other kids. Together we saw the Astrodome and the Galleria go up, and they were also there when a motorcycle—and a few relationships— came slamming down. I could not be prouder of the people they have become, which is a credit to their devoted mother.*

TOP LEFT *With my baby girl Linda, when we still lived in Waco. I worked too hard and missed a lot of their childhood, but however imperfect I may be I love my kids.* | TOP RIGHT *For her 80th birthday in 1992, I sent my sweet mother 80 red roses. She deserved every last one, and many many more.* | BOTTOM *I had my two boys Jonathan and Christopher with my second wife later in life, and they kept me young. Here we are visiting my mother at her home in Jacksonville.*

*I lost track of how many times I asked Laura to marry me, so it was without a
doubt the second happiest day of my life when she finally said yes.
The very happiest day, of course, was when we made it official by walking down the
aisle on August 3, 2002 at St. Luke's United Methodist Church in Houston.
My parents were celebrating in heaven, but happily Laura's wonderful parents,
Joe B. Stoma and his wife Marie, could be with us.*

TOP LEFT *One of the things I love the most about Laura is her commitment to not only her own charity, Houston Children's Charity, but also so many wonderful causes throughout our community. She is the ultimate "Point of Light."* | TOP RIGHT *One of the most recent promotional photos that the TV station used for me. More important than photos or looks is getting the story, and your facts, right.* | BOTTOM *A bittersweet night—May 2, 2017. Following my last 6 p.m. newscast at KTRK, my friends and colleagues at the station all gathered around for a very special photo.*

TOP *After watching 49 straight Rodeo parades trek through the streets of Houston as a reporter, I finally got to be in one—as the Grand Marshal of the 2018 parade.* RIGHT *I was worried Laura and I might have to ride a horse when they named me the Grand Marshal of the 2018 Rodeo parade. Even if I could get up on one, my real concern was staying up there! Thankfully, my friend Joel Cowley offered us a carriage.*

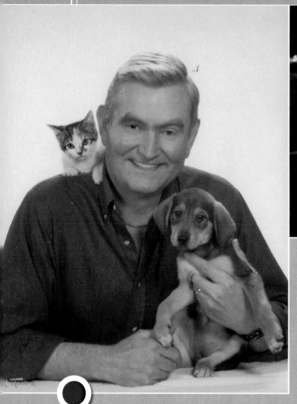

LEFT *There's an old adage that says you should be careful about working with animals, but this photo shoot helping to promote pet adoptions made the scratches and other mishaps worth it.* TOP RIGHT *With my good buddy, A.J. Foyt, in my view the very best human being ever to get behind the wheel of a race car. You name it, and A.J. could drive it—and win.* TOP BOTTOM *Katie Couric was in town to shoot some promos, and we had a nice lunch at Tony's Restaurant.* BOTTOM *Of all the causes I have enjoyed helping through the years, it's always the ones involving kids that give me the most joy.*

TOP LEFT *With a great man and great president, George H.W. Bush, in his post-White House office shortly after his return to private life in Houston.*

TOP RIGHT *Anytime you go to the White House it is a thrill, especially when the President and First Lady are not only friends—but some of the most decent and remarkable people you've ever met. That was definitely the case with George and Barbara Bush at their 1991 Christmas party.*

MIDDLE LEFT *My three co-anchors who followed Dan Ammerman having a little fun with some guy's photo: Gina Gaston, Shara Fryer and Jan Carson. Three pros, and great people too.* | RIGHT *The "Tyler Rose" himself—Earl Campbell. If you saw him play, you will never forget it. I know I won't.*

TOP LEFT *I was a car nut from the earliest age, so meeting a racing legend like Mario Andretti (center) was a real highlight for me.* TOP RIGHT *With our dear, departed friend Arkady "Ariel" Bogoslavsky, who was a fixture at the Bellagio hotel in Las Vegas owing to his supreme talent as a pianist.* | MIDDLE LEFT *My journey on Air Force One was the ride of a lifetime in so many ways.* | MIDDLE RIGHT *Interviewing President Bush was always an honor and a pleasure. Here we are at the Houstonian.* | BOTTOM LEFT *I had the honor of interviewing President Bush on Air Force One.*

For some of the pre-season games, before the team had made their final cuts and was still carrying all of the players trying to make the team, the cabin of that 727 would be jammed with those massive players—some topping 300 pounds—all sitting right next to each other, three seats on each side of the aisle. Literally jammed in there. It was a little better after the regular season started when they had to cut the team down. Then the guys could leave the center seats vacant on most flights.

As head coach, Bum had given Oilers' fans hope that the team could be good, posting two winning seasons in his first three years as coach—but they still had not reached the playoffs. So as general manager going into the 1978 season, he rolled the dice big-time and traded up to secure the very first draft pick that year—which he used claim the Heisman Trophy winner Earl Campbell, out of the University of Texas. The Tyler Rose was coming to Houston.

I suppose everyone has their own view on when the "Luv Ya Blue" era got started, that brief but intense love affair between a blue-collar city and a team that embodied the same grit and determination. I date it sometime during the 1978 season. It started with Bum and the force of his personality. You simply had to love the guy, and his players truly did. He was Texas through and through, and the fans here loved him for that too. By the time Earl came to Houston, we knew the team could be good. They were a good group of kids, who played hard.

Suddenly, things started clicking.

That season, the team won their first-ever game ever in Pittsburgh's Three Rivers Stadium against the Steelers. They won an incredible come-from-behind game against the Patriots on the road, after trailing 23-0. And on a Monday Night Football game for the ages in the Astrodome, Earl Campbell ran for 199 yards, punctuating the Oiler's dominant win over the Miami Dolphins. Then in the playoffs, they won their first two games on the road in convincing fashion, once again defeating both the Dolphins and the Patriots. But in the AFC Championship game, they ran into a buzz saw in Pittsburgh and got whooped 34-5.

Despite the crushing loss, the team returned late that night to an impromptu, massive pep rally in the Astrodome with some 50,000 frenzied fans turning out to thank and congratulate the team for giving us all something to believe in. It was a remarkable, almost unprecedented, display of fan loyalty. "We were not celebrating a loss to the Steelers, but a victory over not caring," *Houston Post* columnist Lynn Ashby wrote. "Now we care. Now almost everyone is an Oiler fan ... Houston has come up from the deepest valley to the mountainside. Next year, we plant the flag on top."

They came oh-so-close to doing just that. At the conclusion of the 1979 season, the Oilers beat the Broncos in the first round of playoffs for their first home playoff win since the 1960 AFL Championship, but in the process Dan Pastorini, Earl Campbell, and wide receiver Kenny Burroughs were hurt. All three would miss the next game against the high-octane offense of the San Diego Chargers and future Hall of Fame quarterback Dan Fouts. The Oilers were massive underdogs going into the game but pulled off a courageous 17-14 upset on the strength of four interceptions and a blocked field goal. "Luv Ya Blue" was at a fever pitch everywhere in town as the team got ready to face the Steelers in a Three Rivers Stadium re-match for the AFC Championship.

The game was a closely contested, back-and-forth affair. Pastorini was playing through injury and pain and managed to find receiver Mike Renfro in the end zone for what everyone thought was a game-tying touchdown late in the third quarter—everyone, that is, except the officials on the field who ruled Renfro out of bounds. It still stands as one of the worst calls in NFL history. The Oilers never recovered, and Pittsburgh went on to win. In fact, Pastorini told me in an interview years later that, after that second Pittsburg championship game, every member of the Steelers came over as he was walking off the field and said, "Dan, you guys really beat us today."

They really did outplay the Steelers that game, but victory was not to be.

After that second AFC Championship loss, we flew back to Houston and got on the busses. As we were coming in from the airport, word came that they had opened up the Astrodome again and let in thousands of people who wanted to see the team. Making our way into town, the highway was lined with people still cheering the Oilers. Arriving at the Astrodome, there was some 20,000 people outside who could not get in—and another 70,000 screaming people inside waving signs and white pom poms. The place pulsated with energy, in one of the most extraordinary outpourings of emotion I have ever witnessed—far more intense than the first rally the year before.

They drove our buses right out onto the field. As we filed off, we were caught up in the moment, taking in the incredible intensity of the atmosphere. I saw players crying, and coaches crying too.

Fortunately, someone had the foresight this time to arrange to have a microphone along with a little platform. Coach Bum maybe had a drink or two on the plane coming back, and when they handed him the microphone he had one of his most famous lines. "One year ago, we knocked on the door," he said pausing before he added: "This year we beat on the door…" The roar of the crowd started to swell.

Bum paused again, and finally growled: "Next year, we're gonna kick the sonofabitch in!"

Utter pandemonium ensued. I don't think I have heard a crowd roar like that before or since.

Looking back, it is amazing to think I saw every game that Bum Phillips coached in Houston; every game that Dan Pastorini quarterbacked for the Oilers; every game Earl Campbell ran the ball here—and there were some unbelievable runs. In one game against Miami in the Astrodome, Earl swept around the right side and scampered effortlessly 80 yards for a touchdown. But Earl was just as likely, if not more so, to run over people. He would simply flatten would-be tacklers all over the field.

After his career ended, Earl underwent surgery to remove a bunch of the screws and the bolts they had put in his body over the years. Bob Allen interviewed him at the KTRK studios shortly thereafter, and Earl brought in a double handful of nuts and bolts and screws—all of the hardware that had been inside of his body all of those years. Just unbelievable. He played the game as well or better than anybody else, but he sure paid a price.

Many times when we'd be on the charter flight on the plane, coming back from wherever we had been, Earl would be so beat up and bruised that they'd give him a liberal dose of painkillers. Clearly, there were times when Earl was feeling the full effect of the medicines, because he would get up in the front of the plane, take the stewardess' microphone, and sing Willie Nelson songs. And not exactly in tune.

After a while, all the guys would start booing and shouting, "Sit down Earl, just sit down! Shut up and sit down!"

There were several other Oilers that I got to know as well. One of them was the place kicker, Toni Fritsch, who signed with the Oilers in 1977. He was from Austria, and he was a soccer player over in Europe. But he could really kick an American football. He was a very good place kicker—easily handling kick-offs, extra points and field goals. Anytime he kicked a winning field goal, Toni would exclaim, "Yeah, I kicka de touchdown! I kicka de touchdown."

Another Oiler who became a good friend was Elvin Bethea, the Hall of Famer. When Hall of Famer Sid Gillman was the coach during the 1973-1974 seasons, normally the radio crew and the sports writers were on the back left side of the plane during our charter flights. Well, somebody told Elvin, who hated flying, that the safest and best seat on the plane was the very back row. So he always sat on the very back row of the plane near us during the Gillman era.

They always seated the radio crew and sportswriters first, and inevitably Elvin would come down the aisle, carrying his suitcase. Reaching his seat, he would look over at us and say, "I see the riff raff are here again this week." To Elvin, we in the media were the "riff raff," but we loved the guy, of course. Everybody did.

After the 1980 season, the Oilers had a disappointing, early exit from the playoffs—losing to the eventual Super Bowl champs the Oakland Raiders. Just a few days later, Oilers owner Bud Adams fired Bum, who ended up going to New Orleans—eventually bringing Dan Pastorini and Earl Campbell with him. They all ended their football careers in New Orleans, but they never reached the heights they did when they were embraced by the entire city of Houston.

After Bud Adams fired Bum, I talked to Bum. He said something I have seen him quoted saying many times elsewhere: "Dave, there are only two kind of coaches in the NFL—them that's been fired, and them that's gonna be fired." He understood the business of his chosen profession, but he knew himself even better. He was one helluva guy.

"He was dumb like a fox," Pastorini later said of Bum. "He milked that persona to his advantage. He's got a lot of country bumpkin. He was sincere, though. It was no ploy. That was how he grew up."

When Bum Phillips died in 2013, it almost seemed fitting that Bud Adams died two days later. Both were ninety years old; both were Houston sports icons. One was universally beloved; the other left a more complicated legacy. But they will remain inextricably tied as architects of the Luv Ya Blue era, a great chapter in Houston's history and a rare chapter of NFL history that has never been replicated since—and may never be, no matter how many winning teams we might have.

One of the grittiest football players who ever took to the gridiron, Dan "Dante" Pastorini. I reported on every game he played during the "Luv Ya Blue" era of the Houston Oilers.

Astrodome, 1974. At this very moment, I already have a broken collar bone and shoulder blade—and that was before the motorcycle landed on top of me.

"BUSTED YOUR ASS"

The Luv Ya Blue Era was a wonderful addition to my life in the newsroom, but as the field continued to develop, my "day job" provided plenty of excitement too. Let's back up a little and look at what was going on in the newsroom. In 1963, the news director at KYW-TV in Cleveland, Al Primo, had instituted what proved to be a radical departure from the original "network" news format when he started using a very heavy rotation of film and videotape during the course of his station's newscasts. As noted in the *Encyclopedia of Television News*, "Prior to this, viewers usually watched as the news anchor read all of the news out loud while looking into a studio camera." Sounds pretty dry to me. Primo's ambition was clearly to *show* his audience the news, not just *tell* them.

Then in 1965, after he moved to Philadelphia, Primo also introduced the first on-camera reporting team. Again, before this new wrinkle, the only faces you saw on your screen during the news were the anchor, the weatherman, and the sports guy. Primo had found a new clause in the labor contract with the American Federation of Television and Radio Artists that covered all reporters which said you could use "any member of AFTRA to write, report, and appear on the air with their story *without paying any additional compensation*." (Emphasis added.) Whereas before reporters would cover a story and write it up for the anchor to read on the air, now these same reporters could present their own stories to the viewing audience—and it would not cost the station more money in the process. That was key.

Of course, TV stations have always been *very* competitive—and as such are always watching their competitors like a hawk. When one station tries something new and it works, the others in that market are sure to follow in some form or fashion. And if it works for the other stations as well, it will quickly be exported to other markets. Al Primo's newscast innovations certainly contributed to my being hired as KTRK's first on-the-street reporter.

This was the advent of the "Eyewitness News" concept that, as it developed going into the 1970s, placed a heavy emphasis on action video, live reporting, the involvement of reporters in their stories, and highlighting the personalities of the news team to viewers. In short order, ABC affiliates around the country joined the "Eyewitness News" movement. When I heard about it, my first thought was, "My God, why didn't I think of that? That's just so obvious! Eyewitness News. We make you an eyewitness to the news!"

(Eventually, someone came up with an "Action News" concept to challenge the "Eyewitness" franchise. At the risk of over-simplifying it, Action News focused on a higher tempo newscast with shorter stories. Most stations ended being a hybrid of the two concepts.)

In the 1970s, the American people, not just Houstonians, developed a huge appetite for television news. They wanted more live news and newscasts, and as a result, news departments started expanding. Not only that, but the time allocated to news grew as well. Where before we were doing fifteen and then thirty minutes of news at 6 p.m. and 10 p.m., we started adding more news programs. Today, in fact, we have news programs starting as early in the morning as 4:30 a.m., and as early in the afternoon as 3 p.m. We have a mid-day newscast, and these days all of this news programming is amplified and supplemented by digital and social media.

In November of 1973, three years after the "horsemen from Albany" arrived, and eleven months after Marvin Zindler joined the team, KTRK's "Eyewitness News" at 10 p.m. finally overtook our competition in the ratings book. By January of 1975, KTRK was winning the 7 a.m., 6 p.m. and 10 p.m. weekday news—as well as most of its weekend newscasts. In time, KTRK's morning news programs were doing so well the station pre-empted the first part of the ABC's "Good Morning America."

Just as a rising tide lifts all boats, our news department's success quickly carried over to other programming, with KTRK winning every "day part" on the daily schedule. Thus began a decades-long run of dominance in the Houston TV market—which may sound like bragging, but there's just no other word to describe what happened here.

With our expanding newscasts and other programming, instead of the station signing off for the night right after the 10 o'clock newscast, we started airing content until midnight. That often meant we had to wait until after midnight to do any kind of extra production work on special reports and feature programs.

One night, the floor crew and I were up until 4 or 5 o'clock in the morning working on a thirty-minute special program that was supposed to air later that week. We pulled together some really good material. After we wrapped up, I finally went home, got some sleep, and went back to work. Arriving back at the station, I ran into our news director, Walter Hawver.

"Mr. Johnson wants to see you in his office," Walt said.

I thought, "Oh wonderful, he's seen the documentary, and probably wants to tell us what a great job we did."

So I walked down the hall, danced into his office, and Ken said, "Sit down David."

Within two minutes, the whole floor crew had gathered in there as well, at which point Johnson commenced to berate us because the night before I had said something funny in "the kicker," the closing segment, and somebody on the floor crew laughed.

"I do not ever want to hear laughter in our studio during a newscast, ever again!" Johnson erupted. Hearing that, I was incensed, but I sat quietly.

Finally, Johnson said, "Okay, that's it. You can all go back."

Well, I bolted. I was going to be the first one out the door, but Ken said, "Not you Dave, sit down." Everybody else left.

"I can tell you're very upset with me," he said. "You're upset about this."

"Well, yes, sir. I am," I replied, still stewing. "Those guys that you brought in here and just berated worked down here all night long, and frankly I thought that's why you were calling us down here—to congratulate us on a job well done. But no, just because somebody giggled, you ripped into us."

"Are you questioning my authority?" Johnson demanded. General managers of TV stations often think they are demi-gods, but in Ken's case I liked him, respected him, and trusted his judgment. "No, not at all," I quickly said. "You're the boss. But those guys are pretty much underpaid. You promoted Chris Curle from receptionist to street reporter, but you're still paying her a receptionist's salary. And Rick Hartley, who shoots film for us all night long, is working on a poverty scale and…"

By then, it was getting close to 5:00, so I told him, "I've got to go get ready to go on the air." So I left and went down to the newsroom, and to be honest I was shaking in my boots. I'm thinking, "God Almighty, you may have really ripped it this time!"

I got my scripts in order and went on the air. After I got off the air at 6:30, the news director Walt Hawver was in the studio. Before I could even get out of the anchor chair, he said "Mr. Johnson wants to see you in his office."

This is it. I'm gonna be fired.

When I walked into his office, Johnson got up from behind his desk and said, "Well Dave, I think you'll be glad to know Chris Curle and Rick Hartley have both gotten immediate pay raises. Now, what other problems have you got?"

I laughed, and said, "Mr. Johnson, thank you so much. I thought I was coming down here to get fired, and I'm glad to know that you've taken what I said in the spirit in which it was intended."

Chris Curle later left us, married ABC News reporter Don Farmer, and they were on the air together as a man/wife news anchoring team on CNN out of Atlanta for a number of years after the launch in 1980. Chris was a great anchor. I'm glad my venting helped her get a little more recognition back then.

I had come a long way from spinning records on the radio. I was part of an award-winning team, and, I was beginning to have some influence at the station. But it snuck up on me. My coming of age in the role first began to come to my attention in a humorous way when I was in Amsterdam covering the first 747.

The so-called "wide body" age in airline travel began in 1969 when Boeing introduced the first 747 aircraft, which quickly became known as the "jumbo jet" owing to its massive size. Its double-decker hump just behind the cockpit made it the most recognizable plane in the world—and around the world it did fly, carrying tremendous volumes of passengers and cargo. Pan American Airlines was the first commercial carrier to put the 747 into service in 1970, and KLM Royal Dutch Airlines added to their inventory in 1975.

When KLM brought their first 747 jet to Houston a few years later, they arranged a special flight for the mayor, the county judge, city council, and other dignitaries. I had the opportunity to go along. We flew to Dallas that day—it must have been New Year's Day because we flew that big, huge plane over the Cotton Bowl, which actually stopped the game so everyone could watch. Nobody had ever seen a 747 down here before. We also did a fly-by over Love Field so that the air traffic controllers there could see this huge airplane.

I had watched those things take off and wondered how in the world does this monster airplane fly. Well, they did fly, and very well at that. Later, on KLM's first flight from Houston to Amsterdam, they invited some news reporters along. Ron Stone went from Channel 2; Fred Hartman, the editor of the *Baytown Sun*, went along; and I joined them as a representative of Channel 13. We spent two days in Amsterdam, going around that really unique city with its canals.

We were walking down one street that was alongside a canal one evening, and at the end of that street, we saw an old movie theatre marquis out front that read "Sex Museum and Live Sex Show on Stage." Well, when the suggestion was made that we go in, the Baptist preacher son in me first resisted. I told the other guys, "Tthis has got to be nothing but a tourist trap." But we went in there anyway—Ron, Fred Hartman and me. It was nothing but a bunch of mannequins dressed up in silly stuff. Then we headed into the theatre, which was very small. It had seating on three sides of a small stage, about eight rows deep.

We were talking after sitting down when a guy two rows in front of us turned around and said, "That sounds just like Ron Stone and Dave Ward." To say we were shocked would be an understatement! No matter how innocent it was, it was not exactly the kind of place you wanted to be recognized—much less have your name shouted. Anyway, we watched the show on stage, and it was nothing. You could put it on TV today and no one would blink an eye.

As we were walking out of that little theatre, we went to the guy who had recognized us, found out he was with a Houston oil company, and told him, "Listen, you don't tell anybody *we* were here; we won't tell anybody *you* were here." Apparently he never did, because we never heard anything about that show from anybody ever again.

I attended another show around that time that had more disastrous results. On March 16, 1974, a successful Houston promoter and good friend, Alan Becker, hosted the Yamaha Motocross Series in the Astrodome. All of the top motocross stars from across the country and around the world would be in Houston to compete for the season-long championship that had started in Daytona. To help promote this big event, Alan thought it would be a good idea to get some television people, radio disc jockeys, and sports writers; put them on 125cc Yamaha motorcycles; and let them run a couple of turns around the track during the intermission of the actual motocross race. It was a celebrity race with really nothing more than vanity at stake.

Having already clearly demonstrated we (1) loved racing and motorized sports, and (2) had absolutely no common sense or concern for our safety, Dan Lovett and I were quick to jump onboard when the invitation arrived. We even went out to the Astrodome the Friday before the race to shoot some TV promos, talking about how we were going to be racing motorcycles there the next night. Then, we put them on the air.

The night of the big event, there were two heats scheduled for the celebrity races during the intermission of the actual professional races, and I was in the first heat along with nine other idiots. Alan had told us you could not hurt yourself on a 125cc Yamaha, but he was wrong. It could be zero-to-death in four seconds on one of those things.

When it came time for our race, I was pumped up and ready to go. When they put the fence down in front of us to start the race, everyone took off at the same time—except me. When I hit the gas, my bike roared right out from under me, in a big wheelie. By the time I got the dancing bear in my hands finally down on the ground, the other bikes were already around the first turn. I was dead last. As it was only a two-lap race, I had a lot of ground to make up with very little time to do it.

Most of the other folks had no experience on motocross motorcycles either, so I started passing them. First, I got into ninth place, then eighth, then seventh—getting past most of them in that first lap. Coming into the second lap, I moved into fifth place, and as I passed another bike I heard a noise. When you're on bike like that with a helmet on, all you can hear is the engine noise. But when I passed the guy in fourth place, I heard a little different noise. I still couldn't figure out what it was.

When I passed the guy in third place, I heard that same noise again, only it was a little louder. When I passed the guy in second place, I heard it really roar loud—and it finally hit me. "That's the crowd," I thought. "There are 44,000 people in the Astrodome, and they are cheering for you, Ward." Well, that was a very dangerous thing, because now I really wanted to win that race.

We came around the last turn, and the guy who was in first place was just ahead of me. I was pulling up beside him and got my front tire about equal with his back tire when we hit the finish line. The only problem was, the finish line was a 4-foot high berm that you had to jump over, but I hit it wrong. My bike flipped end-over-end, and when it came down that bike smashed me like a bug. I remember women screaming in terror, which is never a good sign.

I was sprawled out there on the Astrodome floor with what would turn out to be a broken shoulder blade, a broken left collar bone, and two depressed vertebrae in my back. I had also broken my pelvis in four places. It was pretty grim.

It took a while, but the medical people finally scraped me off the floor. As they were hauling me off, the announcer said, "There goes Dave Ward, they're loading him up on the ambulance," and the crowd politely applauded. The only thing on me that worked was my right hand, so I raised my right hand to wave at the crowd—to let them know I would survive. Maybe. That got a big cheer.

Suffice it to say, they canceled the second heat of the celebrity race that night.

Meeting me at the ambulance was my daughter Linda, who was thirteen at the time. Glendya, Linda, and David Jr. had been sitting up on the third level in the press box area, watching all this unfold. To this day, Linda cannot tell you how she got down there to that exit on the floor of the Astrodome. But she did, and she rode in the ambulance with me as they hauled me out of there. They asked me, "Do you want to go to Ben Taub Hospital, or Hermann Hospital?" Both are great hospitals, but I picked Hermann because I knew Dr. Red Duke was there.

At Hermann, they put me on a gurney and took a bunch of X-rays. Dr. Duke saw those X-rays and the carnage they revealed. Then he walked in, and in that voice of his—which you could hear in the next county—he said, "Well, Ward, looks like you really busted your ass this time!"

I said, "Yeah right, I sure did. But please don't make me laugh. It only hurts when I laugh." My body had been smashed to smithereens, but it was a little harder to damage my sense of humor. It has kept me going through all the ups and downs of my life.

When they finally got me to my hospital room, my right leg was up in traction, and my left arm was strapped to my chest. There really wasn't anything else they could do, so there would be no surgery.

The general manager of the station, Ken Johnson, was out of town that Saturday, but arrived back home the next morning. He grabbed a paper as he jumped in a taxicab at the airport and was reading the *Chronicle* going to his house. When he got to the sports section, there I was plastered all over the front page. A series of photographs showed me flipping that motorcycle over in the Dome. He told me later, "David, if you had been in the back seat of that cab with me on that ride from the airport, I would have fired you right then. I was that angry."

By the time Ken got home, however, he had figured how we could turn this into a positive—not a negative. His idea was to have me doing commentaries on tape, every day, from my hospital bed. There were many days I did commentaries while on strong pain medication, so I have no idea what I discussed. But I did do one commentary that got a lot of reaction. It was on the bedpan. "This ancient instrument of torture," as I called, it. "Surely there must be a better way other than a bedpan."

Of course, with my right leg up in traction, I couldn't get up out of that bed, so I was stuck using the thing. During my eight-week recovery, I had a lot of time on my hands. The only thing that worked, as I said, was my right hand, so I wrote a note to every person who sent me a get-well card or letter.

A few weeks after my accident, a real-deal daredevil Evel Knievel came through Houston to promote one of the many death-defying feats he attempted during the 1970s. Evel (his real name was Robert) was at the height of his popularity, so Channel 13 went out to the airport to interview him. At one point, they asked him about this crazy local news guy who had crashed his motorcycle in the Astrodome in a motocross race. Without missing a beat, Knievel said, "Well, obviously he didn't know what he was doing."

Truer words may have never been spoken.

During my recovery, I had one visitor who came to see me every single day without fail: Alan Becker. Alan and I still kid today that, yes, I had signed the legal waiver, so we know Alan was not acting "on advice of counsel" by coming! He was being the good friend and upstanding guy he has always been.

Another interesting postscript: my hospital bill was covered by workman's comp. The station said that because I was making a personal appearance on behalf of KTRK, my insurance should pick up the whole bill. I was grateful that it worked out that way, because I'm sure it was a doozy.

When I was discharged from Hermann Hospital, the hospital staff gave me a unique, treasured reminder of that popular bedpan commentary that I think I still have somewhere: an engraved bedpan. They polished one up and inscribed it: "Tribute to the Bedpan by Dave Ward."

After being liberated, I spent several more weeks on crutches. Finally, sometime that summer I got back to the studio and on the air. I can promise you I have never gone anywhere near any motorcycles since March of 1974.

Slowing down for a little as I rehabilitated from the accident, I had time to reflect on my family life. Things were not going well there, and I was headed for a crash there, too. Anyone who has ever had kids will tell you that the time passes too quickly before they are all grown up. I loved being a dad and doing fatherly things like teaching my kids how to ride a bike. When Linda and David Jr. were younger, I also taught them how to whistle, and to sing silly songs. Together, we would make kites out of newspaper and sticks, complete with tails. Given my love of flying, I would say paper airplanes were probably my go-to specialty. The kids seemed to like them.

And there were other wonderful moments in our family life. Early on, from our Loch Lohman apartment, our little family could watch the Astrodome rise from the dirt—literally. Afterwards, we'd go to Astro games and the Houston Livestock Show and Rodeo. When the kids were a little bit older, I quizzed them about the music on the radio as we were driving around. What instrument is this? What band is this? The kids were pretty darn sharp, and after a while it wasn't easy to "stump the band."

But I am sure Linda and David Jr. must also feel as if a big chunk of their childhood was spent at the Channel 13 building. If they ever had the day off from school, they'd be there. The much-ballyhooed station swimming pool also received a lot of action from the Ward kids. And in July of 1969, I remember my family was among the crowd watching the moon landing on a monitor in the main area.

Still, I am like a lot of parents that wish I could have spent more time with the children during those early years. In my radio and television careers, at KNUZ for four years and then KTRK for half a century, it seemed as if there wasn't an hour on the clock, or a day of the week, that I didn't work on a regularly scheduled basis at one time or another. We used to put aluminum foil over the windows to serve as low-budget blackout shades because of my weird hours and sleeping schedule. And there were many, many nights I'd get off the air at 10:30 p.m. and head out "prowling" with our late-night photographers.

Looking back, together Glendya and I *had* the kids, but she was the one who really *raised* them to be the wonderful people they have turned out to be. Glendya was always there for our kids, but the truth is I was not always there for her. We had grown apart over the years, which was entirely my fault. I wish I had handled that situation better than I did.

My body healed from the motorcycle wreck, but not long afterward in 1975, Glendya and I divorced after fifteen years of marriage. I was devastated. Glendya and David. Jr. moved to Tyler, while my daughter Linda stayed in the home of a girlfriend of hers from Spring High School.

I had been so busy chasing my career in every fast moving vehicle possible, and it never occurred to me that my family wouldn't be home waiting for me, whatever time I came back. Now they had moved on, and I was alone. It would take me many years and another marriage before I learned enough about relationships to finally become a good partner. In the meantime, I dove even deeper into my work.

And while work was definitely an escape from the pain of losing my family, I found that it also began to teach me more about what really matters in this world. Some of the lessons we learn in life are more painful than others, and some we never master. I am grateful that the love of family is something that can deepen and grow in spite of rough times. All my kids are more of a gift to me than they will ever know. And now, after many years spent learning to truly value family, I am blessed to have my wonderful grandchildren Mark Harrisson Heatley, Michael David Heatley, and Sarah Grace Heatley in my life, young adults who make me so proud, and also Laura's great grown children, Rachelle Rowe, John Wilson Rowe, and Corey Elizabeth Rowe Flores. The presence of each of them in my life helps me keep my work in better perspective every day. And for someone who loves his work as much as I do, that's a big job!

*In 1967, I became KTRK's first on-the-street reporter,
and even after I was tied to the anchor desk I enjoyed getting out
into the community wherever news was happening.*

18

INSTANT EYE

I was on a radio call-in show one time with my respected friend Ron Stone when a caller asked me what turned out to be a little bit of a curveball question. He said, "Tell me, Dave, what is news?"

These days, I know a lot of folks are pondering that very same question.

That simple but penetrating question threw me for just a second, and I started into a rambling answer. "Well, news is…" I said, still pondering, "…it's just…it's whatever's going on. It can be fires or shootings. It's just…what's happening in a given day."

When I got back to the TV station, our news director Walter Hawver was waiting for me at the back door. He just lit into me. "Dave, I listened to that call-in show, and that was embarrassing," he said. "What is news? News is *people*. Whatever is happening to, or for, or about *people*."

I never forgot that.

Going into 1977, KTRK definitely was on a roll but readying for a new conquest: live news. We wanted to take the news even closer to the lives of the people in our viewing audience. We even had a promo campaign complete with a 1970s-ish groovy jingle inviting viewers to "move closer to your world, my friends."

Today, anyone with a smartphone (which would not be me, because I hate the things) can become a live broadcaster in a way, using any of a series of apps and social media platforms. In April of 2016, in fact, our friends at KPRC-TV experienced a total power outage due to severe weather that took out their generator and their backup generator—what the station called a "perfect storm." As a result, the

Channel 2 team was forced to rely on their Facebook page, website, smartphones and iPads to continue their news coverage for a number of hours until they got their power back—a pretty remarkable feat under tough circumstances.

Back in the 1970s, however, the ability to broadcast from any place but the studio was a very tricky, and costly, challenge. But just as Al Primo had been an innovator in terms of the newscast *format*, KTRK in 1977 became one of the first stations to aggressively acquire and employ the latest *technology* to gather and deliver the news. The two specially-equipped, home-built remote vans that were soon roaming the streets of Houston, which we called our "Instant Eye" trucks, provided the most visible evidence of this move by KTRK.

In late 1976 and early 1977, KTRK start heavily touting these investments in live television in a three-minute promotional video I narrated describing how our remote teams delivered "live news" to our viewers. After arriving on the scene, I explained, "the reporter takes off to find out what has happened, while the engineer sets up the equipment. A microwave-transmitting antenna is aimed at a relay point high atop a downtown building, where the signal is re-transmitted to our studios. The photographer, meanwhile, hooks up the 'Instant Eye' camera, pulls cable, and selects a shooting site. Within seconds, working as a team, Eyewitness News can be ready to go on the air live from any location in the Houston area."

Wrapping up the promo, I told viewers that Channel 13 has the best team of professionals working to deliver this "exciting and immediate" form of electronic journalism—and then suggested "that's why 13 Eyewitness News is Houston's choice for news."

To be clear, Channel 13 was not the first station in town to have a 5 p.m. newscast. In fact, Channel 2 had one called "Scene at Five" with Ron Stone. It had been winning the ratings battle in that time slot for years, which was certainly an added incentive for us to find a new and compelling way to set our 5 p.m. newscast apart. In April of 1977, KTRK launched its groundbreaking "Live at Five" newscast with a strong emphasis on this new technology to try and do just that.

"Live at Five" marked the debut of my friend Jan Carson behind the anchor desk. Until then, she had been doing terrific work over several years as a field reporter. Most notably, at least at that point, Jan had covered the catastrophic ammonia tanker accident in the Galleria area on May 11, 1976—which today still stands as the worst truck accident in city history. A tractor-semitrailer carrying over 7,500 gallons of ammonia crashed and fell from the 610 Loop onto the Southwest Freeway where it exploded and released its lethal cargo. Six persons died as a result of the accident, with another seventy-eight persons hospitalized.

Jan was the first reporter on the horrific, chaotic scene together with her photographer Locke Bryan. "I am amazed we showed the dead body," Jan recalled of their reporting recently, "but there was a 'graphic images' warning at the beginning of the story." This was still maybe a year before the station made the move to video, so Locke was shooting in film—which had to be rushed back to the studio and developed before it could get on the air.

Shortly after, Jan, Locke and others on our team had to be hospitalized and given oxygen treatments, but thankfully they were not seriously injured. Their reporting, furthermore, earned them several well-deserved awards and ended up helping change state trucking laws to prevent future such disasters.

When Ken Johnson and Walt Hawver decided to put "Live at Five" on the air, they told me, "We want you and Jan to do it together. It's going to be different." Eventually, Doug Murphy replaced me as the male anchor at 5 p.m., because I was also doing the 6 and 10. But it was meaningful to work with Jan to get that new program going because it really changed the game and set new parameters for taking news out into the community, live, where it's happening now. Imitation being the most sincere form of flattery, KTRK's "Live at Five" concept was soon adopted by dozens of stations across the country.

Of course, with live or breaking news, often you have to ad lib whatever you know—or whatever you've been told about a given situation. It helps if you have a reporter on the scene, so you can throw it to them. Otherwise, you just have to wing it.

One of those earliest live "remote" shots, this one in 1978, stands out. Right before the newscast started, we received news of a robbery and shooting at a dry cleaner over on Dowling Street. Reporter Arthur Wood was near that location with our remote crew in one of our two specially equipped "Instant Eye" vans. Alerted by our assignment desk, they got to the cleaners in about five minutes, and were ready to do a live report at the top of the hour. I opened the program:

"Good evening, friends. There's just been a robbery and a shooting at a cleaners on Downing Street. Let's go live to the scene and our reporter Arthur Wood…"

The next thing you saw, through the miracle of our new technology, was Arthur standing next to a car that had crashed into a building. "Yes Dave, there's been a robbery and shooting here at this dry cleaners across the street," he said, gesturing in the direction of the cleaners. "The robber held up the place, but the owner pulled a gun and shot the robber—but as he was running out, the robber shot the owner. The robber then jumped in his car here and took off, but he crashed into this building—and he's dead."

That was all Arthur had been able to learn in the short time he had been on the scene. In fact, you could see the police just arriving in the background of this live report. So Arthur said, "Let me repeat partially: this is a still developing scene, police are still arriving, ambulance attendants are still treating the dry cleaner clerk or owner, and the robber is *still dead*. Back to you, Dave."

"Thank you, Arthur," I responded. "We'll be sure to check back to make sure that guy ain't Lazarus."

Let me pause right here to make two points. First, even though I have been in the television business for over fifty years, I still have no idea how pictures and sound fly through the air and appear on your TV screen or your mobile devices. And second, when I reflect on the amazing work of our engineers and technicians—the behind-the-scenes men and women who somehow find new and better ways for us to get those pictures and sound on those screens—I have nothing but admiration. It drives home the point that it really is a *team effort* to get the news on the air.

Another technological innovation that made its way onto the news set after we made the jump from black-and-white to color in the 1970s was called "chromakey." Chromakeying is a way of instructing the camera to disregard a chosen color, which then allows the production people to project a moving picture or weather map on a screen of that same chosen color behind a reporter. This visual effect makes it look like you are really standing "in front" of that moving picture or weather radar map—when in reality you're in front of a blank colored screen.

At first, the color everyone used for their chromakey screen was blue, which meant we couldn't wear blue suits, blue shirts or blue ties. One night we were reporting about a fire, and the production team had chromakeyed, or projected, video of the fire on the blue screen behind me so the viewer could see what had happened while I discussed it. Well, the video of this fire not only played on that blue screen behind me—but also my blue eyes. You could see the flames flickering in my eyes, and I subsequently got a card from a woman. "My father always watches Channel 13," she wrote, "but the other night when you were reporting about that fire, we could see fire in your eyes. My father shouted, 'Turn it off! Turn it off! That man is the devil!'"

For the record, I have been called worse.

Eventually, the technical folks realized green was a better color because there aren't too many green suits. When you hear any reference to "green screen," that's what they mean.

We always took our job of delivering the news seriously, but as I've indicated, we also had some fun along the way. The 1970s not only saw the rise of new concepts like Eyewitness News and Action News , but also of consultants who advised management teams on how to build their station's ratings. Out of these consultants came all kinds of research that let stations know how they were faring with the viewing audience. They also made personnel suggestions involving certain male-female anchor teams, and promoted another phenomenon called "happy talk"—the playful banter you see between news personalities as the newscast moves between stories.

I was never a big one for forced "happy talk," partly because I genuinely liked the people with whom I worked. We had an innate chemistry that cannot be forced or drawn up in a consultant's white paper.

One night while I was still co-anchoring with Jan, our outstanding weatherman Ed Brandon came on the air to give his report. I threw it to him saying, "Now here's Ed with the weather…"

"Thank you, Dave," Ed said. "I want to let you folks know that I just got a phone call a little while ago from a guy who's threatening to bomb the TV station."

Then Ed turned around to point at the weatherboard, and he had this red cylinder strapped on his back with B-O-M-B written on it. At one point, the director cut to a shot of me or Jan, and we obviously were reacting to this little stunt. Anyway, Ed finished delivering his forecast, and came back over to the news desk. "Well, that's the weather," Ed said, wrapping up, "and I guess maybe there's no bomb."

At that, I pulled a fire extinguisher out from under the set and said, "Ed, turn around." When he did, PPFFFFTTTT—I hit him with a blast ripped that ripped that fake, cardboard bomb completely off his back—and almost knocked him down. Obviously, we set that up. But no one had to tell us to do that.

Of course, it's a different world these days, with real bombs in the news more than any of us could have imagined back then. There's no way we would ever joke about something like that today. We lived in a bubble then. It seemed like the United States would always be safe from the devastating things that were happening around the world. But even back then, there were tragedies close to home. And the politics of the world were beginning to affect us, too. As technology developed, covering the news meant getting closer and closer to those events.

In August of 1979, Jan Carson left KTRK after signing a four-year contract at another ABC affiliate, KGO-TV in San Francisco. I was sad to see her go. The last piece we covered together was the massive Woodway Square apartment complex fire in late July 31, 1979. It was common during our two years together, especially with big stories, for me to anchor the newscast from the studio while Jan served as a "field anchor" live on location—as we did this time too. Once again using our live remote capabilities, I opened the 6 p.m. newscast as aerial footage of the fire was chromakeyed on the screen "behind" my head: "Good evening, friends. It is the largest apartment complex fire in Houston's history, and it is still burning out on the city's near-west side. Jan Carson has a live 'Instant Eye' camera at the Woodway Square apartments, the scene of a seven-alarm blaze."

The director then cut to a live shot of Jan in the middle of a street, with several fire engines and fire hoses strewn behind her. A haze of dark smoke hung in the air. "Dave, you can see behind me the firefighters are still trying to put out the flames in a number of buildings…"

High winds and fire-friendly wood shingles facilitated that rapidly moving fire, which damaged or destroyed 700 of the 1,100 units in the complex. When the flames were finally extinguished and the smoke had lifted, the blaze left 1,500 people homeless and caused $20 million in damage.

Incidentally, about an hour before that massive fire broke out, Houston's City Council rejected a measure to toughen roofing standards by requiring a fire-retardant asbestos felt be placed under wood shingles. The council quickly reversed course in the immediate aftermath of that blaze and outlawed any use of those cedar-shake shingles in future construction.

I was covering news at home, and news from far afield. Sometime after the Alaska Pipeline became operational in 1977, photographer Wayne Zerr and I went to Alaska to do a special report on it. A lot of Houston companies were involved in that project, and a lot of that oil was going to be coming down here—so it made sense to find out a little more about it. We flew to Anchorage and caught a connecting flight to Prudhoe Bay with the oil drilling companies. There was no way we could get up there on our own. Prior to our arrival, they issued us Arctic weather clothing, including fur-lined parkas and heated gloves to protect us against the harsh temperatures there. At the time, it was as cold as 30 to 40 degrees below zero.

Wayne used an Arcon sound film camera that he had oiled and lubricated with graphite so it wouldn't freeze in the sub-zero temperatures up there, but it still froze up. In fact, everything he shot that was not in a building, he had to shoot from inside the car—rolling down the window. I'd be standing out there doing the stand-up, and at one point even my Bic pen froze. To keep their vehicles operational, once the drivers started the engine, they never turned it off. Those motors ran 24/7.

The last day we were there, I was so exasperated by the freezing temperatures that I said in jest, "I want to shoot something, Wayne." At the time, I was standing there with an old distant early-warning line behind me, and I said something like, "Here we are in Prudhoe Bay (blanking) Alaska. We've come up here to do a story on building of the Alaska Pipeline, but I've got to tell you, there are no Houstonians stupid enough to be up here in this horrible, sub-zero atmosphere. Go ahead Wayne, show them. There's nothing up here but ice!"

After we finished at Prudhoe, they flew us back to Anchorage, and we drove a rental car as far north as we could to film the pipeline. Then we went down to Valdez on the southern coast, shooting more film of the pipeline and interviewing people along the way. Once in Valdez, we filmed the storage tanks and the port facilities where they loaded the oil into these huge tankers to bring all of that oil mostly to the Houston area.

All in all, it was an incredibly interesting and enlightening trip—learning what it took technically to drill in such harsh conditions, and then to pipe that oil all the way to Valdez, and finally transferring it to ships back to the U.S. But it was also the coldest assignment of my life. I don't want to be in temperatures that bitter, so cold you can't turn your car motor off, ever again.

The world was becoming more connected, and the news reflected the good and bad of it. In November 4, 1979, Iranian students stormed the U.S. Embassy in Tehran and took nearly seventy American hostages. Earlier that summer, revolutionaries led by radical cleric Ayatollah Ruhollah Khomeini forced the pro-American Shah of Iran (named Mohammad Reza Pahlavi) into exile in Egypt after thirty-eight years in power and dissolved the government. By then, the vast majority of Iranians had tired of the Shah's rule, bitterly accusing him of either failing to spur enough economic growth and societal progress—or straying too far from the religious tenets of Islam. The Shah's close alliance with the United States, the "Great Satan" in the words of the revolutionaries, was among his greatest sins as they saw it.

In October of 1979, President Jimmy Carter allowed the exiled Shah—who was then very ill with cancer and would die within a year—to travel to the U.S. for medical treatments. The widespread, virulent outrage that Carter's decision caused back in Iran spilled over into the courtyard of the U.S. Embassy on November 4th, precipitating a crisis lasting 444 days and no doubt contributing to President Carter's re-election defeat in 1980.

Four days after the embassy was besieged, Roone Arledge and ABC News launched a new nighttime program on KTRK and its other affiliates called "The Iran Crisis—America Held Hostage" hosted by the network's "World News Tonight" anchor Frank Reynolds. Veteran ABC reporter Ted Koppel soon joined Reynolds as co-anchor, and then took over as solo host in March of 1980. Ted's work on that program, which was re-named "Nightline" a few months later, defined much of his accomplished and respected career.

Meanwhile, shortly after the crisis erupted, like many Americans, I was very upset. But unlike most Americans, I had a public platform for making my disgust with that unacceptable situation known—and even to offer up an idea for doing a little something about it. So a few weeks before Christmas, I wrote and aired this commentary:

> *I have felt the same helpless anger and frustration over the hostage situation in Iran that all Americans are feeling these days. We all know what we can't do, but what can we do? The other day the Iranian Foreign Minister was asked, if our people are still there on December 25th, can we send them Christmas presents? He replied, in so many words, well we recognize and respect your religious holidays maybe something can be worked out. Well, let's work it out. If they won't send our people home then why can't we send Christmas to them? What would happen if every citizen of the United States mailed a small Christmas present or a Christmas card or a letter; anything. Each addressed to an American Hostage, U. S. Embassy, Tehran, Iran. It seems apparent that the only thing those emotionally hyperactive people will recognize or understand right now is an equally emotional expression of our national unity. A demonstration of what 50 lives mean. How better to demonstrate that than to share our Christmas with those poor hostages in Iran? Such a movement could spread to every city in this nation and result in such an outpouring of love and concern that the whole world would stand up and applaud. Millions of Americans each sending the message: Peace on Earth, Good Will Toward Men; the message from the Prince of Peace. Well, I'm going to do it. I'm mailing 50 Christmas cards, each addressed to An American Hostage, U.S. Embassy, Tehran, Iran. The Iranians can scream and shout at us; they can shake their fists at us; but they can't stop Santa Claus. The Ayatollah is no match for the Spirit of Christmas. What do you think? I'm Dave Ward.*

That commentary aired December 7, 1979, on Eyewitness News during the 7 a.m., 6 p.m. and 10 p.m. newscasts, and resulted in a tremendous response. I got more reaction to that than anything I had done before, or after. I was told, and learned later, that several other anchor people all over the United States heard of that, and they made a similar commentary. Most importantly, a lot of people took that commentary to heart, and there was an outpouring of Christmas cards and letters sent to the embassy in Tehran.

When the hostages were finally released on the inauguration day of the new President, Ronald Reagan, some of them commented after they got home about the outpouring of love that came to them before that Christmas.

Sometimes in this business we go beyond reporting and actually impact the news. I hope that the former hostages remember the letters they got at Christmas and how much love from their fellow Americans they represented. I know I will always remember those letters. The response that my short commentary generated seemed to open new doors in my life. In the next phase of my life, I would have the opportunity to get even more engaged with my community, in a couple of significant ways.

Interviewing U.S Senator Lloyd Bentsen for Channel 13's "Issues and Answers" program.
It appears our guest might be straining to hear me over that very loud jacket.

Dr. James "Red" Duke was one of the most accomplished, smartest, funniest and original people I ever met. He was also one of the best medical reporters on TV ever.

"YOU'RE MR. CRIME STOPPERS"

After the 1981 NFL season, I stopped doing the stats for the Oilers' radio broadcasts. By then, Ron Franklin—who had started in the Houston market at Channel 11 in 1971 and moved over to Channel 2 in 1980 (before launching his highly successful run at ESPN in 1987)—was gone. Ron Stone had also left the Oilers' radio team. I was getting busier and busier, and it seemed like it was time for me to move along, too.

One thing was for sure: I didn't do those Oilers games for the money. I had gotten a raise from $15 to $50 a game. They gave me a check for $50 after each game, and I'd just throw it in my briefcase. Early in 1982, the producer for the Oilers Radio Network, Mark Oristano, who was also the sports director for the Texas State Network, called me and said, "Ward, would you please go to the bank and cash those checks from last season."

"What are you talking about?" I asked, clearly having forgotten.

"Texas State Network is up for sale," Oristano explained. "They're going through all the books, and you still have five or six of those Oiler checks you didn't cash—you're holding up a multi-million dollar deal."

So I jumped in the car, went to the bank, and cashed those checks real quick so they could sell the network.

That year, Ken Johnson took a gamble by expanding our 6 p.m. newscast to a full hour. It was seen as risky because other stations had tried a full-hour of news in the same window, only to lose out to game shows and other programming that started at 6:30 p.m. Ken thought a full-hour newscast could work if, among other things, we held Marvin's segment until the second half of the broadcast. He was right.

We also added another iconic personality into that newly formatted newscast: Dr. James Henry "Red" Duke.

Red already was a towering figure in Houston, not only because of his historic role attending to JFK and John Connally in Dallas back in 1963 but also more recently as the founder, in 1976, of the groundbreaking Life Flight operation at Hermann Hospital. Life Flight was a fleet of helicopters or "air ambulances" that Red devised to bring critically injured people from around the region as quickly as possible to the trauma center at Hermann. It has to be one of the greatest medical inventions in human history, especially in light of the number of lives it has helped save.

Even then, Red had a list of medical accomplishments and accolades as long as your arm, which explains why he was later on President-elect George H.W. Bush's short list for surgeon general in 1988.

I had gotten to know Red very well not only from being in the hospital for so long after the motorcycle crash, but also from seeing him often at Kay's where he would tell me story after story about how "we had this guy come in who had been shot three times," or "you wouldn't believe the car crash victim and I had to do so-and-so." When we came up with the idea of Dr. Red Duke's "Medical Minute," or whatever we called it back then, I said, "Doc, you'd be a natural to do this because of your experience, and all the people in Houston who know you and you've treated. It would be a great for us to put this kind of information on television—preventative things, or what to do if you're sick." Red originally agreed to do three medical reports a week in exchange for a $25,000 donation by KTRK to the Texas Health and Science Center.

Once we started airing those Medical Minutes, they were an instant hit. One of his earliest reports covered the topic of kidney stones. The piece opened with Red in a hard hat, a red flannel shirt, and jeans—and he was jack-hammering a slab of concrete on a Houston side street. "You're probably wondering 'What's he doing messing with a jack-hammer?'" Red said in his thick Texas drawl. "By using this same principle, doctors are literally vibrating apart kidney stones in the human body." He went on to cover the widest range of topics: hyperthyroidism, skin cancer, spicy foods, potatoes, bowlegs, fiberoptics, laparoscopy, and on it went.

Red was a true Renaissance man with the widest range of passions, including saving the Texas bighorn sheep, but most of all he was a teacher. He once explained his wide success saying, "I really believe anybody can understand almost anything, no matter how technical, if the language used by the communicator is such that the person is familiar with it."

In time, Red's "Medical Minute" became so popular, they syndicated it and ran it in markets all over the United States. He had to be the best-known doctor in the country for a time, and he took great delight telling me about walking through the Salt Lake City airport with his best friend, Willie Nelson, one day.

"Willie was going to perform, and people were always coming up to Willie, and recognizing Willie," Red said. "Well, in that airport, this woman came up to me, 'Dr. Red Duke, you're Dr. Red Duke! I saw your report, and it helped me save my mother's life.' She just went on and on. I finally said, 'Thank you ma'am. Let me introduce my friend Willie Nelson.' She said 'How do you do, Mr. Nelson?' Willie started giggling."

She did not know Willie, but she definitely knew Dr. Red Duke.

Around this time that we also started another signature feature on our newscasts: our weekly Crime Stoppers "Crime of the Week" reports. Crime Stoppers would become very significant in my life as time went on.

Crime Stoppers got its start in 1976 in Albuquerque, New Mexico, after a university student named Michael Carmen was killed by two thugs during a gas station robbery. Local police investigated the murder for six weeks but had little to go on despite their belief that the perpetrators were locals. They felt that somebody must have some information but for whatever reason was unwilling to come forward. That's when a detective named Greg McAleese partnered with a local television station, KOAT-TV, to air a re-enactment of the crime and set up a hotline for callers to pass on information anonymously. McAleese also arranged for local businesses to finance the costs of the program.

The next day, a caller to the hotline provided a tip that led to the men who were responsible. Within seventy-two hours, police had solved the murder. Not only that, but the hotline also yielded information about many other crimes which had not even been reported to the police.

A couple of Houston Exchange Club members brought the idea to Channel 13 after hearing about it at a statewide convention. Our team loved it from the start and made a deal with the University of Houston Drama Department to provide student actors and actresses to help recreate the crimes. We also partnered with KTRH-AM radio and the *Houston Chronicle*, which both carried the "Crime of the Week."

At the end of each weekly report, I reminded viewers, "Crime Stoppers will pay a $5,000 cash reward this week for information leading to the arrest and charging of the person responsible for this felony crime. Call Crime Stoppers, 713-222-TIPS. Your identity will remain anonymous." The program took off like crazy. We even got calls from inmates in the state prison! They would use the reward they got to pay their attorneys to try to get them out of prison. One suspect the police arrested had the *Houston Chronicle* story of his crime sitting there on his coffee table, as if it was his press clipping.

The drama students we used in these weekly re-enactments were talented—maybe too talented. We were in north Houston one time re-creating an armed robbery, when someone driving by saw the actors and reported what they *thought* was a real crime in progress. Well, three squad cars arrived in a jiffy and, thinking they were going into a potentially deadly situation, the officers all had their weapons drawn. When the actor portraying the robber ran out the front door, with our camera crew following right behind, the officers screamed, "Freeze!!" Staring down five or six loaded gun barrels, that poor drama student just melted into the pavement.

Of course, we tried to find students who fit, as close as possible, the description of the felons and the victims in a given crime. One of the drama students we were using matched the identity of a serial criminal and was arrested by Houston police four or five times before they finally gave him a special I.D. card to avoid such mix-ups going forward.

The Crime Stoppers program has expanded not only all over the United States, but also overseas. Laura and I were in London several years ago, and we jumped in cab to our hotel. When I told the driver the address, he wheeled around and, in his British accent, exclaimed,

"Why, you're Mr. Crime Stoppers!" You could have knocked us over with a feather. At some point, the BBC had come to Houston, taken some of our "Crime of the Week" footage, and aired it in London to help start a Crimes Stoppers program there.

I am biased, but the Crime Stoppers program in Houston really is the most successful of any in the world. In its first thirty-five years, more than 36,000 felony criminals have been caught, clearing nearly 40,000 felony crimes.

In July of 1983, David Glodt unexpectedly, but not surprisingly, received and took an offer to move to ABC Weekend News as head of the Los Angeles bureau. David had done some really terrific work as a reporter at KTRK, winning accolades and awards for his reporting—including his 1979 story "Boys for Sale" following his eight-month investigation into boy prostitution in the Houston area. He had also come to be seen as one of the station's technical geniuses and was promoted to assistant news director. The management team had been grooming David to take Walt Hawver's place as news director, and at the time he was already kind of running the news department—so his loss was a tough one, especially when Hurricane Alicia hit just a few weeks later.

My first experience with a hurricane was Carla in 1961. I was still in Waco at WACO radio, and what was left of that storm came up through Central Texas and dumped a ton of rain. Most of all, I remember that was the storm that "blowed Dan Rather from Houston all the way to New York City." Rather had graduated from Sam Houston State University in Huntsville in 1953 and joined KTRH-AM in Houston a year later. He also was a sports reporter with KTRK before becoming the KHOU news director.

As Carla approached the Gulf Coast, most TV stations did not have their own radar, so Rather took a crew and went to the U.S. Weather Bureau in downtown Galveston which had what was then a state-of-the-art WSR-57 radar console. *The Atlantic* magazine ran a piece a few years ago that picks up the story from there:

> *Seeing the size of the coming storm, he (Rather) convinced the bureau staff to let him broadcast, live, from the office. And he asked a Weather Bureau meteorologist to draw him a rough outline of the Gulf of Mexico on a transparent sheet of plastic; during the*

broadcast, he held that drawing over the computer's black-and-white radar display to give his audience a sense both of Carla's size and of the location of the storm's eye. As CBS plugged into the broadcast, that audience suddenly became a national one.... When Rather aired his broadcast, radar existed; maps existed; but radar superimposed on maps did not. Rather hacked himself a new way of reporting, right in front of people's eyes. His MacGyvered broadcast was the first ever display of a meteorological surveillance radar on television. And the on-the-ground reporting he would go on to do—sloshing among the waves of the Galveston Seawall ("up to his ass," Walter Cronkite would notice, "in water moccasins")—would go on to become the model for the swashbuckling storm reporting so familiar to us today.[8]

Because they were able to see and comprehend the tremendous threat posed by the approaching storm, some 300,000 Texans evacuated from the coast. Many lives were saved by this innovative use of TV reporting, and in the process Rather made a national name for himself. A year later, he made his big move to CBS News in New York.

Very early in my career, I chased hurricanes all the way from Brownsville. Texas on the Mexican border over to Florida, but I never really caught up with one. It got to the point to where my colleagues said that, if a hurricane looked like it might be coming into Galveston, all I had to do was go down to the Seawall, shake my fist at it, and it would turn and go somewhere else.

In 1969, Ben Pearlman, my photographer, and I set out to chase Hurricane Camille—a Category Five killer that really devastated Mississippi. We got past New Orleans driving on Interstate 10 right down by the Gulf. We came up on a section where the traffic was stopped because the storm surge had pushed a 200-foot long section of the four-lane highway some 300 feet up into the trees. If you ever wanted an example of the massive, awe-inducing power of a hurricane storm surge, that was it.

There was another hurricane we caught up with in Louisiana, back when we were still shooting in black-and-white. I had a 18mm Bell

---

[8] https://www.theatlantic.com/technology/archive/2012/10/dan-rather-showed-the-first-radar-image-of-a-hurricane-on-tv/264246/

and Howell hand-wound, spring-loaded camera, and at one point we came to an intersection near a highway. The wind was blowing so hard that the stop sign there was swaying back and forth, and rapidly turning the sign itself from side-to-side. The wind created an effect that looked like a blinking stop sign: *stop stop stop stop stop stop*. I got out and shot it, which got on the air.

In September of 1979, I finally caught up with a big storm. Hurricane Frederic hit Mobile, Alabama packing 145-mph winds. Photographer Greg Moore and I were in a hotel in downtown Mobile, and everybody hunkered down in the basement all night long. When a hurricane rolls over you, it just screams. The wind is so high, all you can hear is the sound of that wind and glass breaking. The hotel suffered damage, but we had taken all of our stuff with us down in the basement so it would not ruin our equipment. Finally, around dawn, it let up a little bit. We had a rental car, which fortunately was unharmed. We left that hotel and started trying to drive, shooting video of the damage—but we couldn't go more than three or four blocks. There were trees down over every street, but we got what we could.

After I became the anchor on the 6 and 10 p.m. newscasts, I didn't get out to chase too many more storms. I was mostly at the TV station. That's why Walter Cronkite coined the term "anchor chair." Years later people asked, "Does that mean you are the anchor of the newscast?" No, it means if you are in the chair to head up a newscast, you are anchored to that chair. You don't get to go out on many stories, and that was pretty much my story too.

Such was the case in mid-August of 1983, when what became Hurricane Alicia formed on Tuesday, August 15th, just a few hundred miles off the upper Texas coast in the Gulf of Mexico. Making landfall on the west end of Galveston Island three days later, it had intensified into a Category Three storm with 115 mph winds. That week, the KTRK-TV Channel 13 news team was on a sixty-hour hurricane watch—constantly reporting on the various facets of the storm, plans for evacuations and sheltering in place, and how Texans were bracing for the storm's arrival, and then the brutal, devastating aftermath. Our coverage featured, of course, our weathermen Ed Brandon and Doug Brown together with my future co-anchor Shara Fryer, as well as a cast of talented, dedicated reporters many of whom are the foundation of the KTRK news team to this very day: Melanie Lawson, Deborah Wrigley, Diana Fallis, Tom Koch, Don Kobos, Don Nelson, and of course Marvin Zindler. Talk about your powerful lineups.

Also a big part of the Channel 13 Alicia team coverage were two other noteworthy members: Sylvan Rodriguez, who had joined KTRK in 1977 and was co-hosting the 7 a.m. news with Don Nelson; and finally the KTRK "Sky Eye" helicopter we acquired in 1981, on which we relied heavily for our aerial coverage of the storm's devastation once the dangerous winds subsided.

A few days later, Walt Hawver and I produced a one-hour special report called "Alicia: Her Story," in which I interviewed Steve Harned of the National Weather Service. Harned said something in that interview that, especially for those who oppose the "Ike Dike" coastal barrier today, bears keeping in mind. I asked Steve what would have happened if Alicia came ashore packing the same off-the-charts ferocity as a Category Five storm like Hurricane Camille did in 1969. "A Camille-type storm would have put in a tide of twenty-five feet... about six to eight-feet above the Seawall," Harned replied. "Then you add on top of that the waves that are generated...it would have put the entire island under water...if you had a twenty-five-foot tide down along the coast, you would be looking at thirty feet or more over the western sections of Galveston Bay and the upper section of Galveston Bay. That would have produced the most devastation... it's incomprehensible."

Walt Hawver retired shortly after our Alicia coverage to teach journalism at the University of Mississippi and later Sam Houston State University. He had come into the TV news business in 1965 after nearly two decades in the world of print journalism. In his words, he "swapped his role as city editor for the *Albany Times Union* to join WTEN-TV as news director...As a former TV columnist often critical of the station, I was intrigued by the possibilities of developing a solid news operation." Shara Fryer accurately describes Walt as our "journalism disciplinarian"—the guy who set the bar high, and held people accountable. During our Alicia coverage, in fact, Hawver got after Shara for using the term "hunkered down," but after she explained her Texas roots growing up in Hallettsville he backed down.

By the time Walt left, he had successfully integrated the newsroom, made our various newscasts perennial winners in the ratings, and built

up a news team staff of seventy-five talented, dedicated professionals—
many of whom are still with the station today. It was a remarkable
legacy of achievement, and if Walt were still with us today I would tell
him, "Ya done good, kid." Thirty-five years later, everyone at KTRK
owes that man a great debt of gratitude—none more so than I do.

Walt was replaced by Jim Topping, who like Walt (and yours truly
for that matter) came to his TV job in atypical fashion. Jim had been
one of our station consultants with McHugh-Hoffman, which was
the very first TV news consulting firm founded in the early 1960s by
ex-Detroit ad executives Peter McHugh and Philip Hoffman.

To be honest, Jim Topping and I didn't get along very well. His
idea of news was very different from mine. I always thought he was
more show-business oriented. For example, one night our lead story
at 6 p.m. was about seven men who were part of a delegation that had
done something—what it was, I cannot recall. At Topping's insistence,
we led into the story with a clip from "The Magnificent Seven." I
was fairly outraged that we might start our newscast showing a clip
from an old movie and was still fuming when I got up off the set. I
walked down the hallway to the little coffee shop, which isn't there
anymore, to get a hamburger. There were four or five other people
sitting around there, and one of them asked, "Well, what did you
think of the newscast, Dave?"

"Listen. We haven't done a newscast since Jim Topping got here,"
I said, "and we won't do one until he's gone."

Unbeknownst to me, Topping was standing right behind me,
having walked in right after I did. I could tell something was wrong
by the horrified expressions on the faces of the other folks. Sensing
what I had done, I tried to lighten it up by saying, "Well, I guess we
have done one or two."

Boy, did that coffee shop empty out quickly after that!

At the top of our game. The Channel 13 Eyewitness news team in the mid-1980s.

THE MINNOW
SWALLOWING
THE WHALE

O ver the course of more than six decades of interviewing people, the law of averages suggests that not every conversation is going to play out as you might think or hope. There are going to be people who curse, or act erratically, or—maybe worst of all—are so dull you cannot possibly put them on the air. In my experience, sometimes even the high and mighty can act awkwardly during a conversation.

During the mid-1970s, Vice President Nelson Rockefeller came to Houston. I interviewed him in a conference room in the Hyatt Regency Hotel downtown and was sitting right across from him almost knee-to-knee. If Rockefeller really wanted to make a point to a question I posed, he would say, "Well, Dave…" Then he would grab my knee and give it a squeeze. He did this four or five times during that interview. Personally, I did not care for it. Maybe he wanted to make sure I remembered him, in which case it worked.

No one else has done that to me, before or since.

In 1984, the Republicans held their national convention in Dallas. The Lone Star State had an elevated profile that year because our own George Herbert Walker Bush was President Reagan's Vice-President, and the Republican ticket was riding into a re-election year with a growing economy that had the political wind at their back. They would go on to win forty-nine states that year against the Democratic ticket of former Vice President Walter Mondale and New York Congresswoman Geraldine Ferraro.

I covered that convention and interviewed the senior U.S. Senator from Texas at the time, John Tower, who had served in the world's greatest deliberative body since 1961—when he succeeded Lyndon

Johnson after his election to be John Kennedy's Vice-President. Anyway, Senator Tower was known to be a free-spirit, a *bon vivant*-type, and on top of that he had announced he was retiring from the Senate when his term expired in January, 1985. So he was no doubt riding high and feeling good about life.

We did the interview sitting on bar stools, and while the technicians finalized our live transmission to Houston I asked Tower a question, mostly to shoot the breeze. "Senator," I asked, "you're retiring now, what are your plans? What are you going to do?"

"Dave," he said without missing a beat, and with more than a little gusto, "I'm going to come back to Texas to drink whiskey and chase..." Let's just say, if you didn't know any better, you would have thought he intended to run after cats.

I thought, *Oh my God, I hope they're not rolling on that back there at the station.* Back then, although derogatory language was still acceptable in some circles, it always caused problems on air. While public officials tried to use appropriate language on air, there were many times when it wasn't clear if we were rolling, and things that should not have been said were recorded. So far as I know, no one at the station caught John Tower's comment, which was as jaw-dropping as it was offensive. Sometimes those statements had much larger ramifications than the speaker would have imagined.

In 1985, for instance, former Houston Mayor Louie Welch derailed his comeback plan to reclaim the mayor's office when he flippantly suggested on a "hot" microphone before a KTRK "Live at Five" interview that one way to stop the AIDS epidemic would be to "shoot the queers." Welch apologized, but he could not un-say it. He went on to lose that re-election bid to the incumbent Mayor Kathy Whitmire.

Another conversation I remember particularly at that Dallas GOP convention in 1984 was one with a bunch of local anchors. We were sitting around the hotel bar one evening after the session, and they got to talking about ratings. One of them said, "Well, Charlie (or whoever it was), how are you doing up there in Detroit?"

"We're number one, a good number one," Charlie said. "For our 11 p.m., we do an eight rating and an eleven share. How are you doing in Chicago?"

"Well, we're doing pretty good too," the next guy said. "We're number one on our 10 p.m. in Chicago, with a nine rating and a twelve share."

This went on with several more anchors from Philadelphia, and New York and elsewhere. "We've got a ten rating." "We've got a fourteen share."

Finally, somebody hollered over to me, "Hey, Ward, how are you doing down there in Houston?"

I said, "Well, in our last November book, our 10 p.m. newscast did a twenty-four rating and a forty-six share."

They all said, "Yeah, right Dave—har har har har!" They did not believe me, for the simple fact that numbers like that had never been done before. In fact, the numbers *were* right, and have *never* been matched since then.

A February 19, 1985 headline over a *Houston Chronicle* piece by TV-Radio Editor Ann Hodges read, "Ch. 13 awesomely controls Houston's ratings." In it, Ann suggested that "ABC owes Ch. 13 a gold medal. The power of that local affiliate is downright awesome— in all categories. According to the trade's TV/Radio Age, Ch. 13 is the strongest ABC affiliate in the country. It delivers 44 percent of Houston's TV audience to ABC throughout the broadcast day...If that pattern holds for February's Nielsens, that should establish Ch. 13 as perhaps the most powerful large market station in the country. Local news is the basic measure, and Ch. 13's record in local news is material for *That's Incredible.*"

In fact, since Cap Cities had acquired KTRK in 1967, just our station had generated $300 million in revenues, which helps explain a related story in papers all across the country exactly one month later. On March 18, 1985, our parent company, Capital Cities Communications, Inc., announced it had agreed to buy the American Broadcasting Companies, Inc. (ABC) network for $3.5 billion. Yes, you read that right. Capital Cities bought ABC, not the other way around. It was the largest merger in broadcasting history at the time. The new company was called Capital Cities Communications, Inc./ American Broadcasting Companies, Inc.—with Cap Cities getting top billing. At the time, it was described in a *Broadcasting* article as "the minnow swallowing the whale...the old order changed last week...a new media giant was announced to the world..."

Our general manager Ken Johnson, who was one of the most respected executives in the Cap Cities universe, was called to New York City for the announcement of the deal. Once the deal went public, he—along with the other station managers—rushed to the airport to get home and report first-hand to their employees. The next day, a Tuesday, Ken gathered the entire KTRK staff together and told us the merger would not affect our jobs, which was an added source of relief and jubilation for all. Ken told us in so many words that our contribution to the strong image of Capital Cities was one of the reasons why ABC Board Chairman Leonard Goldenson wanted to pursue the merger. "Our people should be very proud," Ken said. As it was, the station's phone was ringing off the hook with congratulatory messages from near and far.

The minnow had swallowed the whale, and we were all feeling very strong about our work. We were ready to take on anything. One of the more challenging assignments you can try to tackle in the TV business is hosting a telethon, a word (and programming concept) that literally combines *television* with *marathon*. That's exactly what a telethon is—a televised endurance contest, aimed at raising as much money as possible for a worthwhile cause. Milton Berle hosted the first telethon in U.S. history in 1949, which raised over $1 million for cancer research. Of course, the best-known telethon host and cause was Jerry Lewis, who started hosting telethons for the Muscular Dystrophy Associations of America as early as 1952—and running all the way through 2011. Estimates of what Lewis raised during that incredible sixty-year run top $2 billion put into the MDAA.

Even though telethons are not as popular today as they once were, most news people and others in the media including actors and actresses still find a meaningful cause to get behind, and use their very public platforms to help that cause. For example, I recall just how devoted my very good friend Bob Allen was to the Sunshine Kids, a great organization that provides assistance to kids and teenagers with cancer. In addition to helping countless Houstonians through his "Marvin's Angels" TV features launched in the 1980s, Marvin Zindler's foundation helped make sure kids in the poorest countries received the medical care they needed. But in the 80s, telethons were big news.

In March of 1985, I was going into my seventh year hosting the local, annual telethon for the Gulf Coast Easter Seal Society, a truly wonderful organization dedicated to helping people of all ages with disabilities over a ten-county area in a variety of ways. By then I was also in my second term serving as president of the group. In an interesting twist, however, I hosted these telethons not on Channel 13—but rather on Channel 20, and eventually Channel 39. In 1985, my co-hosts helping to keep the program going were Hank Plante and Ginger Casey from Channel 26 KRIV, then the new Fox affiliate in town, as well as former Houston Oiler Tim Wilson.

Naturally, and most importantly, we also had a phone bank manned by some wonderful volunteers. The 1984 telethon had raised $377,000 in Houston ($26.4 million nationally), and I was over the moon when our 1985 edition netted a substantial increase to $450,000 just in Houston—worth roughly a million dollars today. Part of that was due to the kind generosity of one man: my friend Red Adair. During the years, it almost become part of the script that we would get down to the end of the telethon, and inevitably one of the phone bank volunteers would wave at me and say, "There's someone on the line that wants to talk to you."

It was Red. Every year, he always came up with $25,000 or $30,000 to help bring the telethon to a rousing end, and I thanked him profusely. His response was always the same: "Dave, it's either give it to you and Easter Seals, or give it to Uncle Sam. I'd much rather give it to you."

Red Adair was a Houston original. When he came back from World War II, where he served on a bomb disposal unit, Red joined one of the original oil well firefighting firms Myron Kinley. He founded Red Adair Co., Inc. in 1959, and gained worldwide attention three years later putting out the "Devil's Cigarette Lighter" in Algeria—a gas field fire that had burned for five months. In 1969, John Wayne starred in a movie titled "Hellfighters" based on that fabled episode of Red's life. That made Red Adair the only person John Wayne played in a movie while that person was still alive. I am told The Duke and Red met once in the men's room at a restaurant or club, with Wayne towering over Red. They got along famously.

I got to know Red after I interviewed him and his wife Kimmie at their bay house in Clear Lake, south of Houston. He had this big, long, red cigarette boat called "Blowout." My photographer, Jimmy Priest, and I got in the boat, and Red backed it out. He aimed it toward the bridge headed toward Galveston Bay, and he turned to me and said, "You know, Dave, I just love the feeling of power." Then he hit both of those throttles. With twin inboard engines, that boat leaped. I had been standing next to Red, but the next thing I knew I was rolling back towards the stern of *Blowout*. If Jimmy Priest hadn't grabbed me, I would have been swimming in no time. Collecting myself, I turned to Red, who was howling, he thought it was so funny.

One of Red's greatest achievements came after the first Gulf War in 1991, when Iraqi dictator Saddam Hussein and his humiliated, retreating forces set fire to as many as 732 oil wells in Kuwait precipitating an environmental crisis of unique proportions. It ended up burning nearly a billion barrels of oil, and is believed to have possibly contributed to Gulf War Syndrome. The experts thought it would take a year to put out all of those fires, but Red was part of a consortium of firefighters that put most fires out very quickly. "You could hardly see the sun," Red remembered of the smoke he first encountered there in Kuwait. "It was that thick."

In December of 1986, the station announced Shara Fryer would join me as co-anchor on the 6 p.m. newscast. The pride of Hallettsville, Texas, Shara came to KTRK in 1980 after working for ABC affiliates in San Antonio and Austin. At Channel 13, she had done a terrific job during our Hurricane Alicia coverage, and was already co-anchoring on "Live at Five" with Bob Boudreaux. Just a month before this announcement, moreover, we co-anchored the 1986 election returns that saw challenger and businessman Bill Clements defeat Texas Governor Mark White in his bid for reelection.

I thought it was a great move and was fully on board. Shara is smart and driven and has always had a nose for news—a real professional journalist. I often saw her question producers, associate producers and writers on the details and facts they had written in a given story. She wanted to make sure they got it right, so she—and KTRK—got it right. I always respected her for that.

Our first year as an anchor team was a busy one. For example, on September 13, 1987, Pope John Paul II visited San Antonio as part of a nine-city tour of the United States that year. While in Texas, he got a taste for our Tex Mex fare, received a cowboy hat, and said mass for an estimated 350,000 people at a location in Westover Hills west of downtown. Part of the structure behind the altar at the mass site was toppled by high winds just a few days before the Pope's arrival, but that day the weather element on everyone's mind was the 105-degree heat. *Houston Chronicle* TV critic Ann Hodges aptly noted that all of us news people out there that day were "courting sun stroke and heat prostration," and made a special note of the fact that our Bob Boudreaux was "the only reporter I saw wearing a suit out there in that heat."

As it was truly a historic occasion, the station made the extraordinary decision to, in effect, relocate most of our news operation to San Antonio for the day—so we could bring our viewers as much of the pontiff's movements as we could while he was on Texas soil. We had about eight or nine different live locations between Houston and San Antonio. Shara and I were anchoring our coverage from a terrific vantage point in a parking lot across from the picturesque San Fernando Cathedral. We also thought we really had it pretty good because we had a row of port-a-cans nearby. And we got a good laugh when the crew started calling them "Pope Johns" and "Vati-cans."

The only catch was: our mobile anchor set was in the back of a flat-bed truck…with a metal bed. In that 105-degree heat, that metal flatbed was basically like a frying pan. One of our photographer's tennis shoes actually started melting while standing on it. The tripods for the cameras themselves were as hot as branding irons. Thankfully, someone went around begging stores for cardboard boxes so we could lay them down over the metal flatbed and dissipate some—but not nearly all—of the searing heat. Shara recalls she wore a jacket because, back in that day, that's where you clipped on the microphone—but behind the makeshift anchor desk she wore shorts. I also had a jacket, shorts…and my boots. (An odd fashion statement to make, true, but boots always made my poor, abused back feel better.)

It got to the point that the people around us started taking pity on us, bringing us sno-cones and raspas to take the edge off the heat. Around lunchtime, we had a break while there was some downtime on the Pope's schedule. I took some of that cardboard and made a little place under that truck where I could rest my back and get out of that incessant heat. At one point, everyone started asking, "Where's Dave? Where's Dave?"

Sharing the news often combined the sublime and the ridiculous. The story could be earth-shattering or heart-rending, and we would be dealing with the realities of temperature, porta-cans, or where to catch a few winks. Another story that combined difficult logistics with an important story came just a month after the Pope's visit.

On October 14th, eighteen-month old "Baby Jessica" McClure captured the world's attention when she fell down an eight-inch wide well in her aunt's backyard in Midland. She was somehow still alive after her fall, but she was twenty-two feet below the ground—and the clock on her survival was ticking fast. Midland Police and Fire Departments came up with a plan to drill a second shaft parallel to the one holding Jessica, relying on an army of volunteer oil field hands to help pull it off. News of the complicated, dramatic rescue attempt spread like wildfire across the country and around the world.

As a news organization, we had a decision to make concerning logistics. There were no assets in Midland to get live coverage out of there. We could fly a crew out there, but then you would have to fly them—and their footage—back to get that video to air. We had invested all of this money and effort in a new Sky Link 13 satellite truck, and it would take hours to drive the truck out there—but our commitment to bringing live news to our viewers was such that management quickly made the decision to go. As a result, we were the only satellite truck onsite for quite some time.

When news of the impending rescue broke, ABC News broke into their regular programming to carry a live "Special Report" hosted by Ted Koppel using our feed. Just before Jessica was pulled out, in fact, Ted said, "I should use this occasion to thank our affiliates and our good friends at KTRK in Houston and WFAA in Dallas, Texas. It is their cameras on the scene, their live remote units, that are sending you these live remote pictures that you're watching right now."

After nearly sixty tense hours, live video pictures of paramedic Steve Forbes carrying that sweet child out of the well were beamed around the world—to everyone's total relief.

Count me among those who think it was the first televised miracle.

The 1980s were exciting times. Television news had rapidly increasing technological resources, our station was on top of its game, and we were able to bring important stories to viewers in real time. But the excitement and the success also had a darker underside. There were problems lurking in paradise. Some were industry-wide, and some were closer to home.

During the 1980s, drug use in the workplace became a national epidemic. Cocaine was especially rampant, but marijuana was also of concern. Drinking alcohol was somewhat less taboo, but Capital Cities as a policy always discouraged it on company property.

Early on in my KTRK days, we used to have a spring pool party for the entire staff, with wives and husbands invited. One year, when Jim Masucci was our program manager, I was sitting out there with Jim sipping on a beer when one of the floor crew guys came over, sat down in front of us, and lit up a joint. I was really surprised that he was so bold about it. Then he offered it to me. I told him, "No, what are you doing man? Put that out. You can't do that here on station property."

He gave me a funny look, but he put it out.

Jim Masucci came up to me later and said, "David, that was the exact right thing to do. I'm very proud of you for doing that." It never came up again.

Like many in my generation, I had no interest in marijuana or cocaine. But when I was away from the station, especially in the evening, I was never too far from a beer. Kay's Bar was a key venue for such supply. I was a fixture there like one of the neon lights: always buzzing.

At work, I always—always—did my job. I did not rely on "liquid courage" to discharge my on-air responsibilities. But off the job, it was different. When I would go to a party, it was like I was at Kay's. One beer led to too many.

It was the same at the charity events I emceed.

And at the Houston Livestock Show and Rodeo, though again never while on duty.

And even at family gatherings.

My drinking got to the point that, near the end of 1985, Ken Johnson arranged for an intervention with the help of my buddy Dan Lovett. I went to a therapy center in rural Virginia for a few weeks. It slowed me down for a bit, but after a while, I was still drinking more than was healthy.

The underlying reality was: I had an unhappy and often contentious marriage with my second wife. I did not respect my news director. And my father, who I respected above all others, was in severely declining health. That was a toxic brew. Drinking made everything feel better, at least for a little bit.

In 1985, both my station and I were riding as high as any local station ever has, and yet that was not fulfilling enough. I know now that however consuming a job can be, or however much fulfillment it can offer, the other parts of my life—and most especially the family side—needs to be functioning well for me to really be at peace. I still don't know what I was hoping to find in that endless procession of beers; but, whatever it was, I recognize the responsibility for my behavior was mine and mine alone.

Some people may think going to rehab or getting therapy is like hitting some kind of magical, automatic re-set button, when it's really a process—a gradual evolution. Like the Bill Murray movie "Groundhog Day," every day I got up trying to live the perfect day. I fell short of that goal most days, but I kept trying.

And I am still trying. I think I've finally figured out the alcohol part. I have one vodka most nights—one. It's the cheapest and most watered-down vodka martini you have maybe ever seen, but since my problems were more related to the way I was living my life than to the alcohol itself, that seems to satisfy both my mind and my body, and I don't need any more. The family part, too, is a work-in-progress. But, as I'll tell you more soon, when I met my wife Laura, I finally found a relationship that worked well for both partners. And Laura helps me understand ways to continue to try to be a better father of my grown-up kids. As for my work, I can't say I ever got less consumed with it; but as time has gone on, I have definitely learned to deal with the inevitable challenges that arise in a more productive way than drowning them in beer.

With my friend and colleague Ed Brandon on the news set. We spent some 40 years working together, taking KTRK's news to the top of the ratings ladder.

Henry and Mary Ward in their younger years.
I sure got lucky in the parental department.

㉑

IN ALL WAYS

In November of 1969, I wrote a letter to the editors at *Reader's Digest* to relay an experience my kids, Linda and David Jr., had with their grandfather, the Rev. H. M. Ward:

> *...the kids were searching for a way, beyond a shadow of a doubt, to let me know what they wanted (for Christmas) more than anything else. My father, being a retired Baptist preacher, instantly solved the problem by recalling a verse from the Bible.*
>
> *When the children returned home, they immediately had me look up Mark 13:37. I knew Grandpa had a hand in it when I read... "And what I say unto you, I say until all, WATCH."*
>
> *Two shiny watches were purchased the next day...*

Furthermore, when Linda was growing up, my father used to tell her, "Your daddy is a gentleman." But the way he said it, she thought it was a bad thing, so she cried.

I remember her more than once going around the house saying, rather emphatically, "My daddy is *not* a gentleman."

But the *coup de grace* for my father's antics had to be his imaginary girlfriend named Helga, who would often send my mother flowers with a note telling her what a sweet man she had married, and how wonderful he was. "Helga" would also give my mother presents every once in a while, like a pair of earrings. Of course, my mother knew who Helga really was all along.

As I've mentioned, when I joined KTRK-TV in 1966, Dad was not so sure about my move to television. By 1972, however, he had more than come around. We returned to Huntsville to film a promotional TV ad for KTRK, which you can still see on YouTube. "I've lived in Texas all my life," I said as the video showed my father and I walking around the town square shaking hands with friends. "I spent most of my younger years in Huntsville, our neighbor to the north. My father was the pastor of the First Baptist Church there for around ten years. And not too long ago, dad and I had a chance to walk around the square…Andy Anderson's barber shop is still there, and so is Andy. He used to cut my hair when I was, oh, six or seven. And just outside his shop is where I started my career in journalism. I sold newspapers on the corner…"

Dad just loved being in that ad. During the years, I would send him copies of the ratings when they were living in Jacksonville; and late in his life, he must have been in his mid-80s, my mom and dad drove to Houston. Whenever they came to town, my father would always stop at some little restaurant. "Let's just stop and get a cup of coffee," he would tell mother, who knew just what was motivating him.

"So we'd go in there, and a waiter or waitress would come over," mother recalled. "Dad would say, 'Do you know me?'" When they would say no, he would say, "Well, you know my son," and, anticipating their answer add, "My son is Dave Ward."

"He got such a huge kick out of that," mother said.

It was certainly a point of personal privilege when, on October 17, 1978, I directed my "kicker," or closing commentary, to an audience of two:

And finally tonight, on this date in 1937, a young East Texas Baptist Preacher went to Dallas and married the only daughter of a Dallas streetcar motorman. Tonight Rev. H.M. Ward and his bride, Mary, are celebrating their forty-first wedding anniversary at a hotel in Lufkin. They went there so they could see their son report the news from this chair here in Houston. They don't live in our coverage area, and I don't get to see them very often…so it's really a joy for me to be able to say, happy anniversary, Mom and Dad. I'm sure glad you two got together forty-one years ago today.

One afternoon, my father came to the television station, and walked up to me at my workspace there. I had sent him the latest ratings and explained what they meant. He said, "David, I've been preaching the Gospel of Jesus Christ all over this state, all of my life, and you speak to more people in one night than I did my entire career."

"That may be true, Dad," I responded, "but the message is not the same. Your message is of hope and eternal life; my message, in most cases, is the devil at work on earth."

I've thought about that many times over the years. Dad's comment speaks to the power of television to reach people. Later in his life, my father went back, did the math, and figured out that, as a gospel singer, he had led the music in 109 revival meetings in thirteen states. As a pastor, moreover, he had preached in eighty-three revival meetings over five states. That does not include the preaching he did on a weekly basis, and other lectures he gave throughout Texas. While he touched many peoples hearts and undoubtedly saved many of their souls, the lifetime number of people who actually heard his message was far fewer than those who tuned into the news every night. Having the talents I inherited from my family at the time that television was taking off created an opportunity for me that his generation could never have imagined.

I am grateful that my dad got to see where my decision to enter television led. We both wanted to touch people's lives by communicating with them. And we both had the desire and the ability to stand up before them and share our messages. And while music was no longer part of my daily work after I left radio, he and my mother instilled a love of music in me that has never waned.

We only sang together as a family once in public, at a revival or church meeting in Lufkin in the early 1980s if memory serves. Dad had a tenor voice; mother played the piano and sang soprano; my sister Mary had a beautiful alto voice; and I tackled bass. The song was "Lead Me Gently Home, Father." We rehearsed it beforehand, going over and over and over the lyrics—and it worked. At least they didn't throw anything at us.

Not long after that, my father was being not-so-gently led into the twilight of life. He was going downhill with Alzheimer's disease for the last five or so years of his life. It got to the point where he did not know either one of his daughters, or sometimes even his wife. But he always somehow recognized me when I visited. I can't tell you with any authority why that would be, but I was thankful to still have that connection.

In 1980, my mother had sent me a letter with a typewritten poem enclosed. Some years earlier, my father had written it for a Father's Day sermon he gave in Tyler. "He was cleaning out his desk and found it," my mother wrote. "We read it and both cried a little."

When I had read it, I cried, too.

My Son

> *A few years ago I had a son*
> *In my busy life that rushed along*
> *Days went by and years hurried on*
> *And before I knew it my son was gone*
> *So now I miss my little boy's face;*
> *his teenage daring and his young man's grace*
> *I miss his "Yes Daddy," when I called his name*
> *He's grown up now and gaining his fame*
> *So I seldom see him face-to-face*
> *For this life is a swift and running race*
> *There are miles and miles between him and me*
> *But I'd cover them all, my son to see*
> *For I know 'ere long there'll come the day*
> *When he'll pick up the phone and*
> *Hear someone say*
> *Sorry dear friend, your Dad died today*
> *So I pray, Dear Lord, before that day comes*
> *Please help me in all ways to be good to my son.*

– Henry Ward

I realized that time was marching on, and my father wouldn't be there cheering me on forever. I was busier than I had ever been, but I began to make a more conscious effort to get home to spend time with him. During one of my visits, dad had fallen asleep in his recliner, and I was over on the couch. Out of the blue, he woke up very animated and said, "Oh David, we've got to go home! Go out and hitch up the rig, hitch up the horses!" He had obviously gone way back into his full memory bank. I got up and walked over to him and said, "Daddy, we are home."

He just got this blank look on his face.

"Daddy, we are home," I repeated to be sure he understood. "We're home, and we're okay."

The progression of that insidious disease is a sickening thing to see when it is happening to someone you love, I'll tell you.

Reverend Henry Martin Ward died in Jacksonville, Texas on April 9, 1987, at the age of ninety-one. We buried him in a family plot in Resthaven Cemetery there in Jacksonville. A simple, rectangular gravestone marks his final resting place. My parents also secured a space there for my sister Mary and me too, but I do not want to be buried in Jacksonville. I didn't live there more than about a year-and-a-half finishing up high school. But for my mother and father, Jacksonville truly was their home. That was the only house they ever owned, bought and paid for themselves. All of the other houses were parsonages, provided by the church wherever he was the pastor.

When I returned from Jacksonville after my father's death, I received the kindest cards, letters and messages from viewers and friends offering their sympathies. That really touched me. One letter arrived in a Channel 2 envelope. It was from Ron Stone, who mentioned my father's passing and services in his newscast. In vintage Stone fashion, he had noted in the script he enclosed that my father as a preacher "could shame the devil and summon up God."

Looking back, I can confidently say Henry Martin Ward was "in all ways good to (his) son." But then, he was good to everyone that came into his life. He came from very little and overcame a lot to lead a proud and meaningful life—a respected leader in his chosen profession.

I will always be proud to be his son.

Although it is difficult to go on after the loss of a beloved parent, Houston wasn't slowing down for my grief. I was back behind the news desk right away. It would be a somewhat older and wiser Dave Ward who would share the endless stories generated by the ever-growing city in the next decade.

The Eyewitness News 13 team in the mid-1970s shortly after Ed Brandon joined us from KHFI-TV in Austin. Left to right: Ed Brandon, myself, Dan Ammerman, and Dan Lovett.

THANK YOU, BROTHER

I t fell a day after the Pearl Harbor anniversary, but in Houston baseball history it nevertheless stands as *the* date that lives in infamy. December 8, 1988 brought the announcement that our Astros had somehow allowed the Texas Rangers to acquire the greatest pitcher ever to toe the rubber, Nolan Ryan.

Ryan, who joined the Astros in 1980 and regularly commuted to the Astrodome from his ranch in Alvin eighteen miles away, was understandably angry at the Astros' attempts to cut his salary in efforts to re-sign him. The deal with the Rangers keeping him in Texas still allowed him to commute, albeit by plane, so he could be involved with his two teen-aged sons. When he left the Astros, the "Ryan Express" had 4,775 strikeouts, recorded five no-hitters, and set or tied thirty-eight major league records. News of the transaction once again placed Astros owner John J. McMullen back in the crosshairs of public opinion.

McMullen was a shipping tycoon whose principal residence was still in New Jersey. He headed up a group of investors—including my friend A. J. Foyt and astronaut Jim Lovell—that bought the Astros for $13 million in 1979 from the Ford Motor Credit Corporation. This group is credited with keeping the bankrupt club afloat during the 1970s. To be fair, McMullen had his positives. It was under him that future Hall of Famers Craig Biggio and Jeff Bagwell became Astros. He built up the farm system, and he gave Bob Watson an executive position that led to Watson becoming a Major League general manager in 1993—the only Black general manager in the League and the second in its history.

But after the 1980 season, McMullen came under withering criticism for abruptly firing the widely popular club president Tal Smith, who had been with the club almost since its inception. It was also McMullen's call to change the team's beloved rainbow-colored jerseys. And being a transplant from the Northeast, he never seemed to try to become a part of Houston society or court positive relations with the media.

Like a lot of folks, I was upset by the news that Nolan would be leaving town, but even more incensed when McMullen explained the trade saying Nolan was too old, and over the hill. I was not alone in my feelings. "I would show him the way back to New York" if McMullen showed up in his town, said Alvin Mayor Allen Gray at the time. "I will not attend a Houston Astros game all year in protest."

The Houston Post editorialized: "So Ryan is going to the (Dallas) Metroplex. Well, at least he'll remain a hero and a Texan, which is more than can be said for McMullen."

The night they announced Nolan's trade, I went on the air and directed my "commentary" at the end of the newscast directly at the Astros' owner. "Dr. McMullen, you just got rid of the Houston Astro's Number One starting pitcher, and future Hall of Famer, Nolan Ryan," I started. "This man is *not* an average ballplayer. He is *the* preeminent pitcher…" I cannot remember the entire commentary word-for-word, but toward the end I said, "Dr. McMullen you've proved you're nothing but a Yankee carpetbagger come down here to ruin our baseball team, and we don't need you! Marvin and I will come up with enough money to buy that team from you. We don't need you in this city any more. I'm Dave Ward."

I got off the air and went down to Kay's, and boy were the folks down there were all wound up. "Ward, we can't believe you said that! Wow, that was fantastic!" The next day when I got to the office, however, Jim Masucci came to my little cubbyhole and told me how the Astros had been on the telephone all day talking about all the good that McMullen has done in the city, the donations he has made to charities, and how what I had said the previous night was a personal attack.

"It was a commentary, and I labeled it as a commentary," I tried to explain.

"I don't care how you labeled it," Jim countered impatiently. "To the Astros and Dr. McMullen, it was a personal attack—and they want you to take it back."

People who know me well know that taking things back can be hard for me. But that night, I went on the 6 p.m. news ready to eat crow. I said, "Those of you may have seen my commentary last night about Dr. John McMullen, the Houston Astros, and pitcher Nolan Ryan...Dr. McMullen, I want to apologize to you for calling you a Yankee carpetbagger. That I should not have said..." I said enough to satisfy Masucci, but my heart was definitely not in it.

A month later, I was in Galveston at the Tremont Hotel, sitting at the bar, when in walked Nolan Ryan with his wife Ruthie. I had never met the man, ever, but he walked up—and you would have thought I was his long-lost brother. "I just want to meet you and shake your hand," Nolan said. He never said one word about Dr. McMullen, nor a single word about my commentary. We talked instead about the event we were there to attend.

Afterwards I thought, *I think I've made a friend in this guy.*

In my role, I was constantly meeting new friends of all walks of life, and many of them I still count as friends today. Some were originally people I covered, some were celebrities, and others were colleagues, some so close they are like family. Just as my own life was having its ups and downs, some of my friends were suffering, too. One of my best memories is the return of one of my best friends in April, 1990 after a fourteen-month absence. His return brightened life for all of us in the KTRK family.

During the late 1980s, our outstanding weatherman Ed Brandon had developed a serious cocaine addiction. After hitting rock bottom, he made the courageous decision to seek help. He left the station to go into a rehabilitation program, and once he got himself clean the current Lieutenant Governor of Texas, Dan Patrick, hired Ed to do an afternoon show on KSEV-AM 700. (Patrick started his media career in Houston as a sportscaster at KHOU-TV in the late 1970s, before moving over to KSEV in the mid-1980s as an owner and, ultimately, a popular and effective talk show host especially with conservative listeners.)

While at KSEV, I remember Ed used the song "Afternoon Delight" as his bumper music when he came on the air, but another far more important factor in his budding success during his time at KSEV was a new radio personality named Rush Limbaugh. This rising star came on before Ed's show, and turned out to be a great lead-in.

After about a year or so, Paul Bures came down to me and said, "I understand Ed Brandon is doing very well."

"Yeah, he's got his radio show going," I replied. "He's doing fine."

"We ought to put him back on the air here," Paul said.

I agreed that was a great idea, and since I was a good friend of Ed's, Paul asked me to call him. Just as I had felt when asked to call Marvin, I felt I had been given this gift of an opportunity to help the station. But the significance of this call ran deeper. It was the chance to give someone I loved like a brother, and wanted to see do well, a second chance.

"Ed, how are you doing?" I asked when he picked up. "I just talked with Paul Bures, and we want you back over here to do the weather."

He was ecstatic as you might imagine. "I could be over there tomorrow if you need me," Ed volunteered.

Coming back into the KTRK fold, Ed did a round of interviews with our various station programs, and I also had a chance to sit down with him for a candid "Eyewitness Extra" conversation. "How were you mentally and physically at that time?" I asked him about the time when he was entering rehab. "Where were you at that point?"

"Physically I was almost dead," Ed said, without hesitation. "Mentally, I wasn't much better."

Following his first weathercast back on the 6 p.m. news, Ed took a few moments to address the KTRK audience directly, to try to put his return to the airwaves into context:

The past year, particularly this past week, has been an extremely humbling experience for me. I've been overwhelmed, literally overwhelmed, at the response to the announcement last week that I was coming back here. There is no way I could ever say thank you adequately; there is no way I could ever express the gratitude I feel. But I do want to say this: what I can do is try to live my life a day at a time, in such a manner as to make you feel like I really deserve what you've given me. In the next couple of days, things are going to settle down around here—I hope they settle down. When that happens, I don't ever want to forget that—right here, right now, with these people—I feel like the luckiest person alive. And I'm real glad to be here.

When he was finished, I was sitting next to Shara and reached across the anchor desk, shook his hand, and said, "Welcome home, Ed. It's good to have you back. And in a week or two, it'll be like you were never gone—just watch. Thank you, thank you brother."

I always admired Ed's courage and candor in the way he dealt with a very serious problem. He saved himself, to be sure, but I believe he helped a lot of other people by the honest and sincere way he dealt with his recovery. I also give great credit to the KTRK management for giving Ed that second chance. By then, Tom Doerr had replaced Jim Topping as news director, coming from WJLA-TV 7 in Washington, DC.

Tom recently reminded me that in 1989 I walked into his office and asked him to go to Kay's Lounge, saying it was my "Thursday night hangout place after work." I left out a few other days of the week. I had just gotten off the phone with Houston Congressman Mickey Leland. "For over forty years," Congressman Leland told me, "Kay's was a mystery to someone like me who grew up in the Fifth Ward." He thought it had to be too "redneck"—or something to that effect. Congressman Leland wanted to see for himself, but he said he didn't want to go there on his own. "Too frightening," he said.

So Tom Doerr and I took Congressman Leland there for a drink after the 10 p.m. news soon after that call. Mickey was hilarious. He didn't know what to expect and made some really funny remarks. We stayed for an hour, and I genuinely think he had a great time. To be sure, the regulars in Kay's were thrilled that a real congressman would step into their oasis.

Tragically, that good man died a few months later in August, 1989 in a plane crash on an Ethiopian mountainside at the age of forty-four. He was on a mission to feed the hungry, which he had been inspired to do since a 1984 trip to the Sudan. At that time, Mickey had met a child that, as he described it in a 1985 interview, "looked to be about seventy or eighty years old…a skeleton of a person with a thin layer of brown skin on her, who had just a faint breath of life in her."

As Mickey turned to ask a relief worker about the girl, she died. "I can see her face right now," Mickey recalled. "Every day I see her face."

All I can say is: God bless those who have such courage and devotion.

A few years after Mickey Leland's untimely death, two of the most explosive stories in KTRK history aired on one day, Sunday, December 1, 1991 during our 5:30 p.m. and 10 p.m. newscasts. In them, our terrific investigative reporter, Wayne Dolcefino, aggressively questioned the role then-State Representative Turner played in an attempted multi-million dollar insurance scam. The story centered on one of Turner's law clients, Sylvester Foster, who had drowned near Galveston—but was, in fact, still alive.

This unique saga started on June 22, 1986, when Sylvester Foster allegedly fell overboard during a sailing trip a few miles south of Galveston and was reported to have drowned. No body was found, and a subsequent Coast Guard report concluded that Foster was "presumed dead and lost at sea." With an independent executor, Dwight Thomas, the Foster family moved forward with probating Sylvester Foster's will, which Turner had prepared. Turner had roughly 120 billable hours of legal work he had done for Foster that went unpaid.

Meanwhile, on June 20, 1989, the U.S. Embassy in Spain confirmed that Sylvester Foster was alive in a prison in Salamanca, Spain on drug charges under the alias Christopher Laurent Fostier. By then, Foster's father, Clinton, had already received some life insurance payments. Instead of returning those funds, the elder Mr. Foster filed for bankruptcy.

By the time Wayne's bombshell report hit the air, Sylvester Turner had gone from the Harvard law grad *wunderkind* to be elected to the Texas House of Representatives in 1988. He then jumped into the city's 1991 mayoral race and bested incumbent Kathy Whitmire in impressive fashion to earn a spot in a hotly contested run-off with businessman Bob Lanier. Wayne's first report ran with the run-off election only six days away, and at least one poll at the time showed Turner leading the race going into the home stretch. If victorious, Turner would become the city's first African-American mayor.

The genesis of Wayne's reporting on this story came to life in late November of 1991 when Clyde Wilson, a private investigator whom

Wayne knew well, provided information to the station suggesting Turner was complicit in unlawful efforts to obtain Foster's life insurance benefits. It was later revealed that these same details and allegations were provided and pushed by a member of Bob Lanier's campaign finance committee.

The implications of these tips were serious enough that news director Tom Doerr asked Wayne Dolcefino to investigate. Wayne proceeded to contact all sorts of people, including associates of Foster's and Turner's. He also reviewed the documents from the probate file, and depositions from the two people who had been on Foster's boat the day of the staged disappearance. The picture that quickly emerged of Foster was not a flattering one.

Just prior to his disappearance, Foster had taken out several life insurance policies worth $6.5 million, applied for an emergency passport, been arrested in Las Vegas for his role in a "chop shop" scam, and was indicted for credit card fraud in Houston. A Secret Service agent attempted to take Foster into custody just after the indictment, which was also the night before Foster signed his will in Turner's office. Foster promised the agent he would turn himself in the following day, but instead left on the now-infamous sailing trip.

Foster was considered a fugitive from justice at the time of his disappearance.

During multiple on-camera interviews with Wayne in late November, 1991, candidate Sylvester Turner denied any knowledge of Foster's scheme. Directly contradicting Turner was the court-appointed investigator in the matter, Elizabeth Colwell. She cited multiple reasons to Wayne that she believed Turner was, in her words, "in it up to his eyeballs."

Satisfied they had a story that met high standards for sourcing and truthfulness, Tom Doerr and Wayne moved forward with airing the piece. On Sunday, December 1, KTRK's 5:30 p.m. newscast opened: "We begin tonight with word of what may be one of the biggest attempted insurance swindles in recent Houston history, the apparent conspiracy to fake the death of a thirty-year old Houston man with criminal troubles and millions of dollars in life insurance…What role did Houston mayoral candidate, Sylvester Turner, play in this tale of multi-million dollar fraud?

"Our focus," Wayne said, echoing that infamous line from the Watergate inquiry, "is what did Sylvester Turner know, and when did he know it?"

The story went on to describe the circumstances of Foster's disappearance and efforts to obtain life insurance benefits. "Turner did deal with Sylvester Foster, even after learning he was the target of criminal investigations in early 1986, and they pursued the estate money even after significant evidence of a possible scam in Foster's death had already surfaced," Wayne continued. He included Turner's assertion that he fully cooperated with all of the investigations into Foster's disappearance, but said "at least three investigators very close to this case tell us that's simply not true." The report also included Turner's claim he was left with unpaid legal bills after the probate judge removed him from the case, which made him another victim of Foster's.

After the first broadcast, Turner called a news conference at 8 p.m. to refute the story. Both the presiding probate judge for the Foster case—John Hutchison—and the attorney for the principal insurer contesting Foster's beneficiaries—Jim McConn—attended Turner's news conference. The pair contended Turner's conduct throughout the case had been, in their opinion, thoroughly professional.

In KTRK's 10 p.m. Sunday newscast, neither Hutchison's nor McConn's statements were carried. Instead, coverage of the news conference concluded with the statement: "Reporter Wayne Dolcefino and Channel 13 stand by their story."

The station corrected that mistake the next day by airing Hutchison and McConn's comments on the 6 p.m. news. That same night, our general manager Jim Masucci made the unprecedented decision to give Sylvester Turner three minutes of unedited air time to answer the allegations raised by Wayne before a scheduled debate with Bob Lanier. It didn't help Turner to resurrect his campaign. On December 7th, Lanier won the run-off election by 17,000 votes and a 53-47 margin.

After the 1991 mayoral election, Turner filed suit contending our newscasts deliberately contained false information, and that Wayne and the station's management conspired to cover up the true source of the story. In the trial that ensued, management acknowledged that, at that time, KTRK had no direct evidence that Turner was a knowing participant in the scam. As to whether the information had been provided by a pro-Lanier source, the KTRK team asserted it made no difference where the story came from as long as the facts checked out—which they maintained it did.

Turner argued that Wayne Dolcefino knowingly fabricated his main contention and most of the supporting facts—and had covered-up his actions. Turner also asserted Dolcefino knew there was no estate money because the Foster estate had a negative net worth.

The day Wayne testified in the case, the station management told all of us—Shara Fryer, Bob Allen, Ed Brandon, Marvin and yours truly—to go down to the courthouse as a show of support for our colleague. We later learned the jury felt this was an attempt to influence them. After thirty-three hours of deliberation, that jury reached a 10-2 verdict that Dolcefino's reporting was untrue—and that the station either knew it was wrong or had recklessly disregarded the truth.

That verdict would be appealed—and overturned—in higher court in 1999, but at the time it was a real black eye. That being said, it doesn't change the fact that I think Wayne Dolcefino was the best investigative reporter KTRK has ever had. He went on to do some very fine reporting, and by the time he left the station some two decades later he had a full bookcase of twenty-seven Emmys as proof of his great work.

Things also turned out very well for Sylvester Turner, who went on to have an illustrious twenty-six-year career in the Texas House. He lost his second bid for Houston mayor in 2003 to Bill White, but twelve years later won a very closely fought campaign against businessman Bill King. In my view, Mayor Turner has been doing a great job in office, promoting our great city, soon to become the third largest in America.

In Sylvester Turner's case, the third time running for mayor really was the charm. I can imagine that deep in his heart he feels that justice from that 1991 race was unduly delayed, but in the end not totally denied. Politics in Texas can be as changeable as the weather; and no matter which side you take, you'll usually discover an interesting story.

With my friend and brother, Jeff Bagwell. He has sure always been there for me, as I have tried to be for him. The bumps in the road of life are a lot easier to handle when you have friends like Jeff.

GOOD NIGHT, NEIGHBORS

O f all of the presidents of the United States I have interviewed, George Herbert Walker Bush is, to me, unsurpassed as a public servant. He was the youngest pilot in the Navy when he enlisted and earned his Wings of Gold in World War II as naval bomber pilot. On September 2, 1944, he was shot down in the Pacific Ocean and rescued by a U.S. submarine. Later, after a successful career in the oil business, he became the first Republican elected congressman from Houston since Reconstruction. Afterwards, President Nixon appointed him ambassador to the United Nations and chairman of the Republican National Committee. President Ford named him ambassador to China and then director of the CIA. In 1980, Mr. Bush lost his first bid for the presidency to California Governor Ronald Reagan, who then selected George H. W. Bush to be his vice-presidential candidate. They won in a landslide over President Jimmy Carter and Walter Mondale.

After President Reagan's second term, George H.W. Bush was elected to the Oval Office in his own right in 1988. He was, by far, the most qualified person to become president—certainly in the modern era. But aside from his resume, as brilliant as that is, I also admire the personal qualities of the man I had the privilege of knowing for over half a century. Decency. Integrity. Respect for others. Humility. George Bush was both a great and a good man, the total package.

Going into the fall of 1991, a struggling U.S. economy had surged to the top of most voters' minds as the first volleys of the 1992 campaign were being fired. Already, seven Democrats had announced their candidacies, and had taken to pounding President Bush for every perceived shortcoming. In due course, Republican Pat Buchanan would also challenge Mr. Bush in the GOP primary, and Texas billionaire Ross Perot would mount an independent third-party bid for the White House. It was a surreal chain of political events to watch unfold, especially after the forty-first President's superb handling of Iraq's invasion of Kuwait sent his poll numbers soaring near ninety percent earlier in 1991.

In the midst of this political foment, I had two chances to interview President Bush. The first came on November 1, 1991, at the Houstonian Hotel. The administration at the time was not enjoying the warmest relations with the national news media, so they had taken to arranging interviews with local media whenever the President traveled around the country. That day in Houston, President Bush also spoke with two respected peers: Ron Stone of Channel 2 KPRC, and my former KTRK colleague Sylvan Rodriguez, who had made the big move to Channel 11 KHOU as one of their lead anchors. My conversation with President Bush covered a range of heavy topics—the economy, unemployment, interest rates, crime and family values. Towards the end, I wanted to lighten things up just a little. "One last thing," I said. "The Washington Redskins, Houston Oilers, RFK (Stadium in Washington) this Sunday. Who are you going to be rooting for?"

"I thought that might be the first thing with you," he said, laughing. "No, I've said this publicly since I've been in Houston, and I always start out by saying I've got great affection and respect for (Redskins coach) Joe Gibbs. You better have great affection and respect for Joe Gibbs if you want to live in Washington, even inside the fence in the White House. Besides that, he merits that. Joe is a—God, what he does, the great work he does with kids. But look, (Oilers coach) Jack Pardee is my friend. The Oilers are my hometown club. Warren Moon is a guy not only that I respect, but I believe he'd recognize that we have a friendship, too. And so, I want the Oilers to win it. And I want them to go on and do so well that Barbara and I receive them in the White House as Super Bowl champs."

"So put that one out there," the president concluded, "and I'll go back and take the flak in DC tomorrow."

A year later, on October 24, 1992, I was invited to fly with President Bush on Air Force One. The Bush-Quayle campaign was locked in a tough re-election battle against the Democratic ticket of

Arkansas' Bill Clinton and Senator Al Gore from Tennessee and the independent Ross Perot. We were flying from some campaign stops in Louisiana back to Houston, where the President—even in the midst of a tough campaign—attended the funeral of the Bush family's dear friend Betty Liedtke, the wife of Hugh Liedke, a friend from their Midland days who founded Pennzoil with his brother, Bill.

Once we were airborne, one of the White House press aides escorted me all around and up into what would be the first-class area on a 747. "That's all the White House communications folks," the aide explained, as we walked through. "They can talk to anybody, anywhere in the world…"

As I've mentioned, I like to go up to the cockpit whenever I am on a plane—and I was darn sure not going to pass up on the opportunity to see the cockpit of one of the most state-of-the-art planes in the world. Before the trip, I bought one of those throw-away Kodak cameras, where you just take the pictures, turn in the camera, and they develop your pictures. So I got my little disposable camera, and walked up to the cockpit. The pilot was standing at the cockpit door, and looking in I could see the first officer at the controls.

"Could I take a picture of the cockpit?" I asked the pilot.

"Would it be for publication?"

"No sir," I responded. "It's just for me, using this little throw-away camera."

He agreed, so I took a picture of the flight panel. As I was taking the picture, the pilot told me, "That's the only photo ever taken of the cockpit of Air Force One with the sitting President on board, while we're in the air, and the captain is not in the pilot seat."

Quite a neat little collector's item there.

For the interview itself, we filmed it in the President's spacious office on that airplane. At one point after we finished, I tried my best to convince President Bush to give Ross Perot some role in his administration. By then, it was clear Perot was going to run as an independent candidate. George Bush may truly be the kindest and gentlest person on the planet, but he also had a backbone of steel—as Saddam Hussein and Manuel Noriega found out. He was equally resolved where Perot was concerned—so my suggestion was a total non-starter.

Towards the end of October, 1992, the Bush-Quayle ticket was actually surging in the polls going into the last weekend of the campaign; but the late-breaking news that independent counsel Lawrence Walsh was re-indicting Reagan's defense secretary Cap Weinberger stopped any momentum the GOP team might have had. In the end, Ross Perot took nineteen percent of the Republican vote away from George Bush. That dynamic, maybe more than any other, turned the White House over to Bill Clinton. I thought then, and still do, what a shame it was to see George Herbert Walker Bush, a true friend and one of the finest men I have ever known, get turned out of office like that.

After he left the White House, President Bush only continued to grow in my esteem. Just his physical prowess alone was admirable— evidenced by his feats in the Navy as well as his enthusiasm for parachuting out of planes into his nineties. I was reminded of the degree of fortitude he had when an assignment took me onto a nuclear submarine.

After Marvin Zindler attended the fiftieth anniversary of Pearl Harbor in December of 1991, his fantastic producer Lori Reingold got an idea to do a story on the *USS Houston* nuclear attack submarine and contacted the Pentagon about trying to set something up. She didn't hear back for several months, and when they finally did contact her to tell her they had approved the story, Lori almost said "What trip?" By then, she and Marvin had figured out that, at seventy years old, Marvin couldn't climb in and out of hatches. But I was totally game, so the station sent me out to San Diego instead to put together a series of reports that we also fashioned into a thirty-minute program.

When we first arrived at the dock, Commander G. A. Wallace was there to escort us down the pier. As we chatted, I noticed the official markings on the sub read: SSN 713. When I pointed that out the commander, Wallace said, "Yeah, that's your area code in Houston, dummy!" Our photographer, Bob Dows, was following behind us and cracked up. For the rest of the day, wherever we went to shoot anything, Bob would tell me, "Stand over there, dummy! Give me one more take, dummy!"

He got such a kick out of that.

The *USS Houston* was commissioned on March 21, 1981, when sponsor Barbara Pierce Bush christened and helped launch her out of Norfolk, Virginia. It spent most of the 1980s prowling the Pacific, and in fact earlier in 1992 had been deployed in support of a CIA special operation. In 1989, it had been the featured in the Tom Clancy movie *The Hunt for Red October*, but otherwise had recently had a run of bad luck. During filming, for example, the sub had snagged the line of a nearby towboat, which ended up drowning one of the crewmates onboard.

This would be one of my most memorable assignments; but if you are even remotely claustrophobic, I must say going down on a submarine is not for you. Everything about it is tight, as space is always at a premium.

We went out in the Pacific Ocean, up and down. At one point, we performed the same maneuver you see at the end of *Red October* where this submarine comes roaring up out of the ocean like a breaching whale. They called it an "emergency blow." We were 600 feet under the ocean, and when the captain called "emergency blow" that sub released the water in its ballast tanks keeping the sub under water. After that happened, it was like taking off in an airplane. We came charging up out of the top of the ocean, and then went splashing back down.

When we started going down, all the crewmen in the front part of the sub, they just went weightless and shouted "Woo hoo!" Immediately afterwards, Commander Wallace turned the periscope around and to look behind us. "Look, Dave," he said, offering me a chance to look. "There is the hole in the ocean."

Where we had leapt out of the ocean, the water was just boiling.

Looking back, I never would have been able to do anything like that—like ride in a nuclear attack submarine or fly high-performance jet fighters—if I had not opted for the action of becoming a news reporter over spinning records as a disc jockey. The innumerable gifts of a career in the news are just amazing to me.

In September of 1992, one of the most storied and important TV news careers in Houston drew to a close when my friend Ron Stone retired from KPRC-TV Channel 2. He had been at the station since 1972 but had started at KHOU-TV Channel 11 a decade before then—thirty-eight years as a reporter all together. We had worked together on stories, and then competed against each other as well.

But more than that, we had become friends. We had traveled all over the country as part of the Oilers' radio team. We did a wide range of speaking and charitable events together.

We were also often paired together for the Houston Press Club's Gridiron show, an annual affair dating back to the early 1960s that raises scholarship money to put aspiring journalists through college. The event consists of the local media getting together to lampoon each other and the powerful people they cover. Since the 60s, I had become kind of a regular fixture in the show playing LBJ. But my biggest hit may have been in 1989 when Ron and I co-hosted the show and performed together as the "News Brothers"—a spoof taking off on the John Belushi and Dan Akyroyd as the *Blues Brothers*. Instead of singing "I'm a Soul Man," we did a riff on it called "I'm a News Man."

We enjoyed laughing with, and sometimes at, each other. In 2002, Ron recalled in a column he wrote for *Houston Lifestyles & Homes* magazine how he had come to own a leisure suit in the 1970s. "I bought that chocolate brown, God-awful-looking thing because my friend Dave Ward convinced me it was time to shuck my Brooks Brothers and join the Brave New World," Ron wrote. "Harold In The Heights had talked Dave into one, and Dave sent me out to look. I bought one and wore it on TV one time. The resulting mail was not flattering. One viewer wrote that if I wasn't careful I would start looking like Dave Ward over on Channel 13."

Ron continued:

> *Actually, that has been a problem for quite a while. People confuse me for Ward...One night, Patsy and I left some downtown event, paid the parking fee, and wheeled out into the night. At that time I drove an ostentatious little sports car with the top down. As we reached the first stop light, an enormous, rough-looking man bounded out to the car and began to shout that he was not a crook, not a thief, just a man who needed money to get some gas. I was stunned and frightened, so I handed him the change from the parking garage, a $10 bill. As the light changed and I sped away, I heard him shout: 'Oh, God bless you Dave Ward!'*

Well, Patsy and I have often figured that when I meet my Maker, He will ask why I haven't been as good to the poor people as Dave Ward was.

After Dave had an accident and ended up in the hospital, the parking attendant at the airport told me she'd been praying for me ever since the accident. When I told her that was Dave and I was Ron, she said, 'Well, I've been praying for him then.'

But what goes around comes around. The other day Dave and I had lunch, and he was laughing about what happened to him over the weekend. Seems he'd been at a party and walked out to get in his car. As the valet rushed to retrieve it, Ward realized he had no money save one $20 bill. He was stuck. He could either stiff the guy and have the word spread he was a cheap creep, or hand over the $20. With some reluctance, he handed the parking attendant the $20 bill. As he got in his car, he heard the man say, 'Oh, thank you, Mr. Stone, thank you very much!'

When he signed off for the last time, Ron told his audience on KPRC-TV:

It really is kinda nuts to hear your obituary while you're still around. That way you can add your two cents worth, and that is simply this: Thank you for putting up with me. Thank you for letting me come into your homes—for the letters, the cards, the calls, the thoughts over the years. I always figured that doing local television was a trust, so I never tried to lie to you, never tried to lead you down a false path. I spent 30 years working at two fine television stations in a really fine town. And like the great Notre Dame and Green Bay Packer star Paul Horning used to say, "I feel like I've gone through life on a scholarship." I've been a very lucky man, and now I'm going to find out if there really is life after television—and so far it's looking pretty good. My first job is that I've been given an important task. I'll babysit my 11 month-old baby grandson William...Isn't it great that at 56 I've found meaningful work. Let's keep in touch. Good night, neighbors.

Immediately after finishing his final newscast, Ron was gracious enough to give Shara and me a live interview from the Channel 2 set—which, trust me, does not happen often.

"Television history was made in Houston today when one of our long-time competitors anchored his last daily newscast," I reported that night, leading into Ron's first and maybe only interview on KTRK-TV Channel 13. "For over thirty years, Ron Stone has been a fixture in Houston television…"

When I asked him what he was going to do next, Ron didn't skip a beat. "I'm gonna sit on a porch and take care of my grandchildren, David," he said. "I've got a new La-Z-boy and I'm gonna watch the grass grow." Of course, he was going to launch a production company and keep working on his award-winning "Eyes of Texas" TV-magazine format show, but that answer was vintage Ron Stone: low key and pure class, always.

———————

About a year after Ron's retirement, my own life took a sudden turn. On Sunday, May 2, 1993, I was leaving a neighborhood bar and walking through the parking lot when I slipped and fell. The heels on my boots had worn down, and when I stepped off the curb I hit a slick spot. Both feet went out from under me, and I fell backward as the back of my head hit the curb. I had never before fallen that hard.

Somehow, I got up and managed to drive on home around 8:30 p.m. Later that night, I developed a splitting headache and, by Monday afternoon, the pain was so severe I knew I had to go to Methodist Hospital. There, they did an X-ray and a CAT Scan. Once the results were in, Dr. James Rose came to tell me why I still had a killer headache. He said I had a blood clot about the size of a cherry tomato on my brain just over my left eye. Then he said something that really caught my attention: "Dave, I don't understand how you're sitting here talking to me. I have another patient who fell and hit the back of his head exactly as you did. He ruptured a blood vessel almost exactly where you did; developed a blood clot almost exactly the same size as yours; and this guy has not been able to speak a word for over a year."

Not speak for a year? I earn my living by speaking. Then I wondered, just how am I sitting here and talking to him? They put me in the neurological Intensive Care Unit with all kinds of wires connected to my body. I was in Methodist Hospital a total of ten weeks during which time I received a lot of very thoughtful cards, messages and flowers. One flower was a big, white gladiola blossom. I had nurses coming into my room saying they could smell it down the hall and wanted to see it! Well, I didn't smell anything. One of the nurses held that gladiola bloom right under my nose and I still did not smell a thing.

Dr. Rose later explained, when I hit the back of my head, the olfactory nerves coming out of my nose were severed. The doctor said those nerves can sometimes grow back, but it would take months—and if they didn't grow back within a year, they probably never would grow back. Well, they didn't, and ever since I have had no sense of smell. I can still taste food, but it is really bland because smell and taste are so closely related.

I was off the air to recover from that earthshattering fall for ten weeks. Shara Fryer had been my co-anchor on the 6 p.m. news, while until that time I was the solo anchor at 10 p.m. Well, during my convalescence, Shara and several other anchors, including Alan Hemberger, Melanie Lawson and Gina Gaston took turns covering for me. When I returned, our news director, Richard Longoria, assigned Shara Fryer to be my permanent co-anchor at 6 and now also at the 10 p.m.

I welcomed Shara to the 10 p.m. because, first of all, she's damn good. But it also lightened my workload a little. The whole experience—the fall, the blood clot, the loss of smell (which sometimes can be a blessing)—was like a wake-up call from God. I have never forgotten that. I never will, and the lack of smell just reinforces it all the time.

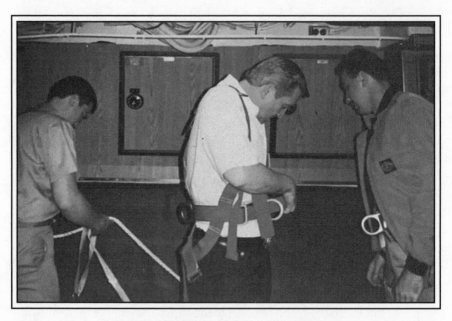

*Aboard the USS Houston Submarine, I'm strapping in
before some pretty hair-raising maneuvers.*

With one of the Navy's public affairs people aboard the USS Houston submarine after an eye-opening, jaw-dropping cruise below the Pacific.

With my sweet mother in the Channel 13 studio after one of our newscasts. Her constant love and support saw me through some tough times in my life.

NOT GOING
TO END WELL

If you have made it this far with my stories, now seems as good a time as any to acknowledge that, on at least two occasions, I have knowingly and willfully dressed up as a woman.

Maybe I should explain.

On March 2, 1994, guests attending one of the *Houston Chronicle's* best-dressed events at a Galleria-area hotel were treated to a unique royal sighting when the program's emcee, Warner Roberts, introduced a distant cousin of the "Dame Edna" character made popular decades ago by Australian comedian Barry Humphries. Hearing her cue, "Dame Edith" came out and sashayed clumsily down the runway in high heels, a red sequin gown, and a white boa—all while singing some silly song about fashion in falsetto.

After Dame Edith finished her outlandish spin around the runway and stepped off, Warner said, "Ladies and gentlemen, please give a warm round of applause for Dame Edith here…who you all know as Dave Ward…"

Well, I turned right around and whipped that wig off—and that place went ballistic! No one had any idea it was me, so apparently the hour or so I spent in one of the hotel rooms getting into that get-up and donning all of that make-up paid off.

More importantly, the event that day raised more than $100,000 for the March of Dimes.

Four years before, in 1990, I was also convinced to portray the fairer sex at a Hou-Dah parade in Galveston, which was a take-off on the irreverent, farcical Doo-Dah parades they started out in Pasadena, California. The Hou-Dah parades usually fell during Mardi Gras season and were corporate Houston's way to poke fun at itself. For several years, I also served as the Hou-Dah Grand Pooh-Bah.

In 1990, they had me dress up like the Brazilian samba singer, dancer and actress Carmen Miranda, who was best-known for wearing a fruit hat in films. In my case, I had a full fruit salad balanced up on my head, and once again the full make-up treatment on my face. When I came walking out of the hotel where we were staying on The Strand, I didn't think there was a chance anyone would recognize me. As soon as I hit that sidewalk, though, I saw a *Houston Chronicle* photographer a block and a half down the street come running in my direction. "Dave! Dave!" he shouted. "Can I get a picture?"

Just unbelievable.

Then they put me in the back of a pick-up truck, gave me a rope to hang onto, and soon we were riding along the parade route. I had insisted that they let me do the parade with a cigar in my mouth, which I am sure looked even odder as I was dancing around back there like a clown. I had that cigar in my mouth the entire parade.

The theme of the parade that year was "Carnaval de Brazil," which explains why they had me dress up like Carmen Miranda. I remember one of the law firms that participated in this parade every year got fifty or sixty people together and marched down the street five or six across in each row like a band, and they all wore big white brassieres. In their front row, they were carrying this big sign that read: "Brazil?? We thought you said Brassieres."

So as I say, I may have done some silly things, but it has always been for a good cause.

Some things I have done, on the other hand, started out seeming like fun but had serious consequences. And often those situations deteriorated because of alcohol. One night in 1995, I went to Kay's. When they closed around midnight, I went over to a friend's place two blocks behind the TV station—which I also did on occasion. You already know what a train geek I am, and this guy had a little N Scale model train running around his living room up near his ceiling. It was a scale model of the Santa Fe Super Chief, and he had taken one of my old business cards that had my picture on it and mounted it up there and made it look like a billboard. I thought that was too neat for words.

This particular night around 1:30 a.m., I was driving home from my friend's house and was just past the television station on Bissonnet going west. At the time, I was living on Newcastle Street in Bellaire, two miles away. Having driven this particular stretch of road hundreds of times, I knew the west-bound lane on the right side of the road had a really bad pothole stretched across that lane. And just before you got to that tank trap of a pothole, there was also one in the left-hand lane. Knowing these massive potholes were coming up, I steered first over into the right lane. After I passed the first hazard on the left, I then steered back into the left lane to avoid the pothole coming up on the right. It was like a slalom maneuver in skiing.

No sooner had I narrowly averted a bent tire rim when I hear *Whoop Whoop Whoop*. The next thing I know a police car is driving up behind me, lights flashing away.

So I pulled over, and the uniformed officer came up to my window asking, "Can I see your driver's license?"

Well, at that time, I did not have a driver's license—which deserves an explanation.

Before the drinks that particular night, I had come under the influence of the famous old attorney, Percy Foreman, who was notorious for getting stopped for drunk driving—so much so they had his own little room up in the county jail. Percy and I were sitting at the Rice Hotel a few years before, and I mentioned something about losing my driver's license.

"Driver's license?" Percy asked, almost indignant. "That's just the state's way to get money from you while keeping a record of who you are and where you're living. If you get arrested driving while intoxicated, the first thing they do is take your driver's license away."

Then he added: "If you get arrested while driving with a suspended license, it's much worse than driving *without* a license—you'll go to jail. If you're just driving without a license, they'll just give you a ticket."

At that point, knowing that I regularly drove with a few beers under my belt, I thought this guy was one of the smartest minds in the legal field—a guy who had seen and done it all. So I didn't renew my driver's license, and in fact went several years without one.

When that officer pulled me over for "weaving," and I told her I did not have a license, she replied, "I'm going to have to get a supervisor." I knew right then and there: *Oh no, this is not going to end well.*

The supervisor came out; they got me out of the car; and they made me blow into a breathalyzer. It registered over 3, indicating that

I was extremely drunk. When the police sergeant arrived on the scene, he said, "Mr. Ward, we're going to have to take you to jail."

My lawyer showed up around 5 a.m. next morning and got me out. And Jack Cato, a former KTRK buddy who was then with HPD, took me out the back of the jail to avoid the reporters out front.

The KTRK brass was understandably upset, but they stood behind me. Masucci said, "You will go on the air at 5, at 6, and at 10 p.m. and you will apologize." I wrote out a script for what I was going to say, which briefly described my arrest. I also added a line in there that I spent the night in jail. The station told me, "You don't need to say that. You just need to say that you were arrested for driving while intoxicated, you apologize, and it will never happen again." So I did this at 5 p.m., then I did this again at 6 p.m.—both times at the end of the newscast. Then, I did it on the 10 p.m.

When I finally finished, Shara Fryer, bless her heart, reached over and patted my arm and said, "That's enough."

It was a humiliating experience. I later learned some bar out in northwest Harris County found and posted a copy of my mug shot up there. Obviously, they weren't Dave Ward fans at that establishment.

I have done some stupid things in my life, and this is perhaps the worst. Flipping that motorcycle end over end in the Astrodome was crazy. There was no excuse for that. But driving as drunk as I was that night in 1995 was the biggest in a series of wake-up calls. After that, I knew I had to change things in my life. Getting arrested with such a high blood volume of alcohol stopped me cold and made me think about the way my life was going. There wasn't anything to laugh about in the story, or any way to deflect that it indicated a problem.

That night, more than all my promises to myself or my time in rehab, changed my relationship to drinking. That's when I began paying attention to the amount I drank and respecting my limits. And that's when I stopped driving after drinking. I could no longer deny that something in my life had to change, and that something was me.

I recently came across a series of letters between my mother and me that sheds some honest light on the state of my life into the early- to mid-1990s. I had always been close to both of my parents, and written to them often, frequently from the station to update them on life, my career and other pursuits. Kids and parents don't write letters nearly as much—if at all—these days. Texts and emails have taken the place of letters, which is a shame because writing a letter, especially to someone you love and trust, can be like bearing your soul to them. You leave a piece of you on the page.

After my father passed in 1987, my mother wrote me frequently as the executor of their estate to update me on the process of probating Dad's will. At one point, she and my sister Shirley were having a disagreement, which weighed heavily on my mother. She shared her concerns in several letters to me and writing her back I tried to be supportive and reassuring.

In the fall of 1991, Mom wrote me a very revealing letter about my marriage to my second wife Debbie, whom I had married fifteen years earlier when I was fifty-two, and Debbie was thirty-eight. We also had two sons: Jonathan, who was almost four years old; and Christopher, who was not even one at the time of the letter.

"I know you are going through a very hard time in your life right now. I know you are very unhappy though you never let on to me that you are," Mom noted, correctly, in her typewritten letter. "I am sure you feel trapped, and maybe feel there is nothing you can do—no way out for you. THAT IS NOT TRUE. You need to act cautiously, carefully, and prayerfully, but you do need to act…I have worried about you—you are under a lot of pressure both on the job and at home, and you are at the right age to have a really good heart attack. That would break my heart…"

Here is a rather long excerpt from my response to her a few weeks later:

> *I don't want the children to feel as though they grew up with a grandfather instead of a father, so I am really trying to keep a young approach with them and that can sometimes be a bit difficult. I'm not a young father…let's face it…but I think I've got enough youth left in me to handle these two boys in the right way, with some help from the Good Lord.*
>
> *I know that you know that Debbie and I clash quite often… much more than I like, and that bothers me. She can be very difficult at times, in many different ways, and all to (sic) often I lose patience with her. I'm working on that, and I think I'm getting better at it, but it's not easy. Let me assure you, however, that we have no plans at all to separate and never will. At least, not on my part.*

> *For the past couple of years, I had been using a prescription drug called Halcion...a sleeping pill...recommended by Dr. Sims. After reading a* Newsweek *article on the medication, and learning about its possible side effects, I no longer use that. They claim the drug can induce violent outbursts for no reason, and with my tempter I certainly don't need any help in that direction...*
>
> *I love you so very much, Mama, and I don't want you worrying about me or our marriage or the children or anything. I'm probably not the happiest guy in the world...you pegged me pretty good on that...but I'm certainly not suffering from depression, mood swings, or anything like that. Working in this same stress-filled job for 25 years would get anybody down from time-to-time, but believe me, I can handle this...Maybe I should share my occasional troubles with you more, but I've just never been one to do that. I don't stuff my troubles inside me. I don't brood and worry over situations that occur. But at the same time, I don't talk about them very much... with anyone.*

Looking back on this exchange of letters, I may have been in denial or protecting my mother. My marriage to Debbie really was pretty much on the rocks at that point. We limped along for another five years until she kicked me out of that house on Newcastle. The divorce was finalized in January of 1997.

Things didn't get better for me in 1997. Later that year, my sweet mother got ill in Dallas, and went to the hospital there so my younger sister Mary could help her. My daughter Linda was also living in Dallas at the time, and she was a big help too. During the course of testing my mother to diagnose her, one of the doctors was convinced he saw something in her brain—a tumor or something. So they operated on her brain, and when they got in there they found nothing wrong.

After they sewed her back up, Mom was recovering for a few days when she threw up. Tragically, she inhaled part of it, which got in her lungs. The infection went rampant from there, and she died on August 24, 1997. I don't know how much longer she would have lived if she had not had that surgery, but I have always blamed that unnecessary surgery for her death. Up until then she was vibrant and active for a person her age.

The day my mother died, while they were still treating her, my sister Mary and I were in the waiting room biding time before we could go back in the room. Growing up, I remember my father always had a distinct aura or aroma about him. I could always tell when my father was close by or in the room because of that. Sitting in that waiting room that sad day, I had that same experience and told Mary, "I can smell Daddy."

"So can I," Mary said, looking back at me equally astonished.

My God, my father has come back for Mom.

By the time we got back into her room, my mother was unconscious. Shortly thereafter, she took her last breath—then she took Henry Ward by the hand and went to heaven. The hospital staff cut off the machines, and that was it.

We buried Mom back in Jacksonville next to Dad, in the plot with her parents. When I was going through her papers afterwards, I found this little gem she had saved. It so perfectly sums up the kind of woman my dear mother was:

> **What I Live For**
> *I live for those who love me*
> *For those I know are true*
> *For the heaven that smiles about me*
> *And awaits my spirit too*
> *For all the human ties that bind me*
> *For the task my God assigned me*
> *For the bright hopes yet to find me*
> *And the good which I can do.*

I had lost my father, my mother, and my second marriage had disintegrated. My dear mom had understood the situation far more clearly than I had. But now, without an emotional rudder, where was I headed?

It's not every day you get to meet your hero, but I did in 1999. A giant in our industry, Walter Cronkite set the right kind of example for accurate, unbiased news coverage that stands to this day.

HUNG THE MOON

On March 12, 1999, my personal hero Walter Cronkite came to Space Center Houston with his wife Betsy to receive the Rotary National Award for Space Achievement's very distinguished Corona Award. The Rotary space awards had been launched in 1987 by Space Center Rotary Club members Owen Morris and Charles Hartman to be like the Oscars for the space community. In 1992, they added the Corona category as a lifetime achievement award recognizing "only the brightest of our nation's space explorers." The inaugural Corona award that year went to engineer and aerospace pioneer Robert Gilruth, often referred to as the "father of manned spaceflight." Astronaut John Young, who among a long list of accomplishments and accolades, was the only human to fly in every spacecraft since the Mercury program, received the second Corona Award in 1997. No one has received an RNASA Corona Award since Cronkite.

I am admittedly biased, but Cronkite deserved it. When people think about his storied broadcasting career, they understandably think of the Kennedy assassination and Vietnam, but from its earliest inception Cronkite had a genuine passion for covering the U.S. space program. When the Apollo 11 mission was launched on July 16, 1969, Cronkite's trademark objectivity abandoned him as he shouted, "Go, baby, go!" He would remain on the air for twenty-seven of the next thirty hours offering detailed explanations of each phase of the mission together with astronaut Wally Schirra. Cronkite's pithy coverage made CBS the most-watched television network for the Apollo missions.

On February 14, 1980, Cronkite announced his decision to retire from the CBS Evening News, and his last day in the anchor chair at the CBS *Evening News* was on March 6, 1981. That evening, he closed out his nineteen-year chapter as America's anchorman when he memorably said:

> *...the person who sits here is but the most conspicuous member of a superb team of journalists; writers, reporters, editors, producers, and none of that will change. Furthermore, I'm not even going away! I'll be back from time to time with special news reports and documentaries, and, beginning in June, every week, with our science program, Universe. Old anchormen, you see, don't fade away; they just keep coming back for more. And that's the way it is: Friday, March 6, 1981.*

The space program continued to be one of Cronkite's main passions for the rest of his life. In the mid-1980s, in fact, he was a finalist for NASA's "Journalist in Space" program, which was modeled after the agency's "Teachers in Space" initiative—but suspended indefinitely after Christa McAuliffe, Dick Scobee and the rest of the Space Shuttle Challenger crew perished in the 1986 Challenger disaster. A decade later, Cronkite recorded voice-overs for the film *Apollo 13*. And a decade after that, NASA made him their only recipient of the Ambassador of Exploration Award who was not an astronaut or NASA employee.

I was so excited about going to the 1999 Rotary National Awards and meeting Cronkite that I splurged and hired a car and driver so I wouldn't have to mess around with parking and risk being late. When I first met Cronkite and his wife Betsy at the reception, I introduced myself and said that I—like the rest of humanity—thought he "hung the moon" as far as television news was concerned. Then I explained that I had been an anchor at Channel 13, the ABC affiliate, for the previous thirty-two years. A few minutes later, Cronkite came back to me later and asked, "Dave, how long did you say you've been on Channel 13?"

"I've been the anchor on the evening newscast for thirty-two years," I said.

Cronkite then told me the always thought he retired too early, after nineteen years as anchor—and so did I for that matter. In those days, CBS had a mandatory retirement age of sixty-five, and even Uncle Walter wasn't spared.

Another Cronkite contemporary I came to know around that time was David Brinkley. Everyone of a certain age knew the *Huntley-Brinkley Report* that aired on NBC from October 29, 1956, to July 31, 1970. They practically helped invent what a modern TV newscast was. It was so influential that, at one point in their careers, most every anchorman in the United States tried to sound like David Brinkley with that very distinct, staccato delivery. His co-anchor Chet Huntley was more of an announcer than a news reporter, but Brinkley had a nose for news. Chet anchored from New York, while Brinkley was in Washington. Their trademark sign-off "Good night, Chet"…"Good night, David"…was particularly memorable and effective, to the point that it was almost a national catchphrase in the late 1950s. "You have to do something to end the program," Brinkley later explained. "I think it was Reuven (Frank, their producer) who thought of the 'good night' line, and insisted on it, and forced it on us. We resisted but gave in—and it turned out to be a real winner. People would shout it at us in the street, so that's when we knew we had made a good decision."

In 1981, Brinkley made the move to ABC News and quickly rose to the top of the Sunday news show dogpile with *This Week with David Brinkley*. Along the way, he had the help of two Houstonians in particular: our former KTRK colleague David Glodt and Dorrance Smith—a Roone Arledge protégé who also helped manage communications in the Bush 41 administration.

During one of the of the Republican national conventions in the 1980s, the Texas delegation ordered what must have been a whole truck load of James Coney Island hot dogs shipped to the arena hosting the event. Somewhere along the way, Brinkley got one of those James Coney Island hot dogs, and fell in love with them. When he moved to Houston after his retirement in 1996, I was driving him someplace in my car and asked, "David, you could live anywhere in the world you want. What made you move to Houston?"

He responded instantly, "The James Coney Island hot dogs, of course!"

He swore to me that was the truth, though I suspect the fact he had family here was part of the draw. I enjoyed spending time with him on the several occasions we got together, and even took him to Kay's at one point. David Brinkley was a great guy, and when he died here in 2003 I felt like I had lost a real friend.

Two years later, in August of 2005, we also lost maybe the most prominent member of the ABC family at the time, Peter Jennings, who succumbed to lung cancer after a twenty-two-year run as sole anchor of *ABC World News Tonight*. That December, Bob Woodruff succeeded Jennings as *World News Tonight* co-anchor with Elizabeth Vargas, who had quickly risen through the ABC ranks and was a mainstay, particularly on the network's *20/20* program.

Tragically, Woodruff was critically injured a month later on January 29, 2006, while on assignment covering the transfer of power in the War in Iraq. He was twelve miles north of Baghdad in Taji when he sustained a traumatic brain injury from an improvised explosive device. The quick action of the soldiers and medics saved Bob's life. Within a few days, he was transferred Bethesda Naval Hospital outside Washington, DC—where he spent thirty-six days in a medically-induced coma. The long road to recovery started there. To his credit—and his family's—he made it.

More recently, in 2017, Woodruff came to Houston for the Crime Stoppers gala event, and I had the chance to visit with him. We talked about his career, and Bob told me he couldn't remember the bomb attack. He was knocked unconscious, and when he came to he couldn't remember what happened or where he was. It had disfigured his face, and he subsequently went through a number of surgeries. Finally, he got back to where he could talk again, and then report again. Bob had originally come to ABC News as a Chinese translator, and ABC sent him back to the Far East. It was a great interview. Bob Woodruff was and is a good reporter and a good man. It's just a shame what happened to him in Iraq, but I admire the way he kept going, kept fighting, and has continued to have a notable career and make a significant impact on others.

There have been and continue to be so many talented people in this business, and I am so lucky to have known as many of them as I have. Closer to home, in March of 2000, KTRK made one of their very best personnel decisions when they decided to bring Dave Strickland back from WAVY-TV in Portsmouth, Virginia as our news director. Another proud product of Sam Houston State University, Dave had started with us in 1984 as one of Bob Allen's producers in the sports department. Later in 1986, we worked together when Dave produced our "Return to Space" documentary following the Space

Shuttle Challenger accident. After that, he was always assigned to be my producer even after he started producing the newscasts. In time, Dave and I became like brothers. I loved him like a brother, and we would sometimes go at it like brothers too.

In the last hour leading up to a newscast, for example, Dave says I could become a demanding perfectionist, which might shock a lot of people who know me. Normally, at home and around the office, I can be a pretty low-key and laid-back guy—at least, that's what I believe. But not before a newscast. When I didn't like something, when I thought something did not belong in our newscast, I would absolutely make my views known. Strickland had strong opinions too, and was certainly no shrinking violet. So we'd be yelling at each other, and if you didn't know any better you might think we did not like one another—not so.

In TV news, the clock is a very severe taskmaster. Every second counts, and you are constantly watching the time. During any given thirty-minute newscast, you normally have around twenty-nine minutes and thirty seconds—give or take—of total time. If you back out the time for the commercials, which you have to run because they pay the bills, you end up with maybe seventeen or eighteen minutes of time for actual news. Well, if a story or segment runs long, which happens more often than you might think, you have to cut something back later in the program. Even during the course of a newscast, Strickland would accuse me of back-timing everything—and obsessing over the clock. Meanwhile, he was inside the control room watching the newscast, but also paying very close attention to the time.

At the end of every newscast, I always liked to have a short little segment we called the "kicker." It might be a joke, or an interesting tidbit, or something strange that happened in the world. I was particularly fond of the "stupid crook" stories. Well, after a couple of decades putting together a newscast, I could tell instinctively when the newscast was running behind schedule—and when that happened, I was always concerned that meant we would have to drop that kicker to end on time. During the commercial, I would bitch at Strickland, and tell him I knew he was going to drop that kicker.

"The kicker's going to be fine, Dave," he would say in my ear.

"No, we're not!" I would shout. "You're going to kill my damn kicker!"

So we'd be screaming at each other, and one of us would end up being right. But as soon as the red light would go off, and the newscast was over, it was time to move on. It was never personal. It was just two guys fighting, and occasionally yelling, for the best newscast we could get on the air. Some nights were more of a struggle than others, but I never doubted Dave's professionalism. We were brothers, as I say, and our station was lucky to have him for as long as we did.

Another reality in the TV news business concerns the month of May. May is the second biggest ratings book of the year, because the ratings you earn in May determine how you are doing versus your competitors which, in turn, affects how much you can charge for advertising for the next six months until the all-important November book. Consequently, lead anchors and reporters are never allowed to take time off in May. This also explains why you were, back in the day, more apt to see one of Wayne Dolcefino's blockbuster investigative pieces during May or November—to help with the ratings.

In May of 1990, I remember Shara Fryer's father, Clifford, passed away from cancer at age seventy-two. They had the funeral at 11 a.m., so our general manager at the time, Jim Masucci, called a friend of the station who had a private plane and flew all of us—Marvin, Bob Allen, me and a bunch of management folks—out to Hallettsville, Texas for the service so we could get back in time for the evening newscasts. I thought that was a classy move by Jim.

"I only took three days off for dad's funeral because we were in the May book, and I needed to get back to work," Shara later recalled. "Then in 2002, I announced my cancer and had to go home to recover from the treatment in mid-May. I was in so much pain, and thought, 'You're not going to get well if you don't go home,' so I did."

Happily, Shara and her doctors caught her cancer, a slow-growing invasive squamous cell carcinoma, early. She didn't have any symptoms, but had gone in for a regular annual exam when her doctor saw something that didn't look right. I have always admired the way Shara took a really tough situation, and with a lot of guts spread a lot of good information about colo-rectal cancer and the importance of getting check-ups.

"I know that cancer does not have to be a death sentence," she said at the time. "I know it helps to face it and march forward."

Marching forward can seem impossible after a significant challenge, but it's our only option. By this time, I had overcome several problems in my life, some of my own making. But I was soon to be tested again. In 2001, I bought a Cadillac El Dorado convertible, which is noteworthy for the simple fact that Cadillac, to my knowledge, has never made a convertible El Dorado. Some company in Florida bought twelve of those things and re-fashioned them into convertibles. The one that I bought was solid black, with a red pinstripe down the side and mag wheels. I thought it was beautiful, but my wife Laura, to put it mildly, really hated it. "That looks like a pimp's car!" she would say.

Well, she didn't have to put up with it for too long. On May 10, 2003, I was driving home from the television station after doing the 10 p.m. news. I was making my way from Highway 59 onto Loop 610 North near the Galleria. Just as I got on to the Loop, a young woman in a Ford Expedition hit some construction equipment and lost control of her vehicle, hit the curb and took out one of the traffic control devices, and at some point careened straight in front of me. I did not see that car until it was just right off my front, right headlight. It's funny. In a split second, as I was assessing what was happening, I remember thinking *Oh Lord! I'm going to mess up my car.*

Did I ever. I hit that SUV just behind the driver's side door, and we went spinning around. Another car crashed into me from the back, and it totaled that Cadillac. In the process, my head hit the rearview mirror, and I was pinned inside that car.

Laura was at home, and sometime after 11 p.m. her son John called from Dallas.

"Mom, is Dave home yet?" he asked.

"No, he's probably running a little late," she answered. "I'm sure he'll be here in a minute."

"Mom, sit down," John replied. "I've got something to tell you. I think Dave has been in a bad car wreck over on the West Loop."

John had a friend who had been to a Houston Rockets basketball game, which was back when they still played at the Summit (the building is Lakewood Church today). This friend got caught in a traffic jam coming out the freeway. Driving past the scene, they could see the man behind the wheel. Rescue personnel were still trying to get him out, and they thought they saw me.

Well, Laura was very concerned. She called a friend of hers, and they headed for the wreck over on the West Loop. They ran into a wreck scene in one of the southbound lanes, just a little bit down from Woodway, and they pulled off. There was an ambulance that was loading up a man, and as Laura hurried up to the crew a police officer said, "Wait ma'am…"

"No, I've got to get in that ambulance," she said. "That's my husband in that ambulance."

"No ma'am," the officer replied. "That man's wife is already in that ambulance, and they're headed for the hospital."

Well, Laura turned around and called to her friend. "Oh, it's a mistake," she said. "It's not Dave! It's not Dave!"

At that moment, the police officer turned to her and said, "Ma'am, are you looking for Dave Ward? He's been involved in a very bad accident on the other side of the Loop up near 59, and they're hauling him off to Hermann Hospital."

Well, after I hit that SUV, I was trapped inside that car for about thirty minutes, and it was very painful. My head had hit the rearview mirror, and I was bleeding like a stuck pig. My right leg hit the gearshift, and it was broken just below the hip joint. They finally got the Jaws of Life on scene, scraped me out of that car, and put me in an ambulance to Hermann Hospital.

When I got there, of course, there was Dr. Red Duke again. "Well Ward, it looks like you've busted your ass again!" he said. After I'd been in that emergency room for twenty minutes or so, Laura arrived. As she was walking toward the E.R., she saw my suit that had been cut off of me. It was covered with blood. When she walked through the door, I could see her and raised up my right hand to tell it was not that bad—and that I would be okay. But when I raised that hand, it too was covered with blood.

The woman who hit me was treated and released that night, but I had broken my hip in two places which required surgery—and that meant I would be sticking around Memorial Hermann Hospital for a few weeks. The station sent our fantastic medical reporter Christi Myers, someone I really liked and respected, out to cover the story. For one thing, it gave me the chance to apologize on camera to anyone who got stuck in that traffic jam caused by the accident.

As a TV newsman, I much prefer covering the news—not actually being the news myself. Leaving the hospital a few weeks later, anxious to get back on the air, I was once again confronted with the magnitude of my good fortune. Another close call. Another set of broken bones and wounds to heal. Yet I had been spared again.

The good Lord still wasn't done with me. And how thankful I was. I had finally gotten into a relationship that was really working, and I still felt on top of my game at the station. I felt like my life was just starting again in many ways. But let me back up a bit and explain how I had gotten there before the accident.

God truly blessed me the day I met Laura Marie Stoma Rowe.

DEPTH OF LOVE

In 1989, I was sitting at my desk at Channel 13 when the phone rang. Nobody at the TV station had secretaries, so I picked the phone up. "Mr. Ward, this is Laura Rowe," the voice said. "I'm the executive director of the Variety Club in Houston. We're having our annual fundraising gala coming up, and I'd like to ask you to be our Master of Ceremonies."

I had heard of the Variety Club but didn't know they had a chapter, or "Tent" as they call them, in Houston. It turns out Tent 34 was founded in Houston in 1949 and specialized in raising money to provide artificial limbs, wheelchairs and funding for a neonatal center at Ben Taub Hospital. By that time, I'd done events for nearly every other charity in town, and being intrigued I wanted to learn more about Variety Club. "I would love to help with your event," I finally told Laura. The date was set for some time in November.

The night of the event, I walked up to the ballroom of the Westin Galleria, and greeted several ladies at a reception desk just outside the door. "I was told to ask for Laura Rowe," I told them.

"Yes, sir, she's by the stage," they said. "She's in a red dress."

It was still very early in the evening, and there was nobody in the ballroom. When I walked in, I saw a woman in a red dress by the stage and headed in her direction. Well, the closer I got, the prettier I realized she was. When I was about ten feet away, the thought just hit me: *That is the most beautiful woman I have ever seen in my life.* (Spoiler alert: she still is.) Nevertheless, we had a show to put on, so I introduced myself—and we went over the program so I could get my scripts finalized. I later learned this was Laura's first major fundraising event of this magnitude for the Variety Club. That debut was a major success, highlighted by the evening's special performers The Gatlin Brothers. At the end of a very fun evening, Laura said, "This was very good, Mr. Ward. Can we call you again next year?"

"Yes ma'am," I replied. "I'd be delighted."

I think I have been the emcee at every one of her fundraising dinners ever since.

There was nothing to this first interaction beyond my helping a great cause. I was married at the time, and so was Laura. It would be another ten years or so before our relationship gradually moved beyond the strictly professional.

Let me tell you a little about the woman who would eventually become my beloved wife. Laura Marie Stoma was born in southern Louisiana, the second of nine children. In fact, the Stomas had five girls in fairly rapid succession before their first son came along. Laura's wonderful father, Joe B., insisted early on that the fact that his girls were growing up in a rural environment did not preclude them from learning about good food, and art, and how to dress properly. He taught his kids how to read a menu, and took them to the Blue Room in New Orleans' Roosevelt Hotel to see the popular performers of the day. His devoted wife Marie (nee Gani), meanwhile, made their children's clothing early on—including the blue dresses for the girls complete with white gloves for Sunday mass at St. Michaels—and regularly cooked three meals a day from scratch.

Together, the Stomas raised a big, welcoming family. When Laura was growing up, in fact, the Stoma household had something of an "open door policy," and was routinely the center of activity—especially big family meals featuring her mother's extraordinary Lebanese home cooking. Those meals normally consisted of kibbe, stuffed eggplants, and the like—but also came to encompass Italian and occasionally Cajun food. Having such a big, inviting family atmosphere growing up will not surprise anyone who has witnessed the effortless way Laura entertains and looks after a large family and her many friends. No one gives more of themselves or tries harder to help others.

Laura attended LSU before moving to Houston in the mid-1970s with her first husband John. She got into fundraising at her kids' private school in north Houston. Along the way, she also helped the

Sunshine Kids, which Bob Allen also helped champion for so many years—trying to brighten the lives of children with cancer.

At the Variety Club—and more recently with the Houston Children's Charity organization she founded with dear friends Gary Becker, Tilman Fertitta, Grant Guthrie, Don Henderson, Charles Joekel, and Bob Ogle—Laura has been very effective at raising money by bringing in big-name entertainers which, in turn, helps her attract great sponsors. Sometimes she has entertainers who are so hot that I haven't yet heard of them. Just recently, in fact, she had a performer named "Pitbull" do her annual gala. I had no idea who that was. He was a very nice guy, but to be honest his music is not my cup of tea. Some of the other mega stars Laura has hosted through the years have been Liza Minelli, Olivia Newton-John, British singer Joe Cocker, Ray Charles; the dynamic duo of Dionne Warwick and Bert Bacharach, and the "Blues Brothers" Dan Ackroyd and Jim Belushi.

One year, Laura had Phyllis Diller and Bob Newhart on stage— one right after the other. Either one of them would have been a great single act by themselves, but I don't think anyone will ever forget having one evening with those two comedic geniuses on the same stage in one night. Phyllis Diller just wowed the crowd, as usual. She wore this outlandish outfit, came out on stage, and just stood there for several seconds and before finally saying, "Ridiculous, isn't it?" From that moment, she had the audience in the palm of her hand. Bob Newhart was just as good.

Without a doubt, the biggest performer Laura ever brought to Houston was one Francis Albert Sinatra in 1997. You know you are a big star when your people can demand that the event organizers install a red carpet for you to walk on through the hotel kitchen on your way to the stage. Anyway, right before his appearance, Sinatra came walking in on that red carpet, and Laura was waiting for him around the corner in the kitchen area. Right before he rounded the corner, she heard him say, "I don't care what that goddamn chairlady wants me to do after this show, I'm not doing it…"

Just then he turned the corner to find Laura waiting. "Well, who are you?" The Chairman of the Board asked.

"I'm that goddamn chairwoman," she responded, smiling her most beautiful smile.

Frank Sinatra ended up doing everything Laura asked, and more. Frank Sinatra, Jr. led the orchestra for his father that night, and it was a thrill just to see such an icon on stage in Houston. In fact, after that he only performed one more show—in Tokyo on New Year's Eve—before he died on May 14, 1998.

In the late 1990s, Laura had one of her Christmas toy give-aways in the grand ballroom of the Hyatt Regency Hotel downtown. There must have been 800 children there that day, ranging in age from infants to teens. Laura put me in charge of the table for very young children, aged three to six years. I guess she thought I couldn't really get into much trouble! There on the table were baby dolls, jacks, balls, and building blocks—basic toys intended for the very young. I had already given away several toys when a nun walked up with a very small little girl. She was about four years-old, and as I watched her feeling around some of the toys I could tell she was also blind.

At one point, the nun said to her, "Oh, look here, dear—here's some alphabet blocks in braille."

At first, I didn't think we had anything with braille on it and was concerned the nun was making a mistake. But sure enough, there were some blocks in a net bag with braille on them along with the letters. Well, that precious little girl took those alphabet blocks as well as a baby doll, and then she and the nun both thanked me very much. After they left, I checked every other set of blocks on the table. Not a single one of the remaining sets had braille on them. The only set, out of the dozens that I had put out on that table, was the set spotted by that nun for that little blind girl. I knew, right then, that what Laura was doing was truly blessed by God. It was one of the most moving experiences of my entire life.

In the fall of 1999, I had been divorced for over two years when, once again, I ran into Laura before another charity event—this one for the Citizens for Animal Protection at the George R. Brown Convention Center. I was, as usual, there early reading my scripts when Laura and a group of her friends walked up and said hi. Houston is a small town in certain respects, and I had heard she was separated from her first husband and in the middle of divorce proceedings. Summoning up a little courage, I used the occasion to suggest we might go out sometime.

"Not as a date, right?" she shot back.

"No, no, no—we'll just have dinner," I said, trying to play it down.

A few months passed, and I finally called Laura early in 2000. I had to emcee the "Women of Distinction" event for the Houston chapter of the Crohn's & Colitis Foundation—also called the Winter Ball. I called Laura to see if she would accompany me, but she politely declined. She had already bought a ticket and was going with a friend. After I hung up, I was sitting there feeling a little disappointed, consoling myself that at least I would hopefully see her there.

Just then, something wonderful happened. Laura called back to say she might be able to come with me if her girlfriend could come too. "Absolutely," I told her and declared I would also get a car service to make getting around easier. A few days later, her friend backed out, so I had the divine chance to go alone with Laura. We ended up having a very nice time—at least I know I did!

After that, we started seeing each other every so often. Laura says now it didn't feel like we were dating in a romantic sense at first. That is true, as I learned quickly she had three pretty firm rules when it came to dating. First, she didn't want to date anyone who worked at night. And second, she didn't want to date anyone who smoked.

Well, I was 0-2 on that scorecard. On top of that, I had not one, but two, ex-wives. I also emceed something every Saturday night. While we were seeing each other, in fact, we had one night a week to go out. We would meet at 7:10 p.m., and I would have to go back to the station by 8:10. That wasn't very relaxing—or romantic. Such are the demands of the job. But, speaking for myself, I would take whatever time I could get with her.

When all was said and done, Laura says I proposed to her over twenty times, which might be a conservative estimate. She was determined not to say "yes" due to her rules, but I was equally determined not to take "no" for a final answer. I later learned her close friend Charles Joekel weighed in on my behalf, telling Laura, "Nobody in the world will ever love you as much as Dave. He will take care of you; but besides that, no one walks away from this depth of love." Our mutual friends Gary Becker and Tilman Fertitta shared similar thoughts with Laura. I will forever be grateful to all of them.

Finally, Laura gave in. "Mom and Dad like you," she said. "My sisters too—everyone likes you."

Before we waltzed down the wedding aisle, however, Laura wanted me to mend some of the relationships in my life that needed fixing— starting with my children. To help with this process, we started going to therapy. It certainly gave me some new perspective on my life and the people for whom I cared.

What did therapy help me realize? One important place it gave me clarity was my relationship with my father. I always loved and respected my father, but when I examined our relationship with some professional help, I could understand that he was not always the warmest man. As a Baptist preacher, his devout faith and determination always to set a good example led him to be a domineering presence in my life. Now I could see that I had rebelled against that to a degree— hanging out with Dash Crofts, for example, and becoming a rock 'n roll DJ. And while I have a deep faith and am grateful to God, I have not been a regular church-goer since my childhood. I figure I spent more time in church as a kid—basically every day—than most people do over the course of their lifetimes.

And I could finally see that my relationship with my dad carried over to the way I parented my own kids. I was always worried that I would not be a good parent, and as a result probably wasn't. The demands of my job certainly made that a complicated scenario, but I guess my own interactions with my father didn't give me a lot of confidence that I was prepared to be a good dad. While I recognize that I can't change the past, I truly regret that I didn't understand these things earlier so I could have perhaps been a better parent when my kids were growing up.

Finally, Laura and these therapy sessions also helped me confront my excessive drinking in a material, lasting way. It was hard to look in the mirror and acknowledge "I am an alcoholic"—but if it took changing to have Laura in my life, then I was damn sure going to change. This is when moderation became the watchword for me, and I began limiting myself to that one weak vodka I mentioned earlier. Laura did not ask me to abstain altogether, but we had to put major boundaries and rules in place.

If you have met Laura, you know she is gracious, genuinely caring and strong. She can be direct when the situation warrants as well. I needed all of these strengths in my life to get me on a better course—

and keep me there. She is, without a doubt, the best thing that has ever happened to me.

It was a blessing beyond measure that, on August 3, 2002, Laura and I were married in the chapel at St. Luke's United Methodist Church in Houston.

That day, it rained so hard that Laura was forced to navigate around high water on the way to the church. We were slightly behind schedule, but frankly I didn't care. When the time came, the chapel was filled with flowers, candles and, most importantly, our closest friends and family. A few weeks beforehand, I called Charles Joekel to see if he would be my best man. "Dave, I won't be your *best* man," he said. "I'll be your *superior* man." So Charles was standing up there waiting for us as the ceremony started. My daughter Linda sang a beautiful rendition of "Ave Maria" as Laura's mother walked down the aisle, and before long it was our turn. The ceremony itself was a blur, but when the pastor announced us "man and wife" I'll never forget the people who stood up to help us celebrate one of the very happiest moments of my life. In fact, I believe the first to stand and applaud was one of my competitors for Laura's affections, Earl Lilly.

Afterwards, we went to the Brownstone Restaurant just a few blocks away for the reception and dinner. There, we enjoyed some truly great entertainment including our favorite piano player Jeffrey Allen and singer Bobby Barrett—who sings Sinatra tunes as well as the original himself. Another wonderful highlight was when Rich Little, the brilliant comedian, did a quick set that included an uncanny impersonation of yours truly.

I had met Rich years before at a charity function organized by Judy Nichols, and we hit it off immediately. Early on, Rich told me the story of his first appearance on the Ed Sullivan Show. "I was standing there backstage waiting for Ed Sullivan to introduce me," Rich explained, "and he comes out and says: 'Now, please welcome this young comedian from Canada, Little Richard!' That threw my timing and everything off! I had to waste thirty to forty-five seconds telling people, 'No, I'm not Little Richard, my name is Rich Little.' So I went on with my routine, got a rousing round of applause, before Ed Sullivan came back on and said, 'Let's hear it again for Little Richard!'"

Rich became a good friend. Laura and I were so pleased he could attend our wedding.

After the reception, Laura and I arrived at the Ritz-Carlton around midnight, but I had a 2:45 a.m. wake-up call because I had to go to Canton, Ohio to cover the Houston Texans' very first football game ever—the Hall of Fame game. Channel 13 has been the Texans' local TV partner since the team's inception, so this was an all-hands-on-deck production for us—and even though I had just married the woman of my dreams, duty called.

Laura says my mistress is my career—my viewers, my TV family. She's right, of course, and when we got married I felt like I was doing some of my finest work at the TV station. Still, a sign of my new priorities was the fact that I started dialing way back on emceeing so many weekend charity events. For one thing, I wanted to be at home, but it was also good for the other talented Channel 13 anchors and reporters to hit the charity circuit too.

A year and-a-half after our wedding, on the Monday after Easter in 2004, Laura was diagnosed with breast cancer. Acting quickly, Laura and Dr. Eva Singletary, her amazing oncologist, put together a plan of attack that included radiation therapy every day for six weeks. Afterwards, as a precaution, Dr. Singletary removed eleven lymph nodes to test them—and originally it appeared Laura might be in the clear. A week later, however, news came that three of the nodes had tested positive. That setback led to six rounds of chemotherapy treatments over the next eleven months. Thankfully, blessedly, this time the treatments did the job—and Laura has been cancer-free since.

Despite her battle against cancer, Laura continued to be very much a hands-on manager of her charity. At their gala in 2004, she had the band Chicago—but neither one of us saw them perform. Laura was not feeling well at all. The chemo treatments she was going through caused her to lose all of her beautiful hair, so she wore a wig that night. When Chicago hit the stage, she couldn't wait to get up to our suite and take that wig off.

My wreck and Laura's battle with cancer, two serious medical setbacks so early in our marriage where each of us required a hospital bed in the house to assist our recoveries, took a toll on us. It got to the point that, everywhere we looked in our first house, there were painful memories. So when Laura suggested we maybe look for a new house, I was fully onboard.

We liked one house that fell through, but while I was in Florida covering one of the Shuttle launches Laura came across another place she really liked. At the time, the Houston housing market was white hot, and good houses were generally sold the day they went on the market—if not before. Well, Laura and her agent drew up a contract, and Laura put some money down—all the while trying to reach me in Florida. I did not have a cell phone in those days, and as it was when I got into a story—especially involving the space program—I was totally absorbed where I was.

When I finally got home, did I ever have a surprise waiting for me! Laura had signed a house contract and put an earnest money check down.

"You must really love this house," I said when I heard everything she had done. So we went over in the morning before I had to go to work. As soon as I walked in, I could understand why Laura was so taken with it. "You will do remarkable things with this house," I told her. And she did. I always tell folks that Laura had a wine room installed that "cost more than my first house," and she made some other terrific improvements. But most of all, it was a chance for a fresh start. A chance to have a real family home.

In November of 2006, I reached my fortieth anniversary at the TV station. The KTRK management gave me a beautiful Tiffany clock owing to my mild—okay, complete—obsession with time. I did not know this at the time, but Laura also suggested they give me a reserved parking spot near the door. After my car accident, I had a few new metal parts in me, and arriving at 1:30 p.m. every day for the production meeting meant I had to park far across the parking lot. Everyone else was already at work. Well, the station very kindly agreed, and I really appreciated that.

Before we got married, I told Laura I wasn't a big traveler, and when I did travel I preferred going by train. She tried the whole train thing, and let's just say she did not cotton to it. But while I did have some ability to get around, I asked her where she wanted to go in the world. She wanted to see Italy, Spain, the Greek Isles. I tried to make sure we hit all of her "bucket list" places at least once. For example, for our honeymoon, we took a cruise leaving out of Monte Carlo going into Venice, where we picked up the Orient Express to London. That was a very special trip for me.

About five years ago, however, I told her, "Sweetheart, you can go wherever you want in the world, and take whoever you want." The truth is I never particularly enjoyed international travel, except when I was with Laura. About five years ago, I decided whatever travel I did going forward would mostly be by train.

After celebrating my forty-fifth anniversary at KTRK in 2011, my dear friend Ed Brandon sent Laura a thank you note for including him in the festivities. In his thoughtful note, Ed wrote, "I believe that without your support and guidance, there would be no 72nd birthday, much less a 45th anniversary on television. As Dave would say, 'You done good.'"

To that I can only say: AMEN!

My favorite photo of Laura on our long-awaited honeymoon on the Orient Express. Without her, where would I be? I hate to imagine it.

It wasn't all serious news and straight faces on the KTRK news set.

SMILE THAT IT
HAPPENED

When he was still in his late eighties, George H. W. Bush once cracked to me that he was "so old that all of my friends are dying in alphabetical order." As I near my own eightieth birthday, I am starting to understand exactly what he meant. If you live long enough, you reach a point where it feels like too many of your dearest friends, respected colleagues and those closest to you come to the end of their time on this good earth.

That was certainly the case for me as the 2000s wore on. In April of 2001, for example, our former KTRK colleague Alvin Van Black died at the age of sixty-one after a long illness. He was quite a character, and in fact helped to pioneer talk radio in Houston starting out on KTRH-AM in the late 1960s. He came to Channel 13 in 1987, and his first assignment was hosting a regular segment called "The World of Alvin Van Black" on our Live At Five newscast. Being a native Houstonian—he attended St. Thomas High School and the University of Houston—Alvin's knowledge of the city was encyclopedic.

After a few years, Jim Masucci conceived a new role for Alvin— social butterfly. Masucci had him wear a tuxedo and cover the night scene around town, and they called this new feature "Alvin at Night." The segment worked, but Alvin left the station in 1998 after management decided we needed to move towards more hard news.

In 2003, Masucci himself died in York, Maine, after a lengthy battle with leukemia. He began his career with Capital Cities in 1956 as part of the production staff at WTEN-TV in New York. In 1970 he had come to Houston as one of the "four horsemen from Albany" and served as our operations manager and eventually developed

"Good Morning Houston," no doubt one of the biggest of his many programming successes. He became the KTRK general manager in 1990 and retired six years later. By then, Disney had bought ABC and affiliates like KTRK from Capital Cities for $19 billion, and with a new regime running the show, Jim figured a forty-year run was a good time to call it quits.

Jim's obituary carried a sentiment worth repeating. It said: "Don't cry because it's over, smile because it happened." While we sometimes clashed, there is no doubt in my mind that Jim Masucci was one of the great minds going during the golden era of television news.

It was Masucci who informed the *New York Times* in a 1994 profile on Marvin Zindler that Marvin was so independent-minded he had closed down the Channel 13 coffee shop three times. "They didn't have a hairnet on..." Jim said starting to explain to reporter Allen Myerson of the *Times*.

"It wasn't just that," Marvin said, cutting him off in mid-sentence. "There was filth under the counter."

The *Times* profile on Marvin was inspired in part by a dust-up a few months earlier between Marvin and ABC News heavyweight Sam Donaldson. In September of 1993, Donaldson aired a report on ABC's "Prime Time Live" ripping into Houston's Methodist Hospital for only spending one percent of its revenues treating the poor. That didn't sit too well with Marvin, who by that time had heart surgery, gall bladder surgery and fourteen cosmetic surgeries all at Methodist. Additionally, Marvin turned to Methodist to help treat people in need who reached out to him.

Marvin was not exactly unbiased where Methodist Hospital was concerned (neither am I, for the record), so he responded to Donaldson's report with a robust, three-night assault on Donaldson calling his piece a "hatchet job." It was highly unusual, to say the least, for a reporter to harshly criticize the work of another reporter within the same network family, so to speak. But Marvin never was your usual reporter.

"Sam Donaldson flies in on an airplane, gets a hotel room, interviews the administrator, does a little stand-up and gets back on his airplane," Marvin told Howard Kurtz, then of the *Washington Post*, a few weeks later. "They come in and {defecate} on the town and leave us to clean it up."

The war of words was on.

"I take a lot of criticism, and you normally don't hear me whining and moaning and complaining about it," Donaldson shot back in the same *Post* story. "What I think is just appalling is that one division of a company has decided that another division's product, properly approved and vetted, is a hatchet job."

Richard Longoria, our news director at the time, noted that "Marvin is a unique reporter. He speaks his mind, and that sometimes gets him into trouble." In fact, Marvin routinely angered companies around town, and those that advertised with KTRK would sometimes threaten to pull their advertising with us if management didn't get Marvin to back off on whatever it was that upset them. The station's management would tell those irate advertisers, "We'll miss you very much," but they didn't cave in to that kind of pressure.

And most of them eventually came back.

Today, the definition of what is news is very much in question. Masucci, Ken Johnson and Walt Hawver always protected the integrity of our newscasts, but Marvin was always very transparent about two things: his cosmetic surgeries, which he encouraged all of us on the KTRK staff to try, and the fact that he thought he was in show business.

"He always calls it that," Masucci said in that 1994 *New York Times* profile. "What he really means is, it's show business with the facts."

"The facts," Mr. Zindler said, snorting. "That's taking it very loosely. But everybody has their shtick. Barbara Walters has her shtick. Sam Donaldson has his shtick…"

Marvin loved to eat lunch at Pino's Italian Restaurant on the west side of Houston. He was friends with Pino, the owner, and had gone to Italy with him. Wherever Marvin ate, he liked to sit where anybody who came into the place would have to go by him. I know this is hard for some of you to believe, but as the white suits and blue sunglasses suggested, Marvin liked to be noticed. But contrary to popular belief, Marvin never let Pino or any other owner give him a free meal. Never. Not even once.

Marvin met his first wife, Gertrude, in high school. They married in 1941 shortly after he got out of high school, and she was with him for the next fifty-six years. In 1997, the couple was in the Jockey Club at Sam Houston Race Track just talking to some people when Gertrude suddenly said, "I don't feel well" and fell over. The doctors later said she was dead before she hit the floor from a massive heart attack. She was a wonderful woman, very easy-going and very understanding.

A few years later, Marvin met a woman named Niki Devine, and they got married in Las Vegas in 2003. Back in Houston, Marvin came on the air and told everybody that he had married a wonderful woman. When he ended, my co-anchor at the time, Shara Fryer, turned to him and said, "Well, Marvin, aren't you going to tell us her name?"

"Oh yeah, her name is Niki Devine," Marvin said. "Kind of sounds like a stripper, don't it?"

Well, of course, Niki was not a stripper. She was a very warm, loving woman—and in fact was a better golfer than Marvin. She told me one time that Marvin's most effective golf club was his foot!

On July 5, 2007, I opened the 6 p.m. newscast on a somber note. "We have some sad news to announce regarding one of our Eyewitness News Members," I said before my 6 p.m. co-anchor Gina Gaston went on explain that Marvin had been diagnosed with inoperable pancreatic cancer that had also spread to his liver. It was typical of Marvin that he kept working despite a really tough prognosis, even filing his restaurant reports from his hospital room at Methodist Hospital. After all, he had signed a lifetime contract with KTRK in 1988, and he was intent on honoring it.

Sadly, as is often the case with pancreatic cancer, Marvin was slipping away quickly, and knowing the end was near he wanted to make a final statement to his viewers. So I went to his hospital room with his devoted producer of a quarter century, Lori Reingold, and his equally dedicated photographer Bob Dows. When we arrived, Marvin was wearing brand new pajamas, and one of his best wigs. Bob started the camera, and after I gave him the cue to start Marvin launched into his statement.

"You may have heard by now I have been diagnosed with *patriotic* cancer..." he said.

Hearing what would likely be Marvin's last in a long line of gaffes on TV, his whole family gathered there in the hospital room started laughing, and I had to stop him. "Marvin, it's not patriotic cancer," I said. "It's pancreatic cancer." We started over, and in the next take he got it right.

When Bob, Lori and I got back to the station, we huddled with news director Dave Strickland on how to treat the statement. It was so perfectly like Marvin to misquote and mangle the pronunciation of his own condition that we aired that little blooper on the 6 p.m. news along with the rest of his comments. In his last appearance on Channel 13, the day before he died, Marvin was still fighting from his hospital room for a man to get his Social Security card.

Marvin Harold Zindler died on Sunday, July 29, 2007. If you ever met Marvin, you will never forget him. On the mausoleum wall where he is interred next to Gertrude, it reads "Marvin was a man for all the people," and he really was. He genuinely cared and loved nothing more than helping kids here in Houston and around the world get the medical treatment they needed. Along the way, he built up a cadre of "Marvin's Angels"—medical professionals who would offer needed treatments because Marvin asked them to help.

"Channel 13 has always had a very strong African-American viewership," Gina Gaston recently observed, recalling our friend, "and it's because of Marvin. There's a train of thought in television, really an over-simplified way of thinking, that Black people will always watch Black anchors and reporters simply because they are Black. But the reality is people will watch the person they think is real, and fair, and cares about them. For many years, KTRK didn't have any African-Americans in the station's core anchor group—and yet we were dominant with Black viewers. Marvin was a big part of that."

The following year, I was hit with the loss of another strong presence in my life.

I was on a radio show with Ron Stone when somebody called in and said, "You two guys are competitors on TV, but you're on the radio station together. How do you do that?"

"Dave is a good friend of mine," Ron answered. "I knew him when he was in radio here. And I've got to tell you, Dave Ward, he could have been an actor. He could have been a singer. He could have been a politician. But no, he chose to go into television and go right up against his old friend Ron Stone."

I cracked up.

On May 13, 2008, Ron Stone died at home at the age of seventy-two following a year-long bout with brain cancer. He was, as always, focused on and surrounded by his wife Patsy and wonderful family to the end.

Born April 6, 1936, in Hanna, Oklahoma, and graduated from East Central State Teachers College in Ada, Ron had launched his legendary broadcasting career as a disc jockey and newscaster on KADA radio. Graduating in 1956, he made the move to television as a news anchor for Ada's KTEN-TV. He subsequently worked at several stations in both Oklahoma and Kansas, but it was while he was working at KVOO-TV in Tulsa in 1961 that Dan Rather, then the anchor and news director KHOU-TV Channel 11 here, noticed Ron's obvious talents and brought him to Houston.

After Dan Rather departed for CBS and New York, Stone quickly moved into the KHOU lead anchor chair and, in short order, the KHOU team with sports anchor Johnny Temple and their folksy weathercaster Sid Lasher—who started at KHOU in the late 1950s—was dominating the ratings. It was also during the 1960s that Ron, a major sports nut, began broadcasting Southwest Conference football games for the Humble Oil radio network.

In 1967, Ron followed Dan Rather to New York as a writer and newscaster for NBC radio, but returned to Houston ten months later. He told me later, "David, when I got to New York, I went down to Rockefeller Center and went into that radio booth and gave my first nationwide network newscast. And, at the end when I said, 'This is Ron Stone, NBC Radio News,' I was ready to come home. I figured I'd just made a mistake." He couldn't wait to get back to Houston and, of course, I don't think Houston could wait for him to get back either.

When Ron came back, he returned to KHOU—so when I was a new anchor, I was up against Ron on Channel 11 and longtime TV newsman Larry Rasco on Channel 2. Maybe that explains why Channel 13 was always in third place at the time. That didn't change when another respected friend, Steve Smith, became the Channel 2 anchor. It was around the time Smith left for Pittsburgh in 1973, and Marvin arrived at KTRK, that we made our move in the ratings. In an interesting twist of fate, when Steve returned to Houston in 1976, Ron Stone was at KPRC-TV Channel 2 and Steve went to KHOU-TV Channel 11.

Ron had retired in 1992, but in my view his passing sixteen years later still left a void that can never be filled. He was that unique. "He wrote and talked to the audience like he was talking across the backyard fence," veteran Channel 2 reporter Phil Archer accurately observed at the time. "Before that, anchormen had been lofty demigods and were up above mere humanity. Ron was your neighbor."

For a quarter century we were competitors, but never rivals. Ron would often ask me, "What is your lead story?" and I would say, "We've got the eight-alarm fire." Of course, there was no eight-alarm fire. And Ron would respond, "Oh, you don't have the midair collision?" And of course, there was no midair collision.

Ron was a magnificent human being, and a truly wonderful friend. To me, he will always be the epitome of what a news anchor should be. I would encourage anyone wanting to enter this crazy business to study and learn from the sterling example set by one Ron Stone.

I frequently describe my early days at KTRK as an on-the-street reporter and later as an anchor going out on night runs with Rick Hartley and Jimmy Priest as "prowling" around town, making crime scenes, shootings, stabbings, and the like. There were times when we went into some pretty rough areas. I don't know if the fact that we had a Channel 13 marked mobile unit kept any would-be thugs away from us. Or the fact that we were usually around police officers possibly kept us out of potential trouble. I know my colleague and friend Jim McNee used to keep a loaded pistol in his car when he went out. So it could be risky business, and there were times when just doing our jobs could really make us wary.

Of course, we were not trying to cover a very messy war like Bob Woodruff, who paid a very high price for doing *his* job in Iraq. And he was the network anchor. I think of other war-torn parts of our world such as Afghanistan, Syria and Yemen where journalists trying to report the horrors of conflict too often become part of its collateral damage. Or even just south of our border in Mexico and elsewhere in Central America, where the drug cartels have been known to "silence" those journalists working to expose the cartel's criminal enterprises and the official corruption that usually goes with it. Every year, dozens and dozens of journalists around the world sacrifice their very lives to make the truth known.

Sometimes the risk is who or what you are covering, and sometimes it is in the way you cover the news. That certainly is the case for our brethren who ascend into the skies to offer audiences an aerial perspective on the world around them. During the 2000s, in fact, there were roughly ten helicopters crashes around the country that killed at least eight individuals. On November 16, 2000, live on the air Shara and I covered the crash of Fox 26 KRIV's SkyFOX helicopter into a small home inside the 610 Loop near the River Oaks neighborhood. The pilot died that night.

The KTRK family was not immune from such tragedy and loss, either.

On Monday, October 13, 2008, at around 11 a.m., pilot John Downhower, forty-three, and photographer Dave Garrett, thirty-six, were in Channel 13's "SkyEye HD" helicopter flying to southern Montgomery County to cover a reported shooting in Magnolia when they crashed in W.G. Jones State Forest just north of The Woodlands. Both men were tragically killed. Garrett left behind a four-year-old son; Downhower, a wife and family.

The nearest airport to the crash site, Hooks Airport, confirmed there had been no distress call before the tragedy. The last images taken from the helicopter showed the craft banking hard to the right. An investigation by the National Transportation Safety Board concluded there was power loss due to an undetermined cause.

Over the years at Channel 13, I met and worked with a number of other very talented, dedicated, and colorful people there in that news department. One I have already mentioned was Jim Priest. I would ride with him late at night after I got off the air at 10:30. We would run car wrecks, police cases, homicides, robberies, fires; you name it— all over the city. I would ride with him sometimes until 3 a.m., and we saw many things that were the stuff of nightmares.

One of the most horrible car crashes I ever saw occurred in the mid 1970s. I was once again with Jim Priest late one night, when a call came over the police radio of a fatal traffic accident just west of Memorial Park on Woodway Drive. We sped over there and when we got on the scene, it was terrible. Police told us there were three young guys in a red Corvette that were going west on Memorial and tried to veer left onto Woodway. Police said they were going well over 100 miles an hour. At that point Woodway splits into Memorial. Well, at the V, that Corvette jumped the curb, went flying into the air over Memorial and it soared about 200 feet through the air and then crashed into the trees on the other side of Memorial. The Corvette was totally demolished. There was nothing left of it, and all three of those young men were killed. Every time I pass that place on the west side of Memorial Park, where Woodway veers off of Memorial, I can't help but think of those three young men who were killed in those trees so many years ago.

Jim Priest was with us at Channel 13 for several years until he developed lung problems. It had to do with our extreme humidity down here, so acting on advice of his doctors he had to move to Arizona, a much drier climate. He seemed to do pretty well out there for a couple of years, but then he died a few years later. Jim was a great guy. We had so many intense experiences together, and I will remember him as long as I live.

Another man I worked with in television who became a good friend was Doug Brown. We first met in Waco during my radio days, where Doug was the weatherman on KWTX Channel 10. I saw his work regularly and knew how good he was on the air. I eventually found my way down to Houston in 1962 at KNUZ radio. A decade later, the famed weatherman on KHOU Channel 11, Sid Lasher, died—so I called Doug Brown, who was still in Waco, and told him there was going to be a job open at Channel 11. He applied for the job, and he got it.

Four years later, in 1976, there was an opening at KTRK, and I called Doug and told him about it. He came over to the station, applied for the job, and once again he got it. He worked on "Good Morning Houston" with Don Nelson, and they became great friends. For the next thirty-two years, they shared the studio together there at ABC 13 and became the nucleus of a news department that would eventually rise to the top of the Neilson ratings.

Doug was such a delightful person, just a really good human being. He brightened things up immensely around the TV station with that big, beautiful smile of his. Four or five years after his retirement, on January 16, 2013, Doug died with his wife Susan by his side. He was seventy-nine years old. I will never forget Doug Brown, his wit and his smile. It was a pleasure knowing him; a pleasure working with him.

I can think of too many other respected colleagues and dear friends now gone, who will always have a place in my heart: Sylvan Rodriguez. Ben Pearlman. Bob Dows. Bob Allen. Willard Walbridge. Guy Savage. Ken Johnson. Walt Hawver. Ray Conaway. Jim Whisenhunt. Paul Berlin. Stephen Gauvain. Ed Brandon.

Every month, I still try to get together with my old Channel 13 friends for lunch. I like to think our dear, departed friends now up in heaven do the same thing. And I like to think they are tuning in, still with us, just in a different way. One thing is for sure, their view is better than ours!

*Another not-so-serious photo of the Channel 13 team—
definitely NOT an official station promo shot!*

A fairly historic interview with four men who walked on the moon:
Buzz Aldrin, Gene Cernan, Jim Lovell and Alan Bean.

LET'S GO FLYING

Thinking about the loss of so many of my friends brings home the facts that time passes quickly, and change is inevitable. For a person like me who loves trains, cars, planes—anything that goes fast— the twentieth and twenty-first centuries are great times to be alive.

My Grandpa Jesse Thurman Warren was born in Osage, Texas in 1888. I remember him telling me when I was a little boy, "David, when I was a boy and you wanted to tell somebody they couldn't do something, you said, 'You can't no more do that than you can fly.' Then, when I was a little older, I saw people fly—and now people fly all the time. These days, if you want to tell someone they can't do something, you say, 'You can't no more do that than you can fly to the moon.' Well, David, I won't live to see men fly to the moon, but you will."

Then he added, "And when that happens, then what are you going to say? You can't no more do that than you can fly to Mars?"

Today, I feel the same way my grandfather did many decades ago. I won't live to see men fly to Mars, but perhaps children alive today will—that is, if our nation ever recovers its sense of daring and makes space exploration a priority again. That is a genuine concern of mine.

As I've mentioned, I got my pilot's license when I lived in Waco in the early 1960s. It has earned me a seat in some pretty neat airplanes. For example, when they were about to open up the new Houston Intercontinental Airport in 1969, later to be called Bush Intercontinental Airport, they had the Navy's Blue Angels come to put on an air show as part of the opening festivities. At the time, they were flying F-4 Phantom jets—huge, twin-engine bomber jets—that saw a lot of service in Vietnam.

I was in the number seven plane flown by one of the Blue Angels pilots, which was the one who specialized in taking news reporters up and giving them an orientation flight. I had my 16 mm Bell & Howell camera with me, and when we took off I told the pilot, "I need to get some film of the new Intercontinental airport."

When we got to 10,000 feet, he said, "Dave, when you're sitting in the back seat of an F4 you cannot see straight out of the airplane. You can only see to the left or to the right or straight up...We're going to come over the airport, so I'm going to invert the airplane, you point your camera straight up through the canopy, and the runways will be down there."

Sure enough, the pilot flipped that airplane over, kept us in a 1G environment all the time. We were kind of going over the top of an arc. I put my camera up and, sure enough, there were the two runways of the new Houston Intercontinental Airport below me. I got great film to show on television that night.

When we came back in to land at the airport, the pilot approached the airport very low and put that plane down at the very start, the very first bit of the airport runway. Then he reversed engines, slammed on the brakes, and we were stopped in hardly any distance at all. While we were taxiing back to where I got out of the plane, I asked him, "Sir, you had a runway in front of you that is about three miles long—why did you slam on the brakes?"

He said, "We're the Gulf Navy pilots. We're trained to make every landing as if we're landing on an aircraft carrier." I never forgot that.

My second ride with the Blue Angels was out of Ellington Air Force Base. By that time they were flying A4 Skyhawks, a beautiful airplane but much smaller than the F4—and much more maneuverable. When we took off from Ellington, the pilot raised the airplane off the runway about ten feet, then he leveled off, raised the landing gear, and pulled up the flaps.

"Let's go flying," he said.

He had the thing at full throttle. He pulled back and put that airplane into a steep climb, going almost straight up. After we'd gone about 500 feet or so, he spun into a 360-degree roll, and then we leveled off.

Around 10,000 feet, I said, "That was an amazing takeoff sir."

"Thank you, Dave," he said. By that time, we were out over Galveston Bay. "Let me demonstrate weightlessness to you."

He then took his cap—not a hat, it was a cap—he folded it and put it on his dashboard in the front on the airplane. In that little A4, I could see straight out the front. He put the plane up and flew in a weightless arc and maneuvered the throttle so that cap of his lifted up off the dashboard in front and he floated it right back to me—right in my face. Just amazing.

Then, over Galveston Bay, we were at about 15,000 feet and he said, "Let's imagine that we have an enemy aircraft about 10,000 feet below us headed the exact opposite direction in which we are going—here is what we would do." Then he flipped the plane up on its back, pulled the stick up, put us into a screaming dive going straight down. When we were somewhere around 5,000 feet, he went "tuckatuckatucka" like a machine gun, then pulled back on that stick, and we came pulling out of that real fast dive pulling about four Gs at the bottom. At four Gs, your body feels like it weighs about four times what it actually weighs.

The pilot came over the intercom and he said, "You okay back there, Dave?"

"Wha…yeah, yeah…I'm okay." I'll never forget that 4 G pull-out.

In my third ride in the number seven plane of the Blue Angels, also an A4, we were out over, flying about parallel to the coastline just southwest of Galveston, when the pilot said, "Mr. Ward, I'd like to demonstrate the roll capabilities of this A4 Skyhawk. He said, "we will roll 360 degrees to the right. And here we go…" He rolled that airplane 360 degrees in about one second. I was flabbergasted! And he came on the intercom and he said, "How was that?"

I jokingly said, "Anytime you're ready, sir!"

A little later I got to fly with the commander of an F101 Squadron based at Ellington Air Force Base just south of Houston. I think that was before the annual air show out there at Ellington. We took this F101 fighter out over the Gulf of Mexico south of Galveston. Two others from his squad pulled up beside us in a formation. They were only a few feet away from us and the pilot said, "Dave, now it's your turn to fly the plane. See what you can do."

He must have nodded at that pilot to the right of our airplane, because that guy immediately moved away about twenty or thirty feet. I took over the stick, and even though I had my pilot's license I was all over the sky. I couldn't maintain altitude—the stick was so touchy. Those pilots, with their training, were able to fly those planes much, much better. We came back, landed at Ellington Air Force Base, and I thanked him profusely for that ride. We, of course, publicized their upcoming air show that evening on Channel 13.

Today, the F4 Phantoms, the F101 VooDoos, the A4 Skyhawks, have all been retired. None of them are in service any more. The one thing that I wish I had done was land in a jet fighter on an aircraft carrier. I never got a chance to do that, and I really, to this day, regret that I did not.

My fascination with airplanes is nothing compared to my feelings about space flight. Although our space program is on hold these days, during its heyday, I was lucky enough to get to know a number of the astronauts who took part in the space program, as well as the technicians and flight directors. Looking back, we were very fortunate to have some absolutely amazing people working on our space program.

One of them was Alan Sheppard, who became the first American to venture into space on May 5, 1961, in the Freedom 7 spacecraft. He was launched on a ballistic trajectory suborbital flight, which carried him to an altitude of 116 miles above the earth's surface. A decade later, he commanded the Apollo 14 mission and walked on the moon.

During the 1970s, the City of Houston hosted its annual birthday dinner, and I was asked to serve as the Master of Ceremonies. They asked me, as the emcee, to wear white tie and tails, so I went to the tuxedo rental store. The evening of the event, I looked like a circus barker—but even worse, I was the only one there in white tie until Alan Sheppard showed up. He was wearing his Navy Admiral's Dress Uniform, which was all white. I told him I was so glad that he came, otherwise I would have stood out like a sore thumb in that sea of black tuxedos.

"You look fine," he reassured me.

Another astronaut I got to know was Gene Cernan, who was the last man to walk on the moon. I interviewed him on his ranch out in

Kerrville in the Texas Hill Country where he raised longhorn cattle. Gene called it his "personal Tranquility Base," and he was very proud of those cattle. So we shot video of the ranch and his longhorns, then I talked with Gene about the space program. I wanted to know where he thought it was going, what he thought about the upcoming shuttle flights and the Mars program. Even decades later, Gene was very passionate about America remaining the leader in space exploration. During the interview, he said he had a message for future astronauts: "Back up on the moon, we left the lights on for you."

In December of 1972, Gene and his crewmate Harrison Schmitt spent three days on the surface of the moon, exploring the Taurus-Littrow mountain range and nearby craters. When the time came to begin their return journey to earth, he wrote his daughter Tracy's initials, TDC, in the lunar dust. Then he climbed the ladder and said: "America's challenge of today has forged man's destiny of tomorrow. As we leave the moon and Taurus-Littrow, we leave as we came and, God willing, as we shall return, with peace and hope for all mankind. God speed the crew of Apollo 17."

Decades later, Gene reflected on those last moments on the moon in an oral history he did for NASA:

> *It's the last steps that are perhaps more memorable to me than that first step, because I'd been in this valley on the Moon, almost living in a paradox. Sunshine the whole three days we were there. Yet surrounded by the blackest black that we can conceive in our mind, and we don't know how to define it, describe it. We pull words out like infinity, the endlessness of space, the endlessness of time, but we don't know what that is. But I can tell you the endlessness of it all exists, because I saw it with my own eyes.*
>
> *So you're in the middle of this. You're part of this unique part of the universe. Everything's [in] three dimension when you look back at the Earth in all its splendor, in all its glory, multi-colors of the blues of the oceans and whites of the snow and the clouds. If your arm were long enough while you're on the surface, it's almost as if you could reach out and put it in the palm of your hand and bring it back close to you and take it home with you. Take it home with you so everybody else could see.*

It always bothered Gene that there was not another astronaut to walk on the moon after him. Later in his life, he also railed against the cancellation of, seemingly, one space program after another.

After my interview with him, Gene flew me back to Houston the next day. He had a twin-engine propeller driven plane, and as we took off and climbed through the clouds it was very bumpy. Right then, a horrible thought crossed my mind. *If we happen to crash this plane and we're both killed, the headlines in the newspaper will read "Astronaut Gene Cernan, Last Man on the Moon, Killed in Plane Crash." And in the story it would say "There was some other guy, a news reporter, with him." No one would know or care who I was.*

Happily, we made it back in good order—and in time for me to anchor the 6 p.m. newscast.

A couple of times, Gene attended Laura's Houston Children's Charity fundraiser in Tilman Fertitta's backyard, and on one occasion some guy said something about how Air Force pilots made for the best astronauts. Well, being a Navy man, that got Gene riled up. "Those Air Force guys got a runway three miles long," he said sharply. "I'd love to see one of those Air Force guys land a jet fighter on a carrier deck at night in stormy weather—they'd never make it!"

Gene Cernan was a great guy.

Another member of the NASA family who is particularly memorable to me is Dr. Christopher Kraft. In November, 1958, when the NASA Space Task Group was born, he quickly accepted an invitation by Bob Gilruth—widely considered to be the "father of the U.S. manned space program"—to become one of the task group's thirty-five original members. Dr. Kraft became NASA's first flight director, and oversaw numerous Mercury, Gemini, Titan missions even into the Apollo Program before he became the Director of the Johnson Space Center. Before his retirement from NASA in 1982, he also played a critical role in the success of the first manned space station (Skylab), the first international space docking (Apollo-Soyuz Test Project), and the first flights of the Space Shuttle.

During the early 1980s, I invited Dr. Kraft to come to the television station. He was getting close to retiring, and I asked him about the technology that's been developed by NASA, how it has just grown and multiplied over the years. "Dave, it is amazing," he said. "We have developed the technology and the capability to put a satellite in orbit around the earth to beam electricity back to the it—solar energy enough to power the entire planet." Then he added: "Now, of course, we're talking about solar transmitting satellite that might be six miles wide and twelve miles long—and when you start talking to people about a gigantic construction project like that in space, their eyes just kind of glaze over."

Naturally, we never pursued that project, and I'm sure it never will be done—at least not in my lifetime. But Dr. Chris Kraft was one of the most forward-thinking and forward-looking men that I ever met with the space program.

His successor as the Director of the Johnson Space Center was Gene Kranz, who started his NASA career by answering a help wanted ad in *Aviation Week* magazine. He started in 1960 at NASA's Langley Research Center in Hampton, Virginia, before moving to Houston in 1964. Throughout his storied career, Kranz took on bigger roles within spaceflight operations. He served as Gemini flight director from 1964 to 1968. Between 1969 and 1973, his other duties included: chief, Flight Control Division; flight director for the Apollo and Skylab programs; flight director for the first lunar landing (Apollo 11); and flight director for the return of the Apollo 13 crew. He also served as the flight operations director during the Skylab program from 1969 to 1974. In 1983, he succeeded Dr. Kraft as director of Mission Operations. In 1994, he retired.

One time, Kranz told me, "Dave, while I was working there at NASA, my children really did not know what I did. The in 1995, this movie came out, *Apollo 13*, where I am played in the movie by the actor Ed Harris. My children looked at me in a whole new light after that film."

Gene Kranz is a great guy too.

Incidentally, I had a similar experience around 1980 when I was out to dinner with my daughter Linda. I saw Neil Armstrong and his wife Janet across the restaurant, and as I waved to him said, "Oh, look Linda, there's Neil Armstrong."

"You know Neil Armstrong?" she asked in total disbelief.

Before she could recover, Neil came over to the table to say hi. I introduced him to Linda, who could barely contain herself. "Oh Mr. Armstrong, I'd love to shake your hand!" She was pretty star-struck.

She told me later that's when it hit her that I knew a lot of important people because of my job.

One of the most memorable interviews I ever conducted took place in March of 2009, when I had the rare privilege to sit down with and interview four space exploration legends: Colonel Buzz Aldrin, who with Neil Armstrong on July 20, 1969, became the first two men to step foot on the moon; Captain Alan Bean, the fourth person to ever walk on the moon; Captain Jim Lovell, commander of Apollo 13, known as the "most successful failure" in NASA history; and Gene Cernan. When the nation was riveted by the idea of American astronauts traveling through space, their story was one of excitement, romance, even sheer celebrity.

It was a very rare occasion to have such notable space travelers together as we talked the past and the future of NASA. Here is just a little bit of how the interview went:

> **Ward:** *Tell me, if you could, what do you guys represent?*
>
> **Lovell:** *Well, accomplishment number one, because we said what we were going to do and we did it.*
>
> **Cernan:** *I think we were the tip of the arrow, you know, we had our pictures in the paper and all that kind of stuff, but the strength, the shaft, the guidance of the failures were the people, the thousands of people who you've never heard of.*
>
> **Ward:** *They tell me that the computer in my car now has more capability than what you had in Apollo 11.*
>
> **Aldrin:** *We got a heck of a lot out of each and every bit that was in that computer.*
>
> **Cernan:** *The technology of Apollo is obsolete, overshadowed by time. You got more technology in the palm of your hand than we had to land on the moon.*
>
> **Ward:** *Well it's been 40 years now since that first landing on the moon. Are you surprised at how far we've come or how far we have yet to go?*
>
> **Bean:** *Well I've been surprised that we haven't done more because I go out to NASA quite often, Johnson Space Center, and I see the people there, they want to do more. They've got the same glint in their eye that we had. They just don't have the money to do it.*

Lovell: *Look at the economic situation right now. I mean we're printing money like it's going out of style and it's going for everything else.*

Cernan: *But Jim, the space program cost every tax payer in this country one penny out of our tax dollar, not trillions of dollars. You tell me we can't afford one penny out of our tax dollars to put a program together to go back to the moon?*

Ward: *Do you feel like the American people have lost the fascination with space travel?*

Aldrin: *Yeah.*

Lovell: *No, no I don't think so.*

Cernan: *They have not. We have a generation of 30 and 40-year-olds who weren't born when Neil and Buzz walked on the moon, or at best were in diapers and knee pants when I made the final steps. I think it's a latent support and passion that they're waiting for us to do something exciting.*

When I saw some video of this interview later, it looked like five white-haired old guys sitting there talking about things they did when they were kids. Before the interview, Laura gave me the best question that I asked in the whole roundtable: what was your favorite moon food? Nobody had ever asked them that before.

Ward: *What was your favorite moon food?*

Cernan: *Oh God, it was horrible.*

Bean: *I'll tell you mine. My favorite food on earth.*

Cernan: *Spaghetti. Spaghetti. How did we know that!"*

Bean: *We had some number of food items you could select from cause they were pasteurized, didn't have any germs and all that stuff, one of them was spaghetti. I wanted to be the first person to eat spaghetti on the moon and I was worried that Buzz and Neil would eat it, but they didn't, thank god. It tasted so bad.*

Aldrin: *How about some hot coffee?*

Cernan: *The things we take for granted on this earth, brush your teeth and have a hot cup of coffee, we didn't have that on the lunar surface.*

Lovell: *You guys are lucky. I just had a frozen hot dog and no coffee.*

Bean: *How about just some heat!*
Ward: *Maybe in future space flights, we'll have hot coffee.*

You might recall that Jim Lovell and his fellow Apollo 13 astronauts had no heat at all. They were practically frozen in space for 13 days. It is a miracle they made it back from that ill-fated mission—but they did. They, of course, did not land on the moon. They went around the back side of the moon, then fired their rockets at the right time to head back to the earth. They had to rig a makeshift air scrubber on their way back so that they could breathe. They also had to cram themselves into the lunar module all the way back to earth and only transferred to the command module just before the retrofire and re-entry. Thank God they made it unharmed.

Lovell's comment about his frozen hot dog broke us all up. That entire interview was a lifetime experience for me, sitting there talking to some genuine American heroes. I will always treasure the memory of it.

*A little politicking as I was getting ready to board Air Force One
and interview our nation's 41ˢᵗ President of the United States in 1992.*

TOP: *About to get one of the biggest thrills and surprises of my life. Laura clearly knows something I do not!* BOTTOM: *I have never been surprised as I was the night Crime Stoppers named their building for me. I am pictured here with Rania Mankarious, Executive Director, Crime Stoppers of Houston.*

IS THIS A TRICK,
OR A TREAT?

O n November 1, 2011, I had the opportunity to say something I
am sure most TV news reporters dream of saying at one point in
their career: "Live from the South Lawn of the White House..." At
the time, I had been in the news business some fifty years, and if I did
have a "bucket list" I can tell you covering the White House—even for
a day—would have been at or near the top. It was a real thrill for me
personally, and an important milestone for KTRK Channel 13 as well.

Why I was one of only ten local news anchors at the White House—
and the only one from Texas—was serious business. Nearing the end
of President Barack Obama's first term in office, his approval ratings
had continued a steady decline into the low 40s—definitely not ideal
going into the 2012 re-election cycle. The Gallup polling organization
found that—with unemployment following the economic crash of
2008 still hovering around nine and a half percent—satisfaction
with the direction of the country was at historically low levels, and
the sagging U.S. economy a top worry on the minds of Americans.
"A second Obama term likely hinges on whether there are signs of
economic progress in the coming months," a Gallup report in late
October, 2011 said.

At one point, every presidential administration gets frustrated
dealing with the White House press corps and tries to "go around"
the Washington media pack to get their message directly to voters
across the country. In the fall of 2011, White House Press Secretary
Jay Carney and his team had started inviting local TV news anchors
to Washington offering access to key members of the administration.
The idea was to tout "how the bipartisan proposals included in the

President's American Jobs Act would create jobs in your community and put money in the pockets of every single American worker and small business owner" as Carney's welcoming letter the day we arrived at the White House suggested.

Of course, the opportunity to interview the sitting President of the United States is something you simply cannot turn down, so our terrific news director Dave Strickland and I jumped on a plane for our nation's capital. On November 1st, we arrived at 8 a.m. at the northwest gate of the White House grounds, and after the Secret Service checked our equipment made our way to the expansive, surprisingly bucolic South Lawn of the complex—a part of which is called The President's Park. We spent most of the day out there interviewing Cabinet secretaries and several White House aides from Houston including a wonderful young man, Brandon Lepow, who sadly died from cancer a few years later.

We had lunch just off the White House Mess in a unique room called—and I am not making this up—the Ward Room. On a warship, the wardroom is where commissioned officers can dine together, and since the small dining facility in the basement of the White House has been run by the U.S. Navy since 1951 when it was first established they applied the same terminology. While the White House Mess seats about fifty people at a dozen tables, the Ward Room is smaller and features darker wood paneling.

It was a chilly fall day in our Nation's Capital, and because I carelessly forgot my overcoat, Strickland, or "Strick" as I have called him for years, lent me his. So I was nice and toasty as I was doing my live hits during the evening newscasts, while poor Dave was shivering away. Every once in a while, it pays to be the on-air "talent!" After a full day out in the elements, I am fairly certain Strick went home with early onset pneumonia.

When you are leader of the free world, time is your most precious resource. Virtually every waking moment of your day is scheduled. To wit, our interview with President Obama was scheduled for 11:24 a.m. in the Cabinet Room, which adjoins the Oval Office and overlooks the Rose Garden. To make the best use of the President's time, the White House media staff had already set up the lights and camera in front of the fireplace at the far end of the twenty-person mahogany table that President Nixon had gifted to the White House in 1970.

One-by-one, the invited TV anchors entered the room and conducted our interviews with Mr. Obama facing towards the row of windows looking out onto the Rose Garden.

Entering the room when it was my turn, I found President Obama to be taller than I expected, with a lean but athletic build and an engaging manner. To break the ice, I told him, "Mr. President, I am by far the oldest person to interview you today, so please forgive an old guy if he fumbles around a little." The president chuckled easily.

Strick and I knew I might have the chance to ask two or three questions at most, so we thought long and hard about what we wanted to cover to make the most of such a rare opportunity. We decided our first question out of the box—which would have most impact for our viewers—should be the energy industry and how that was going to move to the local economy in Houston. Specifically, we wanted to know if the administration intended to move forward with the Keystone pipeline project, which would connect a source of oil sands in the Alberta province of Canada with the refineries down on the Texas Gulf Coast. The project itself would create tens of thousands of jobs, but at the time it was stalled due to its original routing through an ecologically sensitive part of Nebraska.

I could tell the president's enthusiasm for the pipeline was minimal. "We're evaluating that right now," he said. "The State Department has a lengthy process that they have to go through. I think there are a number of factors that we're going to have to look at including whether this threatens the aquifers and drinking water of states like Nebraska where this might run through." In fact, the Keystone was still on hold when he left office some five years later.

Still, the president also told me he was a "big proponent of energy independence," and true to his word later that same day he announced the extension of nearly 1,400 deep water oil and gas leases that had been on hold since the catastrophic British Petroleum oil spill in the Gulf of Mexico the year prior.

As we expected, the interview was over in a flash.

Looking back at what was, for me, a historic day and interview, two other thoughts stick out in my mind.

First, a little over a year later, I was inspired in part by President Obama to change how I referred to myself on the air. It occurred to me that, growing up, President Obama had been known as "Barry" as opposed to "Barack." But after entering politics in Illinois, he managed to make the change to Barack—and make it stick. I don't know why he did it, but assume he thought Barry was too informal, too casual, for a U.S. Senator much less a president.

Well, after fifty years as a reporter in Houston, one day I decided I wanted to go by my real name on air—David. The first night I said, "Good evening friends, I'm *David* Ward…" in the corner of my eye I could see my wonderful co-anchor, Gina Gaston, spin her head in my direction as if to say, "What's going on here?" It was maybe a few days before I was summoned before management and told, "We have a contract with 'Dave Ward' not David. You will use Dave."

So I went back to being Dave. Afterwards the irrepressible *Houston Chronicle* columnist Ken Hoffman wrote about this very brief interlude in an article headlined, "David, we hardly knew ye."

The second thing I remember is, as soon as my interview with President Obama was over, I went back out to the White House South Lawn to interview Commander Christopher Ferguson, who had led the very last Space Shuttle mission just a few months prior. As luck would have it, Commander Ferguson was also there that day at the White House with the rest of his *Atlantis* crew—including pilot Douglas Hurley, and mission specialists Rex Walheim and Sandra Magnus—to meet the president that afternoon.

I was at the Kennedy Space Center on July 8, 2011, to see that final Shuttle launch—just as I had been there on April 12, 1981, for the historic launch of STS-1, the very first Space Shuttle mission. On that maiden voyage, pioneering astronauts John Young and Robert Crippen took *Columbia* up for a two-day, thirty-six-orbit trip to test the capabilities of the first re-usable spacecraft. For the next three decades, NASA's fleet of five Shuttles carried people into orbit repeatedly; launched, recovered and repaired satellites; conducted cutting-edge research; supported the Hubble space telescope project; sent probes to Venus and Jupiter; and helped build the International Space Station, the largest structure in space.

The Shuttles themselves were originally designed to make weekly, inexpensive launches into space—but each blast off ended up costing more than $1 billion. The reason? NASA basically had to rebuild the shuttles after each mission. Added to that, the Shuttles were supposed to be durable enough to withstand 100 missions, but none even got close to fifty flights. Budgetary pressures eventually forced NASA to look beyond the Shuttle, and migrate towards the Orion program that followed. Sadly, thousands of NASA jobs in the Houston area were lost in the process.

Covering that final Shuttle launch three decades later, I got lost in the moment and didn't realize I was jumping for joy as *Atlantis* burst off the launchpad and through the clouds for the last time. There is nothing like the power and majesty of a Shuttle launch, and each time I saw one I was like a kid on Christmas morning. It never got old, that's for sure. Still, there was also a sense of melancholy when the *Atlantis* crew landed that 135th Shuttle mission at 5:57 a.m. on July 21, 2011, after 200 orbits around the earth and a journey of 5,284,862 miles. In that moment, an epic era in manned space flight came to a close.

During our interview on the White House South Lawn, Commander Ferguson expressed his hope that our nation would go back to the moon and this time stay for a year—to show we could sustain a presence there. "I believe we are explorers and will continue to explore because it's in our nature," he explained. He's right, naturally, and like Commander Ferguson I still hope we can find a way to reinvigorate energy and enthusiasm for America's space program. In my ongoing fascination with transportation, my first love had been trains. They were a dinosaur, but the same cannot be said for space exploration. It is the future, and we cannot abandon it.

An interesting postscript for me on the topic of space came four years later when my friend and former Shuttle pilot Scott Kelly blasted off aboard a Russian Soyuz spacecraft from Kazakhstan to spend a full year on the International Space Station. Laura and I were invited down to the Johnson Space Center and Launch Control to watch; and afterwards the NASA team asked several of us who were there if we wanted to say something to the astronauts, to Scott Kelly primarily. I had already interviewed Scott before about being up in space for a whole year and asked him, "What do you think it'll be like? You'll miss a whole year down here, anything you'd like to see happen?"

"Well, I hope by the time I get back they will have finished working on the Gulf Freeway," he quipped at the time. He was, of course, referring to the fact that the Gulf Freeway is a construction project that never ends. Literally.

After Scott blasted off, Laura and I were in front of the camera down at NASA wishing him well and joking about him waving when he flew over us. Finally, I felt compelled to say, "Scott, I am sorry to tell you this, but they're still going to be working on the Gulf Freeway when you come back."

They still were. And they still are.

————————

As the years rolled on, I had the good luck of meeting influential people in all fields. But there was also some more bad luck in store for me. Friday the 13th in January, 2012 was truly a bad luck day for me. I was walking up the steps onto the news anchor set to deliver the 10 p.m. news—as I had done over 10,000 times by then. Melanie Lawson was my co-anchor that night and was already in her seat. I had my scripts in my hands, and walking up said, "Hi, Mel, how you doing?"

Right then, I tripped on the top step and stumbled across the set. As I was careening out of control, Melanie instinctively saw this was not going to end well and shouted with alarm, "Dave! Dave!" Tim Heller, our superb weatherman who took the baton from Ed Brandon when he retired in 2007, was working the weather center with his back to the set. When he heard Melanie, Tim thought she was the one in trouble.

Unable to regain my balance, I fell down the steps and hit that concrete floor hard. Pain shot from my left hip all the way through my left foot. I knew then: *Oh, boy, I've done busted my ass again.* We normally kept a blanket somewhere on the set, so Tim thoughtfully ran and got that to put under my head—to keep me immobilized until the paramedics arrived.

In the meantime, the newscast had to go on—without fail. The floor manager was dutifully calling out the time until we were on air at 10:00. "Five minutes…four minutes…" With time quickly running out, from the floor I told them to move Melanie back into the newsroom, where she delivered the entire newscast while the medical crew tended to me on our usual set. They quickly carted me off to Methodist Hospital, where some talented surgeons repaired the damage and inserted a titanium rod into the bone. Amazingly, they had me up and walking less than twenty-four hours later.

After a few weeks of recovery, I returned home to a stack of get-well messages. For example, our dear friend and former talk-show-host-turned-philanthropist Warner Roberts wrote me a particularly thoughtful card that said, "When Dave Ward hurts, Houston hurts."

Another person went on the KTRK website to write: "With all due respect to Ch. 13 & Mr. Dave Ward, Houston will not let you get off that easy. I suggest you mimic your late colleague, Mr. Marvin Zindler, and report the news from your bed as you recover."

That experience, which was the third time in my career I had to take a "forced vacation" from work, really gave me an idea of how far-reaching the KTRK signal is—and how many people accepted me in their homes for so many years. It was powerful and humbling.

But nothing lasts forever. In 2014, KTRK management told me they were taking me off the 10 p.m. newscast. When I asked why, I was told that, for the previous two weeks, the 10 p.m. newscast had been second in the ratings on Thursday nights. I felt it was because the ABC network program in the time slot leading into the late news had not performed as well as everyone had hoped. That happens in the TV business often. Still, at 10 p.m., the Channel 13 newscast more than doubled the audience in the ratings from the previous show, while our other news competitors in Houston all went down in their audience numbers coming out of the network programming. I tried to make that argument, but it was not enough.

I left that office crushed. I had been on the 10 p.m. newscast at Channel 13 since 1968—for forty-five years—and our newscasts both at 6 and 10 p.m. had dominated the Houston market. Now I felt cast aside. I told my colleagues in the newsroom that I was involved with the decision. I had never before lied to my co-workers; but from my point-of-view at the time it seemed best for the station and my colleagues. Candidly, I was concerned that, if the truth got out to the public, it could harm Channel 13 and its ratings.

Management then made the decision to split the 6 p.m. news into two programs—with me co-anchoring with Gina Gaston from 6 to 6:30 p.m., followed by a new co-anchor team from 6:30 to 7. I was happy to stay paired with Gina, with whom I had worked closely since after Shara Fryer had retired in 2005. Gina is a real pro. A California native, she had come to KTRK in 1992 after working at KTSP-TV in Tampa, Florida; KHTM-TV in Harrisburg, Pennsylvania; and KLTV in my first media market, Tyler, Texas. She co-anchored the morning news with Tom Koch for seven years before leaving for New York and the still-fledgling MSNBC in 1999. Happily, she came back to Houston and KTRK in 2001, and has been with us ever since.

I co-anchored my last 10 p.m. newscast on December 24, 2014. As I wrapped the broadcast up, I touched on some of the highlights of my career:

> *...During my years on our 10 o'clock news, we've seen everything from natural disasters, to economic highs and lows, to political contests that rocked the nation. I've broadcast the election of every President since John F. Kennedy, every Texas Governor since John Connally, and every Houston Mayor since Louis Cutrer. I've reported the launch of every manned spacecraft since the Gemini program—including the 12 Americans who walked on the moon—and was at the Cape to report on numerous shuttle launches, including the very first one and the very last one. Yes, friends, we have seen it all—you and me—right here together, and I will miss that. I have challenged myself every day of these 48 years to give you the very best that is in me, and I hope that you feel that you have received just that...*

After I stopped doing the 10 o'clock news, a lot of people asked me what it was like to leave the television station by 7 p.m. every night. I told them I had to learn what it was like to go to sleep on the same day I got up! That was a unique experience for me. I also had many people say, "Dave, I have a hard time going to sleep. You've put me to sleep at night for over forty years."

Even though I was shaken by the changes going on in my work world, I still was able to laugh when I got to thinking *I've put more people to sleep than Sominex.*

As people in transition often discover, I soon found out that when one door shuts, another opens. On October 29, 2015, Laura and I attended the Crime Stoppers annual gala at the Omni Houston Hotel. Crime Stoppers, as you know, is a cause and organization that means a great deal to me. I had agreed to be the honoree that year, because they said it would help them raise a little dough. Little did I know what that evening would entail.

The evening was filled with one highlight after another, starting with very nice videos from the one and only Barbara Bush, and also astronaut Scott Kelly who was still in the middle of his year-long mission on the space station. One of the most respected TV newsmen ever, my former ABC colleague Ted Koppel, delivered the keynote speech. My KTRK colleague Melanie Lawson—who started at Channel 13 around the time we launched the Crime Stoppers program in Houston—served as the emcee. Steve Tyrell came in from California to sing "You've Got a Friend in Me." Most importantly, almost 600 people attended and helped raise over $500,000 to support the Crime Stoppers mission. That, right there, is already a great great night.

But before the event concluded, there was one more agenda item.

Crime Stoppers' phenomenal executive director, Rania Mankarious, called me up to the stage for a final announcement. I thought it was to help wrap up the evening. Wrong. Instead, I stood there in surreal disbelief as I heard Rania say, "Ladies and gentlemen, it is my honor, it is my distinct pleasure, and it fills my heart to share renderings of a facility which will formally, and forever, be known as the Dave Ward Building Crime Stoppers of Houston."

On the screen behind us, they projected a beautiful rendering of a three-story, red brick building with a very familiar name affixed high atop its exterior wall. Confetti cannons went off, and the crowd responded with enthusiastic applause. It was a powerful moment.

I couldn't believe it—gobsmacked might be the best word to describe it. I was utterly stunned.

"Good evening, friends," I said, still shaking. "I am overwhelmed. I can't...I...this is going to take me several days to really mentally digest this. I...Good heavens...Are you sure?...Now, this is close to Halloween. Is this a trick or a treat? Wow."

Melanie Lawson later said on the air that was the first time she ever saw me that dumbfounded, and I think she may be right.

It was only after that supreme surprise that I came to know what Paul Harvey would call the "rest of the story"—all of the meetings and meticulous planning that went into creating one of the great nights of my life. A year and a half before that night, Laura had been asked to meet with the leadership of Crime Stoppers, who shared with her their plans to raise a lot of money and build the very first headquarters building in Crime Stopper's history. Then, they shared with her their intention to name the building after me, and asked her if she could keep that secret. Boy, did she ever—she and apparently hundreds of people!

When Laura had called my friend Steve Tyrell to tell him about the night and ask him to come and sing a song to me, he immediately accepted. Laura had a particular song in mind to sing—"You've Got a Friend in Me" by composer-singer Randy Newman. The only problem, Steve noted, was that the song was written for the *Toy Story* movie as a duet featuring Newman and Lyle Lovett. But knowing Laura really wanted him to sign that song, Steve's music director Jon Allen called a few weeks later to say he was re-tracking the song for Steve to sing solo.

The funny thing is: in the middle of the reception that night of the big reveal, someone tapped me on the shoulder. I turned around and it was Steve Tyrell. "Hello, brother," I said, totally surprised. I could not believe he was there. That was the first of many surprises to follow. For one thing, the room was positively packed with so many friends: Dan Pastorini and Elvin Bethea, Sylvester Turner and Dan Patrick. The congratulatory videos from former First Lady Barbara Bush, astronaut Scott Kelly, and my colleagues at Channel 13 were huge surprises.

On top of all this, Laura had also asked four of our personal friends—who also happened to be prominent Houstonians—to say a few words. One-by-one, former Texas Governor Mark White, businessman extraordinaire Tilman Fertitta, John Eddie Williams and Edna Myer-Nelson, the founder and CEO of the Richland Companies all went up on stage. That was a pretty powerful lineup, and I continue to be very grateful for their exceedingly kind comments that evening. At the very end of the program, Rebecca Campbell, who was then the president of the ABC owned-and-operated stations for Disney, came up to me with tears in her eyes and said, "Dave, I had no idea you were this loved in Houston."

I can assure you: no one was more moved than me.

More importantly, by the time the last strand of confetti had settled on the floor that night, Crime Stoppers had raised more money than they ever had previously.

The next morning after "The Mother of All Surprises," I joined Laura, Rania, Ted Koppel and others on Main Street in midtown Houston for the ceremonial groundbreaking. The state-of-the-art 28,000 square-foot building—which is standing now on Main Street in Houston—has consultation rooms for victims, families and investigators to meet discreetly. Just as important, police officers now have, for the first time, space to work closely with the dedicated men and women of the Crime Stoppers agency to attack crime in our community. Together, they have helped solve over 35,000 felonies and put some 25,000 felony fugitives behind bars.

After it we cut the ribbon to open the building in January of 2017, they gave me my own office there. I started using it in what turned out to be a pretty brief retirement. As you might expect, I could not be prouder to have my name on that building—and to this day I cannot be more grateful to all who had a hand in making it happen.

And, yes, I have also forgiven those of you who were also keeping it a secret from me!

With Ted Koppel, who delighted me by attending the groundbreaking for the Crime Stoppers building.

After speaking at the annual gala the night before, ABC News' Ted Koppel—one of the really great TV newsmen—very kindly stayed an extra day in Houston to help us break ground for the Dave Ward Crimestoppers Building which now sits on Main Street.

This shot does not do justice to how beautiful the Crime Stoppers building is.

Having the Crime Stoppers building named for me was truly the biggest honor I could have imagined. Here we are at the ribbon cutting.

BY THE GRACE
OF GOD

On Wednesday, June 22, 2016, a unique letter arrived at the station. It was from the Guinness Book of World Records, and it stated that I was, in fact, the longest running local TV news anchor in the world at the same station in the same major market.

It was Texas Lieutenant Governor Dan Patrick who first suggested that we apply to Guinness. He had been in the station some time before and came over to my little cubbyhole to say hello. I knew Dan when he was the sports anchor on Channel 11 back in the late 1970s and early 1980s. Like most Houstonians alive at the time, I will never forget the night in the Luv Ya Blue era when he painted himself blue and went on the air like that. Anyway, Dan asked me, "How long have you been an anchor here?"

"Well, since 1967," I replied.

"What's that, forty-seven, forty-eight years?" Governor Patrick asked. "You ought to apply to the Guinness Book of World Records, that's got to be a record. I'm sure nobody has ever done that."

Afterwards, I mentioned it to the news director, who said, "Why not? Just inquire."

After a quick check, we found some news anchor or television reporter in Peru or somewhere who had been on the air forty-two years at the same station—or something like that. Sensing Dan might be on to something, we got in contact with the Guinness people. They naturally wanted verification, which included letters from at least three co-workers who were there when I went to work at KTRK. I got those, and whatever else they wanted, and we sent it all to Guinness. Three or four months later, the station got that letter making it official. They brought it out to me in the newsroom, and made a big deal out of it.

The entry into the record book read:

> *The longest career as a television news broadcaster is 49 years and 218 days, achieved by Dave Ward (USA), who began working on 9 November 1966 and continues anchoring at KTRK-TV, in Houston, Texas, USA, as verified on 2 June 2016.*

Though I was the longest running anchor, the world was continuing to change around me. In early September of 2016, the City of Houston and I closed a colorful chapter in our common history when Kay's Lounge was sold and shut down to be razed—making way for a new townhome development. The last night it was open, Laura and I had dinner nearby in Rice Village. As we were leaving to go home Laura suggested, "We should go to Kay's."

I hadn't even thought about going there, but Laura insisted, "You need to go by there."

We drove over, and the place was packed. We had to park down the street. When we walked up, people started saying, "Oh, Dave! Dave Ward!" And when I walked in the door—whoa!—the place started cheering. In short order, the nice owner Duane Hefley asked me to say a few words, which I definitely did *not* expect.

"I went to work at Channel 13 fifty years ago this coming November," I said, standing in the middle of the bar. "We discovered Kay's about two weeks after I went to work there, and I spent far too much time here in this beer joint. It was just a beer and wine joint. It was built in 1939, as you all may know, so this place is as old as I am. I just want to thank Duane and everybody for coming out tonight. You young people—you're the future of Houston. And I'm so glad to see so many beautiful faces down here tonight. Thank you for letting me take a couple of minutes of your evening. Have a ball!"

The place went nuts.

As we were driving home, I thanked Laura. In terms of being a regular after-work hangout, I had put Kay's in my rearview mirror years before, but I had a lot of history in that place. Some of those memories are admittedly fuzzier than others, and some of them are of trouble I got into. But when I think of Kay's, mostly I remember the good times and the many friends I made there. Largely thanks to Laura, I was a different person than I had been when I hung out so much at old Kay's. But I was very glad that Laura insisted we go by that last night.

A month before, I had learned another closure was in the works. The station management told me I was also being taken off the 6 p.m. news. My last day on the 6 p.m. news was to have been on Friday, December 9th.

And as I began this tale and you already know, the good Lord, and a clogged artery, had other plans for that timetable.

Once the decision was final in August of 2016, I walked down to the newsroom to inform my KTRK colleagues:

> *I'll make this pretty short. ABC is issuing a press release right about now concerning me, but I wanted you to know about it first because I appreciate, love and respect all of you—my co-workers. My career here at Channel 13…this is pretty emotional for me…is coming to an end. My career here will end at the end of this year. I want you to know I am very proud of the work that I have done here in this news department over the past 50 years. Of the seven guys who were here when I hired on, I'm the only one who is still alive. Our newscast in the evening became Number One in the early 70s, and has stayed Number One for over 40 years. I'm not retiring. There's going to be other things for me to do when I leave here. But I just want you to know how much I appreciate the work that you have done to keep this news department going, and the help that you have been to me in putting these programs on the air. There is more I should say, I know, but I have a Number One newscast to deliver at 6 o'clock—and I need to get my scripts and head to the set…*

A year or so before he died in 2007, Marvin Zindler told me, "Dave, I'd like to do this work until I am ninety, so why don't you sign another four-year contract, and we'll walk out of here hand-in-hand?"

"Marvin, I'll walk out of here with you arm-in-arm," I replied, "but I ain't gonna hold your hand."

I did not have a lifetime contract with KTRK like Marvin, but I always thought I would work at the station anchoring the news until I thought I could no longer do the job up to my expectations. In my perception, I was still performing at a high level. I thought *I'm not through yet, my research is good, our ratings are good.* But at a TV station, management always has 51 percent of the decision-making capacity on their side, and they had a different opinion. It was a particularly bitter pill to swallow, but as the song goes, "You can't always get what you want."

My time as a KTRK anchor did not end the way I had envisioned over the years. But my time there had provided me with so many incredible experiences and taught me so many things that I knew I was strong enough to make the change a positive one. As I looked around at my life, I realized that I had everything I could need. And there were still many opportunities ahead for me to engage with the community I love so much.

––––––––––

Towards the end of 2017, I received word that I had been selected to be the Grand Marshal of the 2018 Houston Livestock Show and Rodeo Parade through downtown Houston—an event I had covered forty-nine times during my broadcasting career. I was surprised and delighted, but one of the first thoughts through my mind concerned whether I would have to ride a horse.

Back in 1948, the star of the Houston Livestock Show and Rodeo was Gene Autry. In those days, the Rodeo usually had just one cowboy star—someone like Gene Autry, or Roy Rogers and Dale Evans. Well, during that 1948 opening where they all ride out on horseback in the rodeo grounds, Gene Autry was so drunk he fell off his horse. That just amazed everybody in the crowd, but he managed to get back up on that horse, Champion, to finish the ride and do his singing performance.

When the Rodeo's call came in, I asked "Do I have to ride a horse?" thinking of Gene Autry.

"We can have a horse for you, or we'll put you in a carriage," said Joel Cowley, the Rodeo's president and CEO.

"You better put me in a carriage," I answered quickly. "I'm not sure I can get up on a horse. And even if I could, I'm not sure I'd be able to stay up on that horse."

"Dave, you reported *on* so many of those parades, we think it only right and fitting that you finally should be *in* the Livestock Show and Rodeo Parade," Joel said.

They changed the Rodeo parade route a few years ago because of the streetcar tracks in downtown Houston. They call it "light rail," but I call it streetcars—like the kind my grandfather used to drive. Anyway, the parade doesn't turn on Main Street like it used to do, but it still goes past City Hall. On the side of the carriage they put us in, they had a sign that read: "Grand Marshal, Dave Ward, and wife Laura Ward."

That was another humbling event, all of those people waving and calling out my name: "We miss you…wish you were still on the air…how are you, Dave? Good to see you…" And on and on and on. I was truly amazed and told Laura how surprised I was that so many people remembered me. I hadn't been on the air regularly since November 29, 2016, and after that only once on May 2, 2017 to tell everybody goodbye.

It just goes to show, once again, the power of television, of news, to connect people. I've seen it time and again. There's really nothing quite like it.

On August 3, 2018, Laura and I went out to celebrate our sixteenth wedding anniversary at Mastro's, which is a great steak restaurant on the grounds of our friend Tilman Fertitta's beautiful Post Oak Hotel. After everything Laura has done for me, and meant to my life, I feel lucky and blessed every day. Additionally, I had just received some positive news about my heart condition—I was out of atrial fibrillation for the first time in a long time—so we had every reason to celebrate that evening.

We were settling into the table for dinner, when Laura announced she had a surprise for me. *What on earth could it be*, I wondered? When she produced my wedding band from her purse, I was overjoyed. I had given it to her the morning of my heart attack, and we both thought it was lost in the chaos of all the surgeries, tests, and different hospital rooms that followed. I had been particularly sad to think it was lost, not only because we had it specially made—a unique and beautiful double-band—but also because of what it represented to me. Getting that ring back, and on our anniversary to boot, felt like a hole in my heart had been refilled.

And there would soon be more to celebrate, when I would regain something else precious to me that I had thought was irretrievably lost. Some ten days later, on August 14, 2018, I returned to the Channel 13 TV station after being away for fifteen months. To be honest, there were weeks and months in the interim when it looked like it might never happen. For one thing, in the history of television news, I don't think it ever *has* happened. It's usually like the title of the classic Thomas Wolfe novel: *You Can't Go Home Again.* Once you walk out the door of a TV station, that's the end of that.

To say I was sad to leave the station after my final May 2017 newscast would be a profound understatement. I was angry, frustrated—you name an emotion, and I probably experienced it. But as always, my viewers lifted me up. Through social media, primarily my Facebook page, I received an unending stream of messages and good wishes. Many of them asked me to share my stories in a book, and candidly it was those messages that got me off my duff to start working on it. Reflecting on the amazing experiences I have had has been a cathartic experience, to say the least, and it made me realize I still had a passion for uncovering and telling the stories of the people and events that have made Houston the great city it is.

When I thought about the last chapters of my career, I had always envisioned eventually transitioning into a scaled-back version of what Ron Stone did after leaving KRPC Channel 2 in 1992. Ron formed his own production company, wrote a few books, and did a number of full-length documentaries usually focusing on Texas history. Like Ron, I am fascinated by Texas history—Houston history, really—but I didn't want to create the long format pieces that Ron did. I wanted to do shorter pieces on Houston history for a feature I wanted to call "Dave Ward's Houston."

After I left the station in May of 2017, ongoing discussions involving key company executives gradually moved in a direction so that my return to KTRK to launch "Dave Ward's Houston" became possible. Those negotiations, in turn, led to an agreement—capped off by a familiar drive on the morning of August 14, 2018. Arriving at the station, Laura and I parked in the reserved parking space they have for me close to the door. If age really does have its privileges—and I have grave doubts about that—that parking space is one of them. We were greeted at the door by the station's director of human resources, Vickie Angenend, to fill out the necessary paperwork. From there we went to a meeting of all the department heads. Wendy McMahon, the president of ABC Owned Television Stations Group, had flown into town and was already in the conference room telling the assembled group that "some special guests" would be arriving soon.

When the double doors opened and Laura and I walked in, the eyes around that full table got as big as saucers. "By the grace of God, and the love of this good woman," I said, gesturing to Laura at my side, "I am somehow still here." Wendy then announced that I would be returning to the KTRK family to do a series of "Dave Ward's Houston" reports. At that, people stood up around the table, and I have to say I saw a few tears. Of course, the entire day, I was fighting to keep my emotions under some semblance of control.

From there, we walked back out to the newsroom where, almost two years to the day before, I had announced my departure. By then, a station-wide email had gone out to the entire KTRK staff, and a press release went out to the media. Laura says that judging by everyone's reaction when we walked into the newsroom, they still were not sure what to make of the improbable information they had just read. They weren't sure if it was real.

Reporter Jessica Willey was among the first to see us approaching and stood up at her desk as if to say *It's really happening*. There, in the middle of the newsroom I had called home for half a century, my colleagues gathered around to greet Laura and me—and in a sense, to take us back into the Channel 13 family. Again, it was hard to control the emotions.

There was not too much time for revelry, however, because I had to go on the set during the 11 a.m. mid-day newscast with my old office cubicle mates Art Rascon and Melanie Lawson to share the day's developments—and to tell the viewers to whom I owe so much about my next project.

As I write, "Dave Ward's Houston" is a series of three-to-five minute pieces covering historical facts about Houston. I hope to touch on interesting topics that not a lot of people know about—things I've learned about this city over all the years of living here. For example, there is the iconic statue of Sam Houston at the entrance to Hermann Park, where it has stood since 1925. It features ol' Sam in his Texian uniform on his horse, Saracen, pointing. But do you know to where he's pointing? The answer is the plains near the San Jacinto River—site of the battleground by the Houston Ship Channel where he defeated the Mexican Army led by General Santa Anna. As for the nearby Mecom Fountain, it was designed by Eugene Werlin—who also designed Miller Outdoor Theater—and given to the city by John and Mary Elizabeth Mecom, who owned the nearby Warwick Hotel, back in 1964. These various pieces will be pre-recorded, and happily our phenomenal vice president for programming Kim Nordt-Jackson is in charge of production.

Over breakfast the day I returned to KTRK, Wendy McMahon, president of the ABC-owned stations, asked me: "Dave, why do you want to do this, to come back?"

"There's a very simple reason," I told her without skipping a beat. "I owe it to the viewers who kept me on the air all those years." I continue to feel I owe this community a tremendous debt—a debt I can never fully repay, but I sure as heck can keep trying.

Back when I was still in radio, comedian Bob Hope came to Houston, and they put him up at the Warwick Hotel—in the penthouse on the top floor. For some reason, I was already in the room when Mr. Hope entered. I remember he walked over to the windows and looked out to the south over Hermann Park and Rice University. "This is the most beautiful view I've seen from any hotel," he said, as if to himself.

I thought, *Wait a minute. This guy has been in hotels all over the world.*

I've always thought Houston was the greatest city in the world—for the simple fact we are the greatest city, in the greatest state, in the greatest nation. But upon further reflection, I think Bob Hope was right. We *are* also a beautiful city—not because we have mountains, or architecture dating back to the days of antiquity, or anything like that.

No, we are a beautiful city because of the hard-working, decent, giving, visionary, resilient, God-fearing, tolerant, forgiving, humble, innovative, compassionate and courageous people who call Houston home. We saw the true character of our people on full display during and after Hurricane Harvey, and we've seen it in a myriad of ways throughout our history. How else could Houston become the fourth largest city in America, and the energy capital of the world? How else could we become the home of the greatest manned space flight program, and the greatest medical center on the face of the planet?

It is you, dear reader—you, and your neighbors, and your colleagues, and countless others who make this city what it is. You've also made me what I am—and that is the luckiest, most blessed, and most grateful person going.

In the midst of the Battle of Britain, when the valor of the Royal Air Force pilots had, rather improbably, succeeded in turning back an all-out "blitz" from the skies by the Nazi German Luftwaffe, Sir Winston Churchill took to the floor of the British House of Commons on August 20, 1940, and declared: "Never in the field of human conflict was so much owed by so many to so few." Well, when I look back at my broadcasting career which has spanned six decades, covering the city I love, I am compelled by the thought that never was so much owed *to* so many by one guy: me.

And so, once again, I thank you.

EPILOGUE

Over time, I have been fairly successful in my field. Good things have happened to me. Doors have opened as if by magic, and I think I know the reason why. There's absolutely no doubt in my mind that what success I have had is a direct gift from God as an earthly reward for my father and mother—two amazing, godly and decent people. I really believe that, and when I get to looking back at some of these things that happened to me I become even more convinced.

For example, when I was still in the radio business in Tyler, I got the idea that I wanted to go to work at KBOX-AM radio in Dallas as a news guy—and in fact got an interview scheduled at the station. It was wintertime, and when I started driving from Tyler up for the KBOX appointment I quickly encountered an ice storm. There was a Continental Trailways bus on the road in front of me, and I decided to follow behind it for some sense of safety. Well, about ten miles out of town, that bus slid off the highway into a roadside ditch. Seeing that I thought, *Well, this is not meant to be.*

I turned around and drove back to Tyler.

Had I made it to Dallas that day, I know I would have gotten the KBOX job, and Glendya and I would have moved to Dallas—instead of eventually getting to Houston. God only knows where I would be today, but I wouldn't be here.

Not too long after that, I also had a shot at a radio job in Austin, but once again for some reason I couldn't get there to talk with the program director on the right day—and they hired somebody else. So there, again, is another reason I ended up in Houston.

And don't even get me going on surviving all of the accidents and dumb things I have done in my life.

It's serendipity. It's fate. And I believe the good Lord had something to say about it as well.

As I write this, I've been in radio and television for over sixty years. As I've said, I still don't know how they make pictures and sound fly through the air. Somehow the technicians, engineers and other wizards make that happen. I have never really spent a whole bunch of time thinking about that stuff. My job has always been to get the story right, and then go on the air and present it in an understandable way to the viewer in as few words as possible. That's what I worried about. I let the engineers worry about high definition, and all that technical stuff.

I never did finish a full, four-year college degree, so the irony is I could not get hired in too many TV stations today with my background. But after six decades as a serial practitioner, I do know if you are going to work in the news business, if you treat it as a profession, and if you respect it as a profession, you'll do well.

If, on the other hand, you treat reporting as just another job, you will not last. Or at least, you should not.

The news business is for those who have a genuine passion for collecting and reporting news. If you have that passion, you're not going to count the days you're asked to work. You're not going to get upset because you're working on Thanksgiving. In this business we've got newscasts every day of the year—so you're going to work holidays, and weird hours. You're going to get called in the middle of the night. To succeed, you need to come in with that expectation.

It is truly a profession, and in addition to expecting to work odd hours, journalists need to understand the paramount importance of conducting themselves with professionalism and integrity.

Over the years, a lot of interns have come through the TV station—a lot of young people studying television journalism. I always asked them, "Why do you want do this? Why do you want to get in this demanding, tough line of work?"

When I hear, "I want to be on TV," I can tell you that is *not* the right reason to do this. Every so often, however, a young man or woman will say to me, "I want to find out what's going on. I want to be in a newsroom where people are actively working to find out what's happening in a community and report on it." *Those* are the people that I always encourage to stay with it.

As for the ones who told me, "I want to be on TV," I suggest learning how to sing or something.

When I was the anchor, I always insisted that our reporters never—ever—referred to our newscast as a "show." Too often, you hear anchors and reporters say, "Later in the show…" It is not a show. It's a broadcast, a program, a newscast—but not a show. We always used to fight with Marvin Zindler, who constantly told people he was in show business. "And if this isn't show business," he would say, his voice rising, "then I'm a fairy godmother!!"

I loved Marvin like a brother—granted, an eccentric brother—but always strongly disagreed with him on that point. And I was not alone. There are still good news people out there who want to do things the right way—as I see it—but there are too many in the industry who try to make it show business.

The thing I hated most in my career, more than anything, was having to come back on the air to correct something we reported that was wrong. Invariably, no matter how closely you check and double-check, every now and then there's going to be a mistake. We're human, but the key is when you learn you have reported something wrong, correct it immediately. I mean, treat that correction like a news bulletin and get it on the air as soon as you can. Why? Because it is absolutely imperative to keep the trust of the people.

Finally, like many people, I am concerned that, at the national level, we currently live in an era of "fake news." As long as there has been a Republic, there have been politicians who have shaded the truth. The modern journalist's sole job is to find the truth and report it. Too often it seems that some of our national news outlets have an agenda and try to appeal to one group of voters or another. Even worse, they don't correct stories that are found to be patently false. That's a shame for them, and more so for their viewers.

At the local level, we cannot get away with that kind of monkey business. I have never had a news director, producer or assistant news director instruct me or anyone I know to cover a story with a particular slant. You couldn't get away with that. Of course, there are two sides to every story, and after gathering facts you have to decide how to weigh the facts objectively and try to present both sides. Trust me: not everyone will agree with how you go through that process. But that's why you do make corrections when appropriate. To me, making a correction is not a sign of weakness, but of a commitment to higher journalistic standards.

Beyond that, the viewers are smart enough to figure it out.

During my time at KTRK, we have reported on countless accidents, crises and other scandals in ways that inspired lawmakers to change laws and launch investigations that end up making ours a better community. I know every reporter in this market, and around the country, shares the same hope—that our work can help make our communities better places to live.

But it starts—and ends—with digging for facts, with fighting to establish truth, and with protecting the integrity of the reporting process.

First, last, always.

Thank you again, and good evening, friend.

Normally, there are no second acts in TV news—at least at the same station—
but in 2018 I decided to return to the station I helped build to a ratings powerhouse.

APPENDIX

As you read about my life, it may seem as if my path was clear from the beginning. Along the way, however, I just took one step at a time, following my interests and opportunities. I could not have told you where all these experiences were taking me. My mother, on the other hand, felt strongly that I was destined for something big. From the day I was born, she saved everything—including the bill from the hospital where I was born. Below are four images that represent to me what my mom had in mind for me and, following, are just a few of the many documents she kept from different aspects of my life. They seem to prove the old adage "Mother knows best." Her faith in me, even in the times when I did not see the path, still gives me strength today. These images bring back so many memories. It's been quite a ride, and I'm thankful that I'm still enjoying the journey.

On November 9, 2016, I was named Anchor Emeritus at KTRH. Then on January 27, 2017, I was named an honorary Texas Ranger, and we cut the ribbon to open Crime Stoppers' beautiful new building, named for me. When I received the key to the City of Houston on May 3, 2017, the day after I had said goodbye to my viewers, I couldn't imagine that my life could ever be fuller. But, as I have seen at every step along the way, if we get back up after the inevitable setbacks life throws at us and keep our eyes lifted to the horizon, we create the possibility for a better tomorrow.

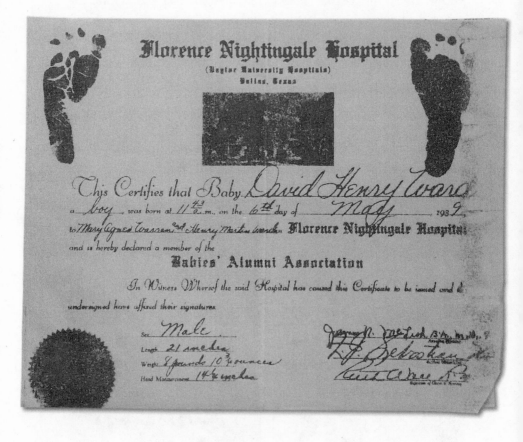

COMMENCEMENT

1957

JACKSONVILLE HIGH SCHOOL

8:00 p.m.

Friday, May 24, 1957

Tomato Bowl

JACKSONVILLE HIGH SCHOOL SENIOR CLASS 1956-1957

Ayers, Jerry
Bacon, Bobby
Baker, Kenneth
*Bass, Paul
Bateman, Arnett
Bloodworth, William
Bolton, Chuck
Broadhead, Gerry
Concilio, Robert
Crane, Richard
Crawford, Loy Dean
*Dublin, Philip
Durrett, Jerry
Dyess, Forrest
Gibson, Donnie
Goodspeed, Donald
Gore, Larry
Gray, David
Haberle, Donnie
Hardy, Bob
*Hassell, Jerry
Henslee, Barry
Holcomb, John
Jernigan, Byron
*Kolb, Larry
Lammons, Frank
Lewis, Tim
Martindale, Billy
*Moore, Jerry
*Moore, Jimmy
McArthur, Robert
McDonald, Mickey
*McFadden, Tommy
Nichols, Lewis
Partin, Billy
*Pate, Barnett
Pearson, Mike
Phillips, Andy
Pope, Danny
*Price, Melvin
*Richardson, Jimmy
*Scruggs, Leldon
Sherman, Earl
Socia, Marvin
Stiefer, Edward
Toland, Ralph
*Warren, Ted
Ward, David
Washburn, Jimmy
*Wiggins, Dicky
Womack, Aubrey

Alexander, Carolyn
Bearden, Beth
Bearden, Patsy
Bolton, Helen
Chancellor, Ann
Chasteen, Pat
Dalby, Theta
Davidson, Anna
Decker, Mary
Firlie, Katherine
Fling, Charlene
Ganske, Gloria
Gothard, Ann
Gray, Barbara
Gresham, Delores
Hensley, Joann
Hunter, Rosalee
Hutto, Nancy
Johnson, Polly Sue
Kersh, Louise
*Leath, Dianna
Lewis, Carolyn
Matthews, Sue
Merrill, Syble
Miller, Rosemary
*Mitchell, Barbara
Morris, Carol
McCarroll, Marilyn
McElmurry, Judy
Nash, Coleen
Odom, Nanette
Pearson, Molly
Pope, Sherry
Porter, Martha
Pruett, Alice
Ratliff, Wanda
Reynolds, Mary
Rogers, Barbara
Rountree, Cloe
Russell, Carolyn
Shuttlesworth, Verena
Simpson, Shirley
*Smith, Daphine
*Traylor, Ann
*Wallace, Peggy
Ward, Mildred
Weesner, Barbara
Wiggins, Patsy
Wiggins, Peggy
Williams, Joyce
*Summer Graduates

United States Navy
Recruiting Service
Landlubbers

HEAR YE: All polywogs, sea serpents, mermaids, octopuses, denizens of the seven seas and all other fishes of the briney deep; all sea gulls, albatross, boatswain birds and all other creatures and constellations of the heavens:

KNOW YE: That __David Henry WARD__ having expressed a voluntary desire to take an active part to insure the continued freedom and rights of the individuals of this great nation, the UNITED STATES OF AMERICA, did the __21st__ day of __June__ in the year of our Lord 19__57__ willingly enter the service of the UNITED STATES NAVY and did swear (or affirm) that he would bear true faith and allegiance to the United States · of America; that he would serve them honestly and faithfully against all their enemies whosoever; and that he would obey the orders of the President of the United States and the orders of the officers appointed over him, according to regulations and the Uniform Code of Military Justice.

F. R. GREGSBY
_____

LTJG, _____ USN
United States Navy Recruiting Officer

NAVPERS-MCNPB 36107

MCNPB 7-701-2060 6-24-55 100M.

Type 1

NAN TRAVIS MEMORIAL HOSPITAL
JACKSONVILLE, TEXAS

Name David Henry Ward Age 17 Admission No. 94875
Address Jacksonville, Tex. 1021 Henderson Phone 6131 Room No. 130 Rate 11.50
Occupation Student Date Transferred: 2-14-57
Bill To Rev. H.M.Ward (Father) Room No. 132 Rate 11.00
Address Same Address
Employer Baptist General Convention
Insurance Blue Cross Grp. #009 Cert.# C9786052
Doctor Dr.R.T.Travis

Admitted: Date 2/10/57 7:25 A.M. P.M. Discharged: Date ___ A.M. P.M.

THIS STATEMENT DOES NOT INCLUDE DOCTOR'S BILL

DESCRIPTION	DATE	REFERENCE	CHARGES	CREDITS	BALANCE
					150.75
COT 2-14-57	FEB 15 57	28,504	1.00		151.75 **
ROOM	FEB 15 57	132	11.00		162.75 **
COT 2-15-57	FEB 16 57	28,521	1.00		163.75 **
ROOM	FEB 16 57	132	11.00		174.75 **
DRUGS M/S	FEB 17 57	27,553	.75		
SUPPLIES	FEB 17 57	48,679	.50		176.00 **
ROOM	FEB 17 57	132	11.00		187.00 **

Honorable Discharge

NAVY DEPARTMENT
UNITED STATES OF AMERICA

from the Armed Forces of the United States of America

This is to certify that

DAVID HENRY WARD   AIRMAN RECRUIT

was Honorably Discharged from the

United States Navy

on the 17th day of JULY 1957 This certificate is awarded
as a testimonial of Honest and Faithful Service

C. H. LUTTINER, ENS, USNR
By direction of the
Commanding Officer

DD 256N (REV. 5-50)

Form ACA 391
(Rev. 8-48)

UNITED STATES OF AMERICA
DEPARTMENT OF COMMERCE
CIVIL AERONAUTICS ADMINISTRATION
WASHINGTON

School Graduation Certificate

This is to certify that _____ DAVID HENRY WARD _____
(Name)

_____ 3623 ETHEL AVENUE, WACO, TEXAS _____ was graduated from the
(Address)

_____ PRIVATE PILOT _____ curriculum of the

_____ WACO FLYING SCHOOL _____
(School)

_____ WACO, TEXAS _____ Airman Agency Certificate No. 2-07-11
(Address)

on SEPTEMBER 15, 1961 _____; that he has successfully completed the instruction required
(Date)

by the Civil Air Regulations and is eligible to apply for a _____ PRIVATE PILOT _____

Certificate and SINGLE-ENGINE LAND Rating as issued by the Administrator of Civil Aeronautics.

The record of this graduate is as follows:

Flying time:		COURSES SATISFACTORILY COMPLETED	GRADE
Dual	23:20	METEROLOGY	
		NAVIGATION	
		RADIO	
Solo	18:00	RADIO NAVIGATION	
		AIRCRAFT	
Total	41:20	ENGINES	
		CIVIL AIR REGULATIONS	
Final flying grade	90%		
		WRITTEN EXAMINATION	86%

I certify that the above statements are true.

_____ WACO FLYING SCHOOL _____
(School)

H. D. Basinger

By _____ HOWARD D. BASINGER _____
(Signature)

_____ OWNER - OPERATOR _____
(Title)

Date issued SEPTEMBER 15, 1961

16—S127-3   U. S. GOVERNMENT PRINTING OFFICE

Place of discharge	RECRUIT TRAINING COMMAND, USNTC, SAN DIEGO, CALIF.
Authority for discharge	Art. C-10305 BuPers Manual & BuMed Inst. 1910.2A
Serial or file number	521 18 09
Date and place of birth	6 May 1939 (Date) Dallas, Texas (Place)
Date of entry into active service	21 June 1957
Rating at discharge	High School Airman Recruit
Total service for pay purposes during this enlistment	00 YRS 00 MOS 27 DAS
Service (vessels and stations served on)	RECRUIT TRAINING COMMAND, USNTC, SAN DIEGO, CALIF.

Remarks

C.H. LUTTINEN, ENS   *U.S.N.(R)*
By direction of the
Commanding Officer

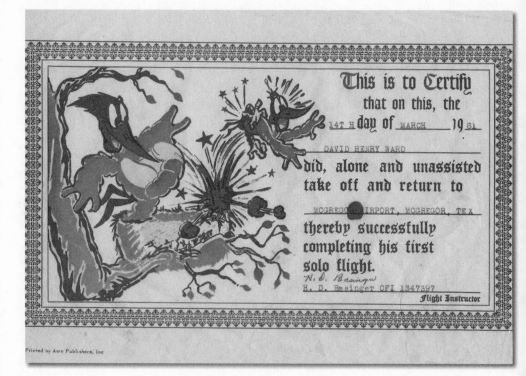

Jet Flight Certificate

PRESENTED FOR PERSONALLY EXPERIENCING
HIGH SPEED · HIGH ALTITUDE FLIGHT
IN THE
LOCKHEED "T-BIRD" JET AIRCRAFT

DAVE WARD

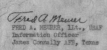

FRED A. MEURER, 1Lt., USAF
Information Officer
James Connally AFB, Texas

U.S. AIR FORCE T-33
U.S. NAVY TV-2

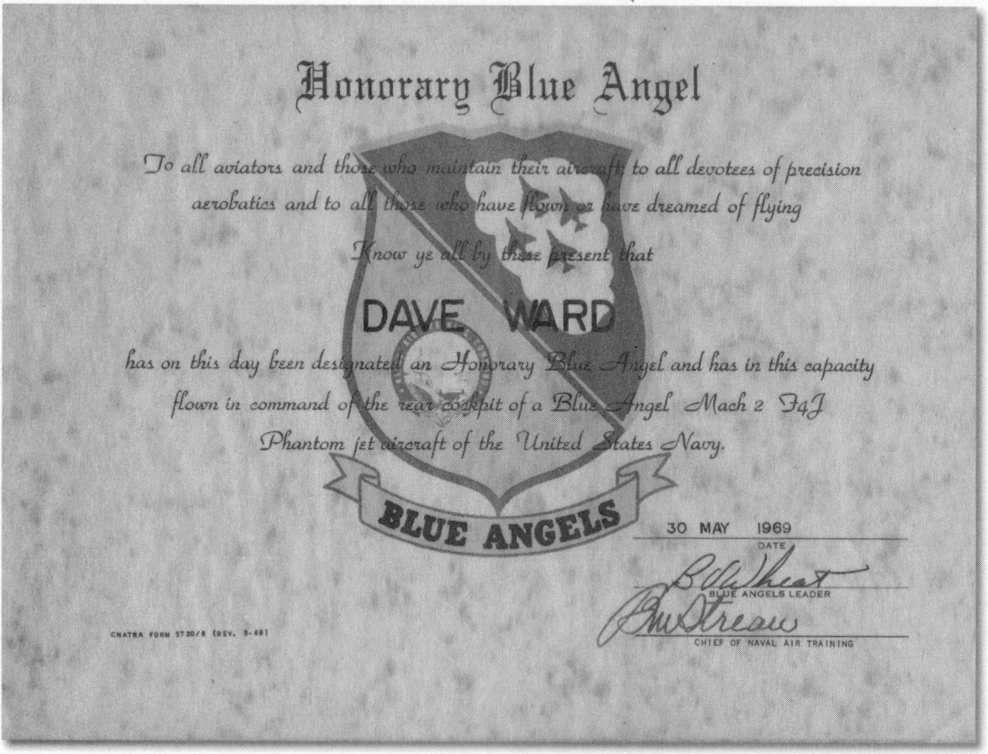

Honorary Blue Angel

To all aviators and those who maintain their aircraft, to all devotees of precision aerobatics and to all those who have flown or have dreamed of flying

Know ye all by these present that

DAVE WARD

has on this day been designated an Honorary Blue Angel and has in this capacity flown in command of the rear cockpit of a Blue Angel Mach 2 F4J Phantom jet aircraft of the United States Navy.

30 MAY 1969
DATE

BLUE ANGELS LEADER

CHIEF OF NAVAL AIR TRAINING

CNATRA FORM 5720/8 (REV. 5-69)

THE "REPUBLI-CRAT" CONVENTIONS. .OR,
THE PLIGHT OF INDEPENDENT RADIO

By Bill Jay
K-NUZ News Director

Now that the conventions are over, David Ward, assistant news director, and I have been asked to give an accounting of our experiences for K-NEWS readers. The days we spent at the Republican National Convention in San Francisco and at the Democratic National Convention in Atlantic City were so packed full of excitement and activities that we can only hit a few of the high spots in our limited space.

We will both testify to the fact that coverage of these two historical events was one of the most interesting experiences of our radio careers.

Right off the bat, let us say that a round of applause goes to the sponsors who made possible this coverage for Texas Coast Broadcasters, Inc., operating K-NUZ and K-QUE (FM) in Houston, and KAY-C and KAY-D (FM) in Beaumont.

Sponsoring firms for both conventions were Mosehart and Keller Ford and Sonny Look's Sir Loin House (Houston) and Rainbo Bakery and American National Bank (Beaumont).

(Continued next page)

Setting up for the Republican Convention in San Francisco here are Assistant News Director Dave Ward (seated) and K-NUZ/K-QUE News Director Bill Jay. Coverage resulted in more than 90 reports for Houston listeners.

Telephone contacts with Texas delegates proved invaluable to K-NUZ/K-QUE convention team. Here Bill Jay, news director, was snapped by a photographer while in the midst of securing materials to be relayed to Houston.

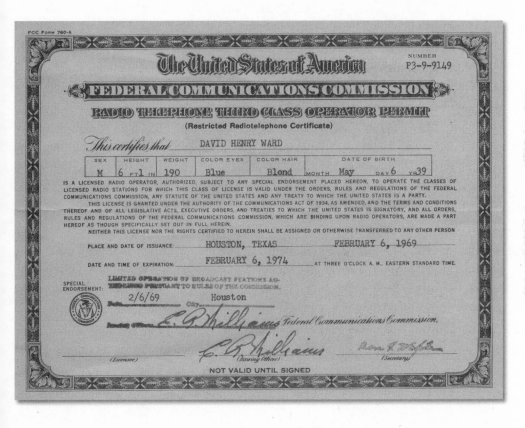

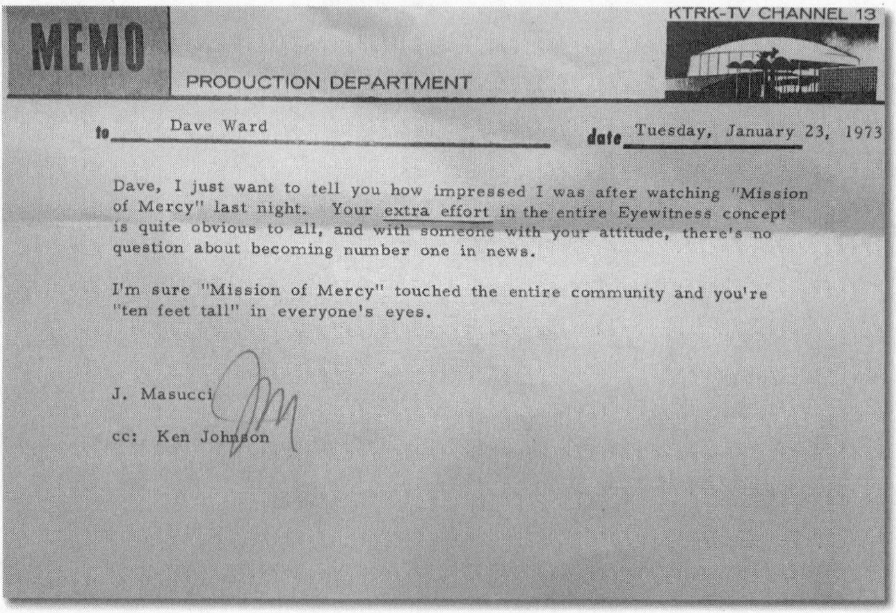

MEMO

PRODUCTION DEPARTMENT

KTRK-TV CHANNEL 13

to _____ Dave Ward _____   date _____ Tuesday, January 23, 1973

Dave, I just want to tell you how impressed I was after watching "Mission of Mercy" last night. Your extra effort in the entire Eyewitness concept is quite obvious to all, and with someone with your attitude, there's no question about becoming number one in news.

I'm sure "Mission of Mercy" touched the entire community and you're "ten feet tall" in everyone's eyes.

J. Masucci

cc: Ken Johnson

CHANNEL 13 IS PROUD TO PRINT THE FOLLOWING COMMENTARY, WRITTEN AND PRESENTED BY DAVE WARD ON THE DECEMBER 7TH EDITIONS OF EYEWITNESS NEWS AT 7AM, 6 AND 10PM.

" I HAVE FELT THE SAME HELPLESS ANGER AND FRUSTRATION OVER THE HOSTAGE SITUATION IN IRAN THAT ALL AMERICANS ARE FEELING THESE DAYS. WE ALL KNOW WHAT WE CAN'T DO, BUT WHAT CAN WE DO? THE OTHER DAY, THE IRANIAN FOREIGN MINISTER WAS ASKED, IF OUR PEOPLE ARE STILL THERE ON DECEMBER 25TH, CAN WE SEND THEM CHRISTMAS PRESENTS? HE REPLIED, IN SO MANY WORDS, 'WELL, WE RECOGNIZE AND RESPECT YOUR RELIGIOUS HOLIDAYS. MAYBE SOMETHING CAN BE WORKED OUT.' WELL, LET'S WORK IT OUT. IF THEY WON'T SEND OUR PEOPLE HOME, THEN WHY CAN'T WE SEND CHRISTMAS TO THEM? WHAT WOULD HAPPEN IF EVERY CITIZEN OF THE UNITED STATES MAILED A SMALL CHRISTMAS PRESENT, OR A CHRISTMAS CARD, OR A LETTER, ANYTHING. . . EACH ADDRESSED TO: 'AN AMERICAN HOSTAGE, U.S. EMBASSY, TEHRAN, IRAN?' IT SEEMS APPARENT THAT THE ONLY THING THOSE EMOTIONALLY HYPERACTIVE PEOPLE WILL RECOGNIZE OR UNDERSTAND RIGHT NOW IS AN EQUALLY EMOTIONAL EXPRESSION OF OUR NATIONAL UNITY. A A DEMONSTRATION OF WHAT 50-LIVES MEAN. HOW BETTER TO DEMONSTRATE THAT, THAN TO SHARE OUR CHRISTMAS WITH THOSE POOR HOSTAGES IN IRAN. SUCH A MOVEMENT COULD SPREAD TO EVERY CITY IN THIS NATION, AND RESULT IN SUCH AN OUTPOURING OF LOVE AND CONCERN, THAT THE WHOLE WORLD WOULD STAND UP AND APPLAUD. MILLIONS OF AMERICANS, EACH SENDING THE MESSAGE, ' PEACE ON EARTH, GOOD WILL TOWARD MEN'. . . THE MESSAGE FROM THE PRINCE OF PEACE. WELL, I'M GONNA DO IT. I'M MAILING FIFTY CHRISTMAS CARDS, EACH ADDRESSED: ' AN AMERICAN HOSTAGE, U.S. EMBASSY, TEHRAN, IRAN.' THE IRANIANS CAN SCREAM AND SHOUT AT US. . . THEY CAN SHAKE THEIR FISTS AT US . . . BUT THEY CAN'T STOP SANTA CLAUS. THE AYATOLLAH IS NO MATCH FOR THE SPIRIT OF CHRISTMAS. WHAT DO YOU THINK? I'M DAVE WARD."

13 EYEWITNESS NEWS

DAVE WARD

Klein PTA Sets Variety Show

Klein High School PTA will present "Variety Show '73" on March 17 at 7 p.m. in the beautiful new Klein High School auditorium. Dave Ward of Channel 13 will be master of ceremonies.

Klein high school or intermediate students who have an act to perform are invited to audition on March 7th and 8th at 4 p.m. in the Klein Intermediate School cafetorium.

There will be a bake sale following the variety show with proceeds going to the Dr. Randall Simpson Memorial Scholarship Fund.

Refreshments will be on sale after the show in the high school cafeteria and proceeds will go toward additional scholarship funds.

Remember the show on the 17th of March at 7 p.m.

KLEIN PTA VARIETY SHOW 1973

MARCH 17, 1973

7:00 P.M.

INTRODUCTIONS..............Sylvester Turner
          Klein High School Student Council President

MASTER OF CERMONIES........Dave Ward
                    Channel 13 News

****

JUDGES....................Mary Wehrung
          Northhampton Music Teacher

          ....Mary Laird
          Klein Int. & Middle School Choir
          Director

          ....Laura Cline
          Klein High School P.E. Department

          ....Ernestine Jackson
          Greenwood Forest Music Teacher

          ....Bill Chambles
          Klein High School Choir Director

          ....John R. Robinson
          Klein Int. & Middle School Band
          Director

          ....L. Thompson
          Klein High School Ass't. Band Director

SCREEN ACTORS GUILD RESIDUAL PAYMENT

THE GUILD is pleased to send you the enclosed check, covering television
residuals due under the Guild's television contract with the producers.

Date

MAR 1 1 1974

Name	Dave Ward	464 56 7120	Company	Universal

*Series	Episode	Run	Amount
WORLD PREMIERE	My Sweet Charlie	3	141.12

Check No.	1370691	Net Amount	99.00		Gross Amount	141.12

* "F" PRECEDING SERIES TITLE INDICATES PAYMENT IS FOR FOREIGN TV EXHIBITION. "TE" INDICATES THEATRICAL EXHIBITION
ALWAYS NOTIFY THE GUILD WHEN YOU HAVE A CHANGE OF ADDRESS
KEEP FOR YOUR INCOME TAX AND UNEMPLOYMENT INSURANCE RECORDS

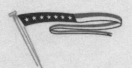

COMMANDING OFFICER
USS HOUSTON (SSN 713)
FPO San Francisco, Ca. 96667-2393

April 6, 1992

Dear Mr. Ward,

Welcome Aboard USS HOUSTON (SSN 713). My crew and
I stand ready to assist you in all respects.

The meal hours for this underway are:

Lunch	1100-1200
Dinner	1700-1800

Meal items are listed in the Plan of the Day.
Costs for the meals will be taken by the Supply
Officer, LTJG Leff.

The following areas are designated for smoking on
board USS HOUSTON, Forward Compartment Lower Level
and the Chief's Quarters.

Athletic equipment is located in the Sonar
Equipment Space and Engineroom.

If you have any questions, please do not hesitate
to ask.

Sincerely,

G. A. WALLACE
Commander, U. S. Navy
Commanding Officer

Texas Radio Hall of Fame

Dave Ward
Honored Inductee

2016

Est. 2002
www.TRHOF.net

Josh Holstead
Operations Manager

From the desk of
and
From the heart of

MARY WARD

God bless you this day!

MY SON

A few years ago I had a son
In my busy life that rushed along;
Days went by, and years hurried on
And before I knew it, my son was gone.

So now I miss my little boys face,
His teenage daring,
And his young man's grace;
I miss his "Yes Daddy" when I call his name,
He's grown up now and gaining his fame.

So I seldom see him face to face
For this life is a swift and running race;
There are miles and miles between him and me,
But I cover them all, my son to see;
For I know ere long will come the day
When he'll pick up the phone and hear someone say
"Sorry, dear friend, your Dad died today".
So I pray:"Dear Lord, before that day comes,
Please help me in all ways,
To be good to my son".

.........Henry Ward

From the desk of
and
From the heart of
MARY WARD
God bless you this day!

David, I read the following little poem to/on you
the phone on your 46th birthday - May 6, 1985.
It expresses my feelings about you in a fine
way and I wanted you to have it to keep.

A happy day it was when you were born,
A son entered my life on that special morn.
A son who grew up with cuts and scuffed knees,
A son who played ball, rode a bike, and climbed trees.
A son who makes me happy to be living,
A son who has his own way of giving.
A son who has grown up to be a fine man,
A son who has made me as proud as he can.

With all my love,

Mom

Walker's Point

June 5, 1996

Dear Mary Ward,

Thanks so much for your special
message. It was kind of you to write and share
your sentiments, and I so appreciate your having
been in touch.

With all best wishes,

Warmly,

Barbara Bush

Mrs. Ward - Your son is a wonderful
man and gives so much to
Houston. He is truly a "Point of
Light."

CONSULADO GENERAL DE NICARAGUA
1925 SOUTHWEST FREEWAY
HOUSTON, TEXAS 77006
TELEPHONE (713) 528-6563

Yo RODOLFO GARCIA M. Consul General de Nicaragua en

Houston, Texas, Estados Unidos de Norte America con-

cede permiso provisional al Sr. DAVID H. WARD

CANAL 13 T.V. Houston

Quien se dirige a Managua sin pasaporte, por el es-

tado de emergencia y quien presta ayuda medica a la

ciudadania. Dirigiendose por via aerea.

Houston, Texas, Diciembre veinte y cuatro de mil

novecientos setenta y dos.

Rodolfo Garcia M.
Consul-General

SUPER COWBOY SEEKS SUCCESSOR
Dave Ward Is the Gridiron Show's LBJ
—Post Photo by Jerry Click

Dave Ward is a human being too.

Anchorman Dave Ward's warmth and spontaneity on Eyewitness News is only natural because he doesn't try to be stiff and formal. The proof of Dave's professionalism is his authoritative approach to the news, along with his easy-going personality. It makes for an easy way to digest hard news, and moves you a lot closer to your world.

Eyewitness News Six & Ten

*I am honored that the Crime Stoppers' building bears my name
and also that at the entry there are tribute walls commemorating my career.
I just wish my mother could see it!*

*This is the day I returned to my TV home in order to stay connected
with my viewers through "Dave Ward's Houston." I have spent
more than half a century reporting the news here.*